NO WORSE ENEMY

"As well as being the best book from the front lines so far, it is the first which shows the real down and dirty story behind the headlines and upbeat assessments. A superbly written, considered piece of war reportage, it will stand comparison with the very best of the last half-century. Unlike any book before it, this one asks us to see the British and American soldiers through the eyes of the bewildered and all-too-often bereaved eyes of Afghans. *No Worse Enemy* will do for Afghanistan what Michael Herr's *Dispatches* did for Vietnam."

Frank Ledwidge – author of *Losing Small Wars: British Military Failure in Iraq and Afghanistan*

"Ben Anderson has written an account of his time in Helmand that is both extremely readable and useful, in that he presents lots of the detail that usually gets lost. *No Worse Enemy* has the benefit of the author having spent his time in the country on the ground, on patrol, taking risks and always patiently listening to what was going on around him. If you want to understand how the war in Helmand is really being fought, buy this book."

Alex Strick van Linschoten – author of *An Enemy We Created: The Myth of the Taliban*

"Compelling and brilliant ... Ben Anderson presents the reader with an extraordinary account of the tragedies in the Afghanistan war. This is a first-hand look behind the headlines at the reality of the difficult challenges British and American infantry face in modern, bloody counterinsurgency warfare operations."

Regulo Zapata – Green Beret Special Forces (Ret) and author of *Desperate Lands: The War on Terror Through the Eyes of a Special Forces Soldier*

"*No Worse Enemy* provides the very rare first-hand account of the realities of the war in Afghanistan, a gripping narrative derived not from just one or two trips to large forward operating bases, but from multiple embeds with a variety of different units in the most austere reaches of Afghanistan's restive Helmand Province. The book provides a candid and honest insight into what is really happening on the ground, an invaluable perspective for both military practitioners, as well as those who have never set foot on a battlefield but who want to know the real story. A great addition to the books out there on Afghanistan."

Ed Darack – author of *Victory Point: Operations Red Wings and Whalers*

NO WORSE ENEMY

THE INSIDE STORY OF THE CHAOTIC STRUGGLE FOR AFGHANISTAN

BEN ANDERSON

ONEWORLD

A Oneworld Book

Published by Oneworld Publications 2011

Copyright © Ben Anderson 2011

The moral right of Ben Anderson to be identified as
the Author of this work has been asserted by them
in accordance with the Copyright, Designs and Patents Act 1988

ISBN 978–1–85168–852–4 (Hardback)
ISBN 978–1–85168–857–9 (Paperback Travel Edition)
ISBN 978–1–85168–863–0 (Ebook)

Typeset by Jayvee, Trivandrum, India
Cover design by BoldandNoble.com
Printed and bound in the UK by TJ International Ltd.

Oneworld Publications
185 Banbury Road
Oxford OX2 7AR
England

Learn more about Oneworld. Join our mailing list to
find out about our latest titles and special offers at:

www.oneworld-publications.com

For Nanny Butch, who endured more bombs than I ever will, and despite weighing less than a jockey, even helped the anti-aircraft guns shoot back. She was the toughest, but most humble, person I've ever known. I'll remember her, and the example she quietly set, forever.

Vi Anderson 1924–2011

CONTENTS

Acronyms and abbreviations ix

Maps xi

Prologue xiii

Introduction xv

A note on translations xxi

PART I: THE BRITISH ARMY, JUNE TO OCTOBER, 2007
QUEEN'S COMPANY, THE GRENADIER GUARDS 1

PART II: US MARINE CORPS, JULY TO AUGUST, 2009
2ND BATTALION, 8TH MARINES 59

PART III: US MARINE CORPS, FEBRUARY TO MARCH, 2010
1ST BATTALION, 6TH MARINES 77

PART IV: US MARINE CORPS, JUNE 2010
1ST BATTALION, 6TH MARINES 175

PART V: US MARINE CORPS, DECEMBER 2010 TO
JANUARY 2011, 3RD BATTALION, 5TH MARINES 189

Afterword 251

Recommended further reading 257

Acknowledgements 259

Index 261

ACRONYMS AND ABBREVIATIONS

ABV	Assault Breacher Vehicle
ACOG	Advanced Combat Optical Gunsight
ALP	Afghan Local Police
ANA	Afghan National Army
ANCOP	Afghan National Civil Order Police
ANP	Afghan National Police
A-POB	Anti-Personnel Obstacle Breaching System
ASF	American Special Forces
CAO	Civil Affairs Officer
COC	Combat Operation Centre
COIN	Counter Insurgency
DC	District Centre
DFC	Directional Fragment Charge
DFID	Department For International Development
EOD	Explosive Ordnance Disposal
FOB	Forward Operating Base
GIROA	Government of the Islamic Republic of Afghanistan
GPMG	General Purpose Machine Gun
IED	Improvised Explosive Device
ISAF	International Security Assistance Force
KIA	Killed in Action

LAW	Light Anti-tank Weapon
LTTs	Lines To Take
MEDEVAC	Medical Evacuation
MIC-LIC	Mine Clearing Line Charge
MRAP	Mine Resistant Ambush Protected
MREs	Meals Ready To Eat
NAAFI	The Navy, Army and Air Force Institutes
NATO	North Atlantic Treaty Organisation
NCO	Non-Commissioned Officer
NDS	National Directorate of Security (Afghan Intelligence Service)
OMLT	(pronounced 'omelette') Operational Mentor and Liaison Team
PAX	Passengers
PB	Patrol Base
PID	Positive Identification
PRT	Provincial Reconstruction Team
Psy-Op	Psychological Operation
QRF	Quick Reaction Force
RC	Regional Command
ROC	Rehearsal of Concept
ROE	Rules of Engagement
RPG	Rocket-Propelled Grenade
R&R	Rest and Recuperation
SAW	Squad Automatic Weapon
Semper Fi	*Semper Fidelis* ('Always faithful' – the motto of the US Marines)
WMIK	Weapons Mount Installation Kit (mounted on a roofless Land Rover)

MAPS

Helmand Province   xviii
Operation Mushtaraq (Marjah)   120
The Sniper Hole (Marjah)   161
Pharmacy Road (Sangin)   222

PROLOGUE

You knew that this was going to happen one day. And now you're going to die in the cold wet mud of a ditch in Afghanistan because you chose to join a bunch of American marines as they were dropped like kittens into the middle of a perfect ambush.

You deserve to die for just floating along again. Not thinking, not making a decision, just stumbling slowly forwards until you couldn't turn back.

It was so bad I imagined a tiny black-eyed dormouse, frozen with terror in the corner of a glass tank half-filled with a huge, languid, grey and black snake, its tongue and eyes gradually moving closer; so slow and arrogant it was repellent.

I had other strange visions: nothing peaceful, no floating towards a white light, just a quick flash of me and the Marines, curled into foetal positions, pressing ourselves as far as we could into the cold, dark mud. Above, a huge cartoon Taliban face, hundreds of feet tall, turbaned, dirty, brown and sweaty with a wiry beard and a wart, grinning maniacally down at us, growling with joy.

Even the fucking ditch was America's fault. They had built it over fifty years ago to make the desert bloom, win hearts and minds and counter Russian influence. But being American, they had to build it in a perfectly straight line, in a land where nothing is straight. So as I dived into the ditch and slid towards the putrid water at the bottom, I was still an easy target for the Taliban fighters who did the same.

I wanted to wrap my arms around something but there was only freezing mud and a few dehydrated reeds. I went limp, resigned to the fact that metal was about to enter my body. Cus D'Amato's old saying about how no boxer ever got knocked out who didn't want to get knocked out suddenly made sense. *OK, I lose, there's no way out, just put me to sleep so that this ordeal can end.*

A rocket whooshed over my shoulder and exploded against the wall behind me.

'AW FUCK, I'M HIT, I'M HIT', screamed the marine next to me. As he rolled on to his side I could see his right leg was covered in bright red blood that gushed from beneath his knee.

'WHAT THA FUCK', he moaned.

'I'm hit too', screamed the marine on my other side, holding the back of his left leg. 'Am I bleeding?' he asked, moving his hand away briefly.

'No, you're good', I told him, sounding calm for a second. I rolled on to my back, expecting to feel pain, or a warm wet patch, somewhere. *Please don't let it be between my legs. Please let me keep my legs.* But there was nothing, except knuckles bloodied from the scramble into the ditch. The bullets clattered above us in murderous clouds and the screams and the faces around me all said the same thing: we don't know where it's coming from and we're all going to die.

INTRODUCTION

Everyone who has covered the wars in Afghanistan over the last thirty years has a few – possibly apocryphal – stories that perfectly sum up the struggles of foreign forces. One of my favourites came from a chance discussion with two American soldiers, whose home for twelve months – a dingy concrete arch – I was sleeping in.

I was in the Arghandab Valley, just outside Kandahar City, in October 2010. There hadn't been any fighting for a few weeks, so I was reading a book, written by a Russian journalist, about the Soviet invasion of Afghanistan. The author described a foot patrol with a wily old Russian commander when suddenly they had found themselves surrounded by a passing flock of sheep, guarded by their shepherd. Why, the reporter asked, had the sheep not been sheared? It was the middle of summer, when temperatures often top fifty degrees. The commander told him to grab a sheep and feel its belly. He did – and found several rifles, strapped underneath the animal, totally hidden from view. The commander grabbed another and found more. I was so amused by this story that I read it out loud to the two American soldiers. 'MOTHERFUCKER!' one of them screamed. 'We saw shitloads of sheep not too long ago and I remember thinking the exact same thing – why haven't they been sheared?' The likely answer to that question kept him angry for hours. We never seem to learn from history.

I've been travelling to Afghanistan, and in particular Helmand – the country's most violent province and the focus of first Britain's, then America's, military effort – for five years. When I was first there, what I saw raised continuous and obvious questions that I thought were too stupid to ask out loud. All those bombs are for five guys in sandals, with AKs? And they escaped? Those roofless old jeeps are all you have? Those junkies and thieves are the good guys? If the Taliban have been routed, why do all these IEDs keep popping up around us like mushrooms? If the people are so happy to have been liberated, why do they look so angry?

With each trip, the war became less recognisable as the one being described from podiums in Kabul, Washington and London. A positive spin could be expected but there was often such a gulf between what we were told was happening and what I was seeing with my own eyes that I sometimes questioned my recollections. Only when I watched the hundreds of hours of footage I'd gathered did I realise the situation was even more calamitous and our ambitions more fantastic than I had at first thought. And my shock only increased when I got accurate translations of what the Afghans I'd filmed were actually saying.

Each time I returned, there were new policies, new forces, new ambassadors, generals, planes, drones and even tanks. And there was a surge, because a surge, we were told, had turned things around in Iraq. On each visit, I was told that the Taliban were on their last legs, the Afghans were almost ready to provide security for themselves and the government was almost ready to govern. Mistakes were made in the past but now we're doing it right. Even the increasingly audacious attacks by the Taliban were seen as proof of their desperation. The tipping point was close.

I was deeply sceptical. I had to keep going back to see if I was wrong. Billions of dollars were being spent. Brilliant minds were dedicated to the project. The credibility of a superpower and NATO hung in the balance. Such an effort, with such high stakes, couldn't result in so little.

This is a simple book, written chronologically, about what I've seen: an honest account of what the war looks like on the ground. As it drags on and public interest evaporates, I don't think I have anything more important to offer than that. Apart from a tiny handful of quotes taken from my notebooks, every word spoken here was transcribed directly from my many video tapes.

In the months following the 9/11 attacks, the Bush administration thought they had bombed their way to a swift and brilliant victory in Afghanistan. Some even thought they'd invented a new way of fighting wars, from twenty thousand feet, where none of their blood need be shed.

The Taliban, we now know, hadn't been defeated. They had merely stepped off the stage, to watch what happened next. Many had been willing to play a part in the new reality, which would have been entirely consistent with the history of conflict resolution in Afghanistan. But they were snubbed. What happened next, after vital resources had been diverted to Iraq, was simply a return to predatory power politics and the rule of the warlords. To a place where the corrupt and vicious thrived and the most able and honest were side-lined. The state of affairs that had allowed the Taliban to sweep to power in the first place. The 2005 elections, which might have led to a truly representative government, were a sham, with some observers claiming that fraudulent votes outnumbered the genuine.

So the Taliban gradually returned, slipping back over the border from Pakistan as easily as they had left. As fighters, they were surprised to discover that beyond Kabul, there was no one around to stop them. Soon they were operating in every province of Afghanistan. In the countryside, where most Afghans live, they began to provide better security, justice and employment (often through participation in, or the protection of, the opium trade) than the government itself. Sadly, this wasn't difficult.

This eventually led to the deployment of NATO forces beyond Kabul. In the summer of 2006, just over three thousand British troops (of which only six hundred or so would actually be out on patrol and in contact with Afghans) were sent to Helmand province. Helmand, together with neighbouring Kandahar, was the Taliban's historical power base. At first, the Brits didn't wear helmets, handed out toys to children and were only tasked with 'facilitating reconstruction and development'. The defence secretary even

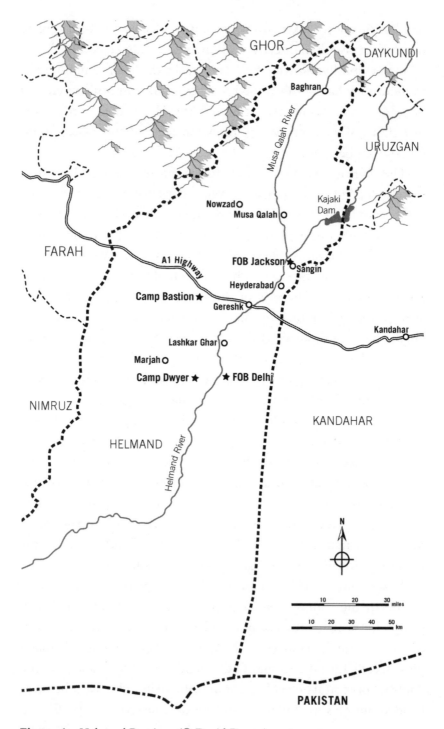

Figure 1   Helmand Province (© David Berger)

hoped they could complete their mission without firing a single bullet. Our good intentions, it was thought, would mean that we would be welcomed. Soon afterwards, the war in Afghanistan really began. The Brits found themselves fighting off waves of attacks against their tiny and isolated patrol bases.

I first started travelling to southern Afghanistan in the summer of 2007, when the hopelessly under-manned British forces were struggling to hang on to what little ground they had. Since then, I've spent a lot of time with British, Afghan, and American troops, often during key operations, as they tried to carry out the latest policies. I stayed with them for weeks on end as they fought their way into towns and villages with the aim of establishing a permanent presence. I spent as little time as possible on the main bases, where not much ever happens. Staying with the infantry also meant I got to talk to Afghans far more than is thought possible when you're on embeds and to see how the war has affected their lives. The stories and exchanges recorded here are not anomalous. I've made an effort to exclude any that are. They show what happened many times. Some of the people represented here might feel cheated. They might argue that things eventually improved after I left. While this may be true, the overall picture continues to worsen considerably.

I have travelled elsewhere in Afghanistan but I have chosen to focus on Helmand province, where the war has always been fiercest. Helmand also offers the benefit of seeing how the two largest contributing forces – British and American – coped in such unforgiving terrain. The Brits eventually had eight thousand troops there but it was nowhere near enough. The Americans ended up sending thirty-three thousand and even then, their small gains were described as 'fragile and reversible'. I was able to directly compare the two in Sangin, where a third of British casualties occurred, which was taken over by the US Marines in 2010. It was no coincidence that I came closer to being killed with almost every visit. Apart from a few square kilometres of land – and it was never more than that – being cleared and secured here and there, the only thing I ever saw happen was an increase in troop numbers and a corresponding increase in casualties, military and civilian. This, I was told, was further evidence of the Taliban's desperation and proof that the insurgency was in its last throes.

Ben Anderson
10/9/11

A NOTE ON TRANSLATIONS

Most of the time, I have transcribed in English what Afghans said in Dari or Pashtu. I worked from over 170 tapes and had everything translated as carefully as possible. In the process, I often found that what people were actually saying was radically different to what American or British troops were told they were saying. I have only included the interpreters' words or phrases in Dari or Pashtu when mistranslations and miscommunications were particularly revealing.

I have had to be sloppy in using the word 'Taliban' to describe all opposition fighters in Afghanistan. It would take another book to explain the many different motives of the many different groups currently fighting, ranging from angry farmers to former Mujahadeen commanders. It is safe to say that a great many have no relationship with the pre 9/11 Taliban and even fewer have any link with or affinity to Al-Qaeda. Many are just angry local men who feel obliged to fight government or foreign forces. It's often said that this is simply the way they are, but in many cases they took a considerable amount of persuading. These are the men I'm referring to when I say 'Taliban'.

PART I

THE BRITISH ARMY
JUNE TO OCTOBER, 2007
QUEEN'S COMPANY
THE GRENADIER GUARDS

The British Army, it was thought, would be perfect for Helmand province. From their extensive experience in Northern Ireland, they knew how to interact with people, and with their self-deprecating, informal approach, should be brilliant at winning hearts and minds. They first deployed to Helmand in 2006, when they were the only major military force in the province. They expected to stay no longer than three years.

The Ministry of Defence had kept reporters away from the fighting. But when the soldiers started releasing their own footage, shot on hand-held cameras and mobile phones, showing fierce fighting from tiny, isolated and almost derelict outposts, they were forced to change their policy. After over eighteen months of negotiations, I was finally allowed to join the troops in the summer of 2007.

The MoD weren't the only ones who didn't want me in Helmand. The BBC had also shown little interest. The trip only happened at all because I'd been supported by one executive, who had commissioned me before. Everyone else thought there was nothing to say or learn about the war in Afghanistan, and even less public interest. Only when I returned with hours of footage of battles that lasted for days was I given a slot in peak time.

CHAPTER 1

'My conscience is clear because it was a genuine mistake. You know and I know the Taliban were keeping those people there because it was a target', said Lieutenant Colonel Richard Westley, the Commanding Officer of the Worcestershire and Sherwood Foresters. He was holding a *shura* (a meeting of elders) with Dur Said Ali Shah, the Mayor of Gereshk, the second-largest town in Helmand province. 'I would like to make a goodwill payment to help with the cost of the funeral. This is not compensation. Nothing can compensate for the loss of a whole family. But it might just help with the payment for the ceremony, the funeral and the guests that have to be entertained as part of Afghan protocol.'

The Mayor nodded.

'I will rely on your judgment and wisdom to tell me when the best time to do that is', said the Colonel.

The Mayor nodded again but remained silent.

On the day that I first arrived in Helmand province, twenty-five civilians had been killed by a 500lb bomb dropped on a building from which the Taliban were firing. Only after the bomb had been dropped and the fighting stopped did the British soldiers who had called for the air strike realise their mistake. As well as around thirty fighters, they found the bodies of civilians, including nine women and three children. They had been hiding in a small room in one corner of the compound.

'The intensity of fire from that building was such that trees and branches were being knocked down by it, and the risk to my

3

soldiers was so great that we engaged with an aircraft and dropped a bomb', the Colonel explained.

Every senior British soldier I spoke to was certain that the people had tried to flee but were prevented from doing so.

The Colonel said that even the man whose family was killed blamed the Taliban.

'He was vehemently against them and holds them responsible for a pretty deceitful and cynical incident where they rounded his family into a building, then fought from that building, knowing that we would respond. We killed all the Taliban but unfortunately, and unknown to us, we killed all the civilians that the Taliban had been incarcerating there. We were duped. And frankly, that rather hurts because we like to think we're a little bit cleverer. While we are deeply deeply regretful about it, it is some comfort when people come up and say "look, we don't hold you responsible, we know who is bringing about the evil in the valley and it isn't ISAF (International Security Assistance Force)".'

President Karzai denounced the incident on television, saying that the 'careless' killing of innocents will wipe out any goodwill generated by everything else foreign governments are trying to do in Afghanistan. 'Afghan life is not cheap and should not be treated as such', he said, more angry than I had ever seen him. The deaths took the toll for 2007 to almost 250, more than the number killed the previous year. It was still only July.

The Colonel addressed the Mayor directly. 'It is my promise to you that we will not again strike buildings unless we are absolutely sure that civilians are not in the area. I will find the Taliban and I will destroy them. But if I kill ten Taliban and one civilian, that is a failure.'

Afghan homes are surrounded by high and impenetrable walls. The actual living quarters are hidden from view. The pilot who dropped the bomb had flown over the building twice and seen nothing but Taliban fighters with weapons. That there were no civilians to be seen is hardly a surprise – they were unlikely to stand out in the open after the Taliban had gone into their homes and started firing. It is impossible to know that there are no civilians in a compound unless someone can go in and check every room, which they can't do in the middle of a fight. The bomb had been dropped at night, in complete darkness.

I asked if there would be a change in tactics.

'No. We just have to apply the tactics we've used in the past with a greater degree of certainty. Individuals have to be targeted directly, without buildings being hit. We need to be that bit more certain there are no civilians in the area.'

And if this happens again, I asked, do you stand any chance of winning the support of the local people? The people of Gereshk, he explained, were pragmatic. They would sit on the fence and see what happened before choosing which side to take. (Or whether to take sides at all, I thought.)

'I think we're at a fairly critical stage. I don't think another incident of that nature would undermine the good that we've done. But I'm just not prepared to take that risk', he said.

It wasn't chance that the first meeting I saw between Coalition troops and Afghans was about civilian casualties. The subject of damage to people's homes, or security in general, dominated the vast majority of discussions I saw. More than a year after entering Helmand, the British effort, which was supposed to be about aiding reconstruction and development, had become overwhelmingly military. The soldiers were struggling to protect themselves and the measures they were taking were costing the Afghans dearly.

The Mayor's phone rang with a tune that sounded like a theme from a Super Mario game.

'Good ring tone, good vibe', said Westley, nodding his head slightly to the rhythm.

The *shuras* took place every week and were open either to the public or to elected Afghan officials, who were supposed to be consulted on military operations and development projects, while being mentored on how to govern. But with the British faces changing every six months, Afghan officials often simply went along with whatever was being said and took what they could. The long-term deals were done elsewhere.

Lieutenant Colonel Westley and Mayor Ali Shah sat on cushions at one end of a long, old carpet, in a small room just outside the soldiers' accommodation in Forward Operating Base (FOB) Price, the main British base just outside Gereshk. Below them, on the carpet itself, were an Afghan National Army (ANA) commander, a police chief, three British soldiers, 'Lucky' the terp (interpreter), and two American Special Forces soldiers, sporting thick beards, who never spoke.

'How are the people in the town feeling about security at the moment?' asked the Colonel.

The police chief said that the people wanted the Taliban out but they didn't want these big operations. The people didn't understand why the Taliban had to be fought in their midst. They wanted to know why there couldn't be another front line outside the town. Colonel Westley promised that would happen one day. The Afghan Army commander said the Taliban hid their weapons under their scarves and hid themselves among the people. They took shovels and pretended to be working in the fields. 'And as soon as you're gone, they throw away the shovels', he said.

'That's what insurgents do', said the Colonel, 'but with your help, the NDS (the National Directorate of Security – Afghan intelligence) and fingerprinting equipment I'll soon have … we'll be able to see if these people have fired a weapon and if they are locals or Punjabis, Pakistanis or Chechens.' There had been intelligence reports and rumours about foreign fighters, including British Pakistanis (one with a Midlands accent), Arabs and even a sixteen-year-old female Chechen sniper.

'Between us we will sort them out', said Westley. He ended every statement with a sentence like this, always using the words 'we' or 'us'. A reminder that this was supposed to be a team effort. It was a sentiment or illusion that the Afghans didn't seem to share. They always said 'you'.

* * * * *

A few days later, after a heated argument with my Ministry of Defence minder, I attended another *shura* with some local farmers, about more civilian casualties caused by air strikes.

'Where apologies are required, they will be made', said Captain Patrick Hennessey. He was a well-spoken officer (you can usually identify a British Officer just by hearing them speak) from the Grenadier Guards, attached to the battle group commanded by Lieutenant Colonel Westley. 'Then, the process of reparations will be looked into. Compensation is a big thing in the Afghan culture, in a way that we find quite strange. There's a very clear financial compensation defined for the loss of a daughter, a son or an uncle and it's something that we will go into in this meeting in depth', he said.

The strikes had mostly been American, and been called by the Brits, but everyone defending them was from the Afghan government; the first and only time I saw any representatives from the central government in Helmand. Captain Hennessey and an American soldier – who'd appeared from nowhere – sat at the back of the room but were soon fast asleep in their plastic chairs.

An official, the head of the anti-crime department of the Gereshk district police, stood up to speak. A small man, with a neatly-cropped beard that had started to turn grey, he was as emotional as the men he addressed and struggled not to break down. 'The ISAF operations are not useful', he said. 'They leave and the Taliban come back, so we will always have these problems. Local commanders, ex-Mujahadeen, can establish security, not outsiders. They are indiscriminate. They see no difference between women and children and the Taliban.' His finger trembled as he raised it in emphasis. I thought he was going over the top, trying to let everyone know that he empathised with them. But then I realised that he too had lost several family members to an air strike. 'You can ask anyone about how honestly I have served the government and if I have any links with the Taliban', he said, almost in tears. 'But they have hit me so hard that I am stunned. What can I do? I have lost four of my brothers. How can I look after their families now?'

Neither the other officials nor the farmers reacted. The fact that this had happened to a senior government official surprised no one. 'After the bombing, no ground troops came out at all. They could have come but no one did. I don't have anything else to say, my only request is that in future operations, civilian casualties should be prevented', he said, although the only two people in the room with any connection to air strikes were fast asleep.

The elders raged about the bombings, saying that the Taliban were often far away by the time the bombs were dropped, that security was getting worse and that people would soon start joining the Taliban. 'Life has no meaning for me any more', said one man, 'I have lost twenty-seven members of my family. My house has been destroyed. Everything I've built for seventy years is gone.'

Metal containers were brought in, placed on tables and opened. The elders were given bricks of five hundred Afghani notes, signing for them by dipping their right thumbs in ink and making fingerprints. Captain Hennessey thought that millions of dollars were being handed over: $100,000 per person killed. The actual amount was closer to $2000. The men were told the money had come from the president himself. As he handed it out, the ANA commander said, 'May God give you the fortitude to bear this and protect you from such sorrows in the future.'

The money, a huge amount in Helmand, was handed out in front of the Afghan National Police. I worried that the men (who carried the money wrapped in sheets and would bury it somewhere in their compounds) might soon be receiving another unwelcome visit.

Afterwards, I spoke to some of the men who had received compensation.

'I lost twenty people and I was given two million Afghanis [about $46,000]' said one man, explaining what had happened. 'It was before 12.30 at night when your forces came to our area. They were involved in a fight but the Taliban retreated. I had put everyone, all the family and the children, into one room but after the fighting was over we brought them outside to their beds. Later, a jet came and dropped bombs on our house. Two rooms were destroyed. In one of the rooms, my two nephews and my son were there. My son survived. I rescued him from the debris. In the other room were six of my uncle's family. All became martyrs. They were buried under the soil. I moved the children away and came back to rescue those under the debris. While we were trying to do that, the children were so frightened they started running away. The plane shot them one by one.

'All we want is security, whether you bring it or the Taliban. We are not supporting war. We support peace and security. If you bring peace and security you are my king. If they bring security they are our kings. I want nothing. I don't want a post in the government. All I want is to be able to move around.

'I was given this money for the martyrs but it means nothing to me. I wouldn't give one person for all the money I've been given. I'm grateful that the president has paid attention to us but if you gave someone the whole world it wouldn't bring a person back.'

He was in tears by the time he'd finished speaking. I couldn't ask him any more questions.

CHAPTER 2

A week later, I awoke at 5.30 a.m. to go on a reconnaissance patrol with the Grenadier Guards into the upper Gereshk valley. The valley is part of what's called the Green Zone, a narrow strip of some of the most fertile land in Afghanistan. It follows the Helmand River from the Hindu Kush all the way to Iran. In contrast to its fortified Baghdad namesake, the Helmand Green Zone is where most of the fighting takes place. Its irrigation ditches, hedgerows and high-walled compounds are perfect for guerrilla warfare and the Taliban had created a network of trenches, tunnels, booby traps and weapons caches. The American Special Forces called it the 'Heart of Darkness' but its neatly arranged green fields, thick bushes and hedgerows make it look oddly like the English countryside.

The patrol was to a village, Zumbelay, from where six families had recently fled, saying they'd been forced out by fifteen Taliban fighters. After walking less than a kilometre, we saw other villagers running away. This usually means they know there are Taliban close by and there will soon be fighting. Suddenly, a single shot ripped the air around us. Then came dozens more, so loud and so fast that it felt as if we were being attacked from every tree and bush in sight. I lay down in the grass next to Glenn Snazle, whose bulk, tattoos and cleanly-shaved head made him look like a classic sergeant major. An awful burst of popping filled the air above our heads. That isn't the sound of guns being fired. It's the noise of bullets breaking the sound barrier. It's a sound you're never supposed to hear, because it means you're far too close. I gripped the earth with both hands as if it that might lessen the impact of being shot.

Four or five RPGs (rocket-propelled grenades) whooshed over our heads, sometimes exploding, sometimes sinking into the wet mud around us. We ran to one side and crouched next to a wall. An RPG exploded on the exact spot where we had been lying. Some of the Afghan and British soldiers charged towards the direction of the gunfire and soon there was so much noise it was impossible to tell who was firing what and at who. Two bullets hit the wall next to us with such velocity that we instinctively flinched. I heard someone report a casualty over the radio; an Afghan soldier, with a three-inch hole in the back of his neck, staggered past supported by two of his colleagues.

The Taliban were attacking from three positions and trying to get another group to move west, to surround us. ('They draw you in, then the horns of the bull come down on either side of you', is how one soldier described the tactic.) We heard a series of howls, followed by deep thudding booms. I was told these were Chinese 107 rockets, being fired from yet another position. There was an awful wait as the rockets arched through the air, then landed hundreds of metres beyond where we crouched.

After almost an hour, I heard an F16 fighter jet roaring towards us. 'That is the sweetest sound in the world', said the heavily-sweating soldier next to me. I saw the underside of the plane, white like a shark's, as it passed overhead and fired missiles into a building a hundred metres or so ahead. Everyone went quiet as they waited to see if the missile strike had been accurate. The Taliban were also quiet, either because they were desperately trying to find a ditch to dive into or because they'd been killed. Air strikes were called for with few restrictions, so the mere presence of planes or helicopters in the air – a show of force, as it was called – was often enough to scare the Taliban into retreating.

Everyone was ordered to start moving back, believing that eighteen Taliban had been killed, mostly by the air strike. Lance Corporal Jack Mizon and Lance Sergeant Jason McDonald, who had charged forwards with the ANA, re-appeared, soaked in sweat and bouncing with adrenaline. 'It was a bit too close with the RPGs whizzing over the wall', said McDonald, with a humble, gap-toothed smile. The ANA also re-appeared, some sprinting in all directions and others standing still, in plain sight of the remaining enemy fighters who had tried to flank us. 'Get them shaken out into a defensive posture, get a grip of these fucking idiots', screamed Major Martin David.

'One of them was stood up', said McDonald, 'when there was RPGs winging straight over our heads. I was on my belt buckle and he was stood up, eating an apple and laughing at us.'

'Very good soldier, my soldier very good', said the ANA's commanding officer, almost singing with laughter as we pulled back. I hadn't seen him since, on the way in, he'd made one of his soldiers carry him over a stream so that he didn't get his boots wet.

When we got back to the patrol base, the ANA found the Taliban's frequency on their radios and listened to them talk (this is called 'i-comm chatter'). Anyone with a normal CB radio could listen in as they were doing. I heard such ridiculous things – four hundred fighters are about to storm the base! We have taken forty casualties in the ditch! Thirty suicide bombers are about to detonate themselves! – that I assumed the Taliban knew they were being listened to and were being deliberately misleading. But i-comm chatter was treated as if it were the most sophisticated covert surveillance, so secret and so valuable that if I ever mentioned it I'd be aiding the enemy. The ANA either hadn't got that message or were ignoring it, as they immediately started talking back, taunting the Taliban about the battle they had just lost.

'Come back to the same place tomorrow without the planes and helicopters and we'll show you a fight!' replied the Taliban.

'We'll kick your ass the same way', said one ANA soldier, causing the others to roar with laughter. 'And fuck your mother.'

The Brits weren't so jubilant. They carried the heavy equipment back to the base. They knew that the ground they'd just cleared would have to be fought for again.

* * * * *

The fighting in Zumbelay was part of an effort to expand a relatively secure area, optimistically designated the 'Afghan Development Zone'. It formed a triangle between Gereshk, Lashkar Gar
(the provincial capital), and Camp Bastion, the huge and rapidly-
expanding British base, complete with landing strip, safely
positioned in the Helmand desert. As part of a wider policy, the
'comprehensive approach', this area was supposed to be the focus
of an intense nation-building and reconstruction (or construction, as some soldiers were quick to point out) effort. It was hoped
this effort would quickly convince the local population that the
Afghan government, with the 'support' (no one was allowed to say
the effort was British- or American-led) of the international community, could provide a much better way of life than the Taliban.
The local people would then side with the central government and
reject the Taliban, making it impossible for them to operate. It was
classic counter-insurgency, called 'draining the swamp', or 'hearts
and minds' in past campaigns, although to find an example that
actually worked, you had to go back over sixty years.

The comprehensive approach looked perfectly feasible in a
PowerPoint presentation, when the beneficiaries, who weren't consulted, were viewed as automata. When applied to an actual soci-
ety, especially one as fragmented, traumatised and complicated as
Helmand's, it rarely lasted longer than the first ten minutes of a
shura. An anthropologist would struggle to understand the competing interests of local power-brokers, often motivated by long-
running tribal, political and drug-trafficking rivalries. A few seemed
to understand but the security situation meant that they were rarely,
if ever, there when they were needed. Instead, soldiers had to do
what they could.

To begin to understand how hard it was for the British to attempt
to carry out this policy, imagine an Indian dropped into Chicago, or
a Brazilian dropped into Islamabad. Imagine asking them, without
speaking the language or having any idea who to trust, to create,
staff and monitor an entirely new system of government. What's
more, imagine asking them to do this within six months, while

13

fighting a war and after having killed several hundred civilians by mistake.

And this task had fallen to soldiers, untrained for many of the roles they were asked to perform, because so few people from the Department For International Development (DFID) or the Foreign Office ever set foot in Helmand. This surely guaranteed it could never succeed. It could only have had any chance of succeeding if it was truly Afghan-led. And led by the right Afghans, which it certainly was not.

When I asked soldiers about the comprehensive approach, I often had to start by explaining what it was. I never got an answer that wasn't full of scorn or sarcasm. One lieutenant colonel said that if I saw any of the Foreign Office or DFID individuals in charge of all this reconstruction, would I please point them out to him, because he hadn't seen any.

I joined Lieutenant Colonel Westley a few days later for another *shura*. Among the many problems being addressed was a hospital whose generators had stopped because they had run out of diesel fuel, even though the director had been given the authority to order more whenever he needed it.

'The point is this, Mr Mayor. Forgive me, but you need to tell the director of the hospital that he needs to take control of this issue. He was at this meeting a week ago and he has done nothing about it.'

'What size shoes does he take?' the Colonel asked, gesturing towards the Mayor. There was confusion. 'I'm going to give him a pair of these boots' – he tapped his army-issue boots a few times – 'so he can go and kick the hospital director up the ass and tell him to start doing his job.' Everyone laughed.

The Mayor suggested that he should get a shirt and tie, so he could do his job properly too.

'You must not lose your character, your turban and your *shalwar shameez* (sic) you must not lose …', said the Colonel insistently, not realising that the Mayor had also been joking.

There were other problems. There were far more police on the payroll than actually existed. Some of those that did exist had been found setting up unofficial checkpoints where they taxed locals until they had enough money to get high. The British police officers (all six of them) who were training the ANP told me they had pulled up at one checkpoint to find a fifteen-year-old with an AK-47 in charge, while the actual policeman lay nearby in an opium-induced coma. Stories of young boys being abducted and raped were common. 'Ninety per cent of crime in Helmand is committed by the police', I was told by one of the British police mentors.

I followed Lieutenant Colonel Westley and the Mayor on a tour of Gereshk, the second-biggest town in Helmand. As our convoy pulled on to the main road, the top gunner put his hand in the air, stopping all oncoming traffic. 'Dominate, dominate, dominate', said one of the soldiers in the vehicle, 'don't let these fuckers in.' As we drove on, all oncoming traffic was waved to the side of the road until we'd passed. The gunner waved furiously at every vehicle until it pulled off the road. 'It's just a measure against any vehicle-borne IEDs', he said. 'Sometimes we have to use mini-flares, which we fire about ten feet in front of the vehicles. That generally does the trick.'

We pulled up to a two-storey, U-shaped structure that was going to be a police station. Lieutenant Colonel Westley was happy. 'It looks like there's some development going on here already', he said energetically. Other projects had stalled because contractors had been intimidated. At least one had been murdered.

'We are building a new jail too and soon a court', said the Mayor.

'This is really important stuff for what we call security sector reform', said Westley. 'You'll have the police, the NDS, the police checkpoints, the jail and the courthouse in the same area. It means we can have a proper process of law.'

The NDS was established during the Russian occupation and modelled on the KGB. They had an awful reputation for torture and murder, often of tribal or drug-trafficking rivals. To describe them, the police and their checkpoints as a proper process of law was astounding.

Lieutenant Colonel Westley kept on talking and asking questions enthusiastically, as if he were being conducted on a tour of the Mayor's brilliant development projects. He offered the Mayor a stage but the Mayor was not willing to take it and rarely even spoke. 'And this fits in with our overall plan that we're looking for in Gereshk, doesn't it?' asked the Colonel.

'We need a fark too', said Lucky the terp, translating what the Mayor said.

'A fark? What's a fark?' asked the Colonel, baffled.

'A fark, with grass and trees.'

'A park, Lucky, with a P.'

The police station stood alone on a barren patch of ground. Inside, the contractor complained that he hadn't yet been paid. We looked at a cluster of compounds in the distance. Most were hidden behind high grey walls but one seemed deliberately designed to ridicule the tradition of privacy. It rose high above its surrounding walls and was elaborately decorated, with brightly-coloured tiles and roof slates. It looked like a Chinese restaurant designed by Liberace.

'Who owns that rather grand building over there?' asked the Colonel.

'It's government land that we handed over to the people', said the Mayor, wearily. Garish palaces like this one, often owned by drug lords were usually referred to as 'narco-tecture'.

The Mayor had to be asked three times who owned the building.

'Haji Amidullah', he eventually said.

'And what does he do?'

'He's a shopkeeper', said the Mayor.

'A very wealthy shopkeeper', said Lieutenant Colonel Westley, looking at him cynically. There was a long pause.

'He has much poppy', the Mayor finally conceded.

'Much poppy, interesting', said Westley. 'Are you going to show me where the park's going to be?'

The Mayor pointed to a row of houses that had been flattened. 'These people made a protest and complaint against me to the Governor. He moved me to Lashkar Gar and I was there for three months. When I came back, the people approached me and said they have no more problems.' The obvious implication was that the houses had been demolished in retaliation for the protests but Lieutenant Colonel Westley didn't press the point, perhaps thinking that things like that would stop once 'security sector reform' was complete.

'It's a really exciting future that you are driving here for the people of Gereshk', said Lieutenant Colonel Westley. 'The time is just right, now, Mayor Ali Shah. You have the people behind you. We'll deal with the Taliban and keep them away. We can work with you but this is your vision. This is your ...' He struggled to find the right word. 'This is your thing that you are giving to Gereshk.'

We drove to the NDS headquarters, a row of rooms along the back wall of a yard that wasn't fit for animals. Outside the gate – or rather the gap between two walls where there should have been a gate – lay a large pile of used hypodermic needles. A short old man, in police trousers pulled up above his huge belly by braces, walked up and stared at us, as if he wasn't sure we were real. Even Lieutenant Colonel Westley's enthusiasm was dimmed. It was, he said, 'dire'. But he still believed it was possible to turn things around. 'There is a firm belief that Afghanistan can be won. It isn't by any means a hopeless cause. The people believe in us being here. And most of my soldiers, if they were honest, would say they would rather be in Afghanistan than Iraq. I think it has a future.'

* * * * *

Just north of Gereshk, the Brits had established a row of three small patrol bases on top of a Russian-built trench system that straddled the Green Zone, forming the only visible front line I'd seen in Afghanistan. Three days before I arrived, a car bomb had been detonated close to the patrol bases. When a motorcyclist got too close to the burning vehicle, he'd been shot dead. One of the soldiers admitted the man hadn't been a suicide bomber and hadn't been carrying weapons but he also said that he was probably up to no good anyway and may have been a dicker: a spotter for the

Taliban. Anyone who stood and watched, especially someone with a mobile phone, was suspected of being a dicker. Most people stood and watched when convoys passed and many had mobile phones.

A few hours before I arrived, the ANA had seen a man creeping around in some nearby abandoned houses. They were well on the way to beating him to death when a British soldier intervened and told them to arrest the man and take him to the main base for questioning. They agreed. But then they dragged him a bit further away and, I was told, 'no one was quite sure what happened after that'. The sentence was delivered with such an intentional lack of conviction that it was clear everyone knew exactly what had happened. I climbed up into a watchtower and asked the ANA soldier on guard what they had done with the man. He drew his finger across his throat and laughed.

Later, one British soldier told me that the man had been executed but another said he'd been taken to the nearest base and arrested. The soldiers were in an awkward position, eager to tell you what they knew but nervous about getting into trouble. The Ministry of Defence had a huge 'Media Ops' team who schooled soldiers in what to say. They issued 'LTTs': lines to take when speaking to journalists. You can soon recognise the LTTs within few words, especially on big issues like equipment, morale and civilian casualties. They are predictable and banal and most soldiers visibly flinched when they said them. Often, when the camera is off and the notepad is packed away, they'll say: 'and now I'll tell you the truth'.

Jacko, a platoon sergeant from the Worcestershire and Sherwood Foresters, led me along the top of the old trenches. We looked into the green zone and its many hiding places. 'It hasn't been touched for twenty-five years', he said. 'The Paras and Marines didn't push into it. No one's been in there since the Russians.' Jacko was typical of the Non-Commissioned Officers (NCOs) I met in Helmand province. Brave and honest, he couldn't take himself too seriously even when he described the night he was shot in the back and was saved by a radio battery he was carrying.

I noticed a bayonet strapped to his body armour and asked, half jokingly, if he'd ever had to attach it. 'It's come to the point once or twice where we've had to fix bayonets', he said, smiling, 'because it's been that close with the enemy.'

I sat down next to young private, Paserelli, who'd been keeping watch while Jacko and I spoke. He told me he'd lost two friends already, one nearby and another in Lashkar Gar. I asked if he thought the mission was worth dying for. 'I don't think it is, personally. Being out here is just a job. It doesn't really feel right losing a mate to a country that, to be honest with you, I don't really care about. It's never had any effect on my life.' His attitude had only changed when his friend was killed. 'It gave me a bit of a boost, thinking "right, the fucking bastards have shot my mate, so we're gonna go and get stuck in so he didn't die for nothing".'

CHAPTER 3

In the few weeks I'd been in Helmand there had been increasing talk among the soldiers about a big operation that was coming up. Most of the battle group was about to enter the Green Zone or block escape routes from it. Then, they had to not only clear it but to hold a large section, including several villages north of Gereshk.

Jacko and his men had a brief morale boost when four Mastiffs – huge bomb-proof trucks – arrived. The Mastiffs were as big, safe and expensive as the trucks the Americans drove. But when they realised the trucks only carried eight men, that only four (of the sixteen ordered) had arrived and that anyway, they were too big and heavy to be taken into the Green Zone, their spirits sank back. One of the soldiers whose tent I shared nicknamed the mission 'Operation Certain Death'. My legs and genitals felt hopelessly fragile as I constantly imagined how easily they could be separated from my body if I stepped on an IED.

Simon Butt was the Worcestershire and Sherwood Foresters Company Commander; a bear of a man who looked like he'd just played a series of particularly tough rugby matches. Simon told me that RPGs, mortars and bullets weren't a major worry, because you can do something about them. But everyone feared the IEDs (improvised explosive devices), which were scattered over the Green Zone. He'd also had intelligence reports about five suicide bombers – two Afghans and three Pakistanis – thought to be walking around Gereshk wearing explosive belts.

Simon had already lost a few men but as Company Commander, couldn't be seen to grieve. He said that had to wait until he got home. And when he did, the first thing he had to do was meet the families of his men who had been killed. When Simon spoke, his eyes didn't leave mine for a second and I don't remember seeing him blink. He said there were teenage soldiers in his company, on their first tour of duty, who had already killed twenty men. That, he said, is called 'growing up fast'.

* * * * *

Before the big operation, I managed to meet a unit of twelve men from the Queen's Company, the Grenadier Guards. The Guards, who had the reputation of being one of the last relics of the British class system, were sometimes unfairly dismissed as being better suited to performing ceremonial duties outside Buckingham Palace in their red tunics and bearskin caps, rather than fighting. These Guards were living with the ANA, sleeping in cots under mosquito nets, in a small and decrepit base built by the Russians in the 1980s. They formed an OMLT (Omelette – Operational Mentor and Liaison Team), tasked with training a unit of Afghan soldiers, whom they described as 'below average students'. Sitting on a wooden bench and encouraged by each other's laughter, they talked on, until they had left me with an image of the ANA as a heavily-armed, badly-dressed version of the Keystone Kops. On drugs.

The ANA were exceptionally brave, said the Guards, often sprinting towards the Taliban when they attacked but showing no interest in any other aspect of soldiering, sleeping through their shifts on watch, and often stoned. The national desertion rate was around twenty per cent but according to Sherard Cowper-Coles, the former British Ambassador to Afghanistan, was as high as sixty per cent in those deployed to Helmand. New recruits were put on buses before they were told where they were going.

The Afghan troops often watched the British showering and openly engaged in varying levels of camp or homosexual behaviour on what had become known as 'man love Thursdays'.

('Thursday night is the start of the weekend, so it's a party', explained an Afghan friend.) Cultural sensitivity training had told the Brits not to let the ANA see their men's magazines, for fear of causing offence. But the ANA begged for them and often only worked if they were bribed with 'sexy mags' like *Nuts*, *Zoo* or *FHM*. Just before I arrived they had been told to stop smoking weed, so they sat in a circle, piled their stashes in one big heap and set it on fire, inhaling the fumes. When they were caught, one of them ran outside and tried to escape in a jeep; he was so stoned he reversed into a canal instead.

* * * * *

A few nights before the operation, I was drinking tea outside the Naafi (a British services shop) when a young soldier sat down and introduced himself. His eyes were glazed and he swayed slightly, struggling to stay upright. I thought he was stoned, or drunk, looking to start a confrontation. But he just said, 'I'm scared.' I told him he'd be lying or mad if he thought otherwise but my words carried no impact. He said that on the last big operation, his friend, lying next to him, was shot through the eye and died instantly. The attack was so heavy that no one could move, so he had to stay there, next to his dead friend, for an entire hour.

'I hate my job. I can't function, can't sleep and I'm totally scared about this big op coming up.' He had just turned eighteen and this was his first tour. One of his superiors had reluctantly agreed to let him see a psychiatrist – but made it clear that if he was lying about his condition he'd be crawling around the camp until his hands and knees bled. The soldier, who was still just a boy, told me he was praying for malaria or a bullet in the foot so that he could go home.

After dinner that night the fire alarm went off but as we got up to leave there came an order to sit down again. Lieutenant Colonel Westley appeared at the front of the tent and announced that Captain Sean Dolan, his close friend, had been killed. He had been on attachment with American troops and had taken a direct hit from a Taliban mortar.

I walked outside and shuffled about on the black plastic decking, not quite knowing what to do with myself. Afghan workers, in Kellog, Brown and Root t-shirts, lowered the flags. 'Those fucking flags spend more time at half-mast than they do up', said one soldier as he walked past.

The flags stayed at half-mast the following day. The Grenadier Guards I'd spent the night with had been hit by a suicide bomber as they drove back to Gereshk. One of them had been killed and four injured. The bomber had wrapped the explosives on his body with newspaper, glue and hundreds of ball-bearings the size of marbles, making himself into a human cannon as well as a bomb. The stumps of his legs landed twenty metres apart on the road, together with his entire jaw, including his beard.

The bomber had leapt on to the vehicle from behind a fruit and vegetable stall, giving the gunner no time to shoot. Company Sergeant Major Simon Edgell and Lance Corporal Jack Mizon had been in the only other vehicle. They'd had to treat the casualties themselves. 'Sergeant Dave Wilkinson died straight away', said Mizon, 'and Lance Sergeant Shadrake got a piece of shrapnel in his neck. But there was five casualties. One bloke had a head wound, someone lost his ear and Sergeant Jason McDonald had lacerations to his neck and his back. So there's two of us dealing with five casualties and then we started taking small arms fire. We managed to get them on in the end. But Dave didn't make it.' Locals, he said, stood by and watched them struggle. The small arms fire may have been ammunition boxes catching fire in the jeep.

I said that the intelligence reports of the five suicide bombers in Gereshk must have been correct. 'What reports?' Mizon said. Nobody had told the Grenadier Guards.

Later that evening, as I sat on a trestle bench with the other Grenadiers, a truck dumped the charred carcass of the WMIK on the ground. Soldiers in rubber gloves pulled the kit out of the jeep and laid it on the floor. Most of it was burnt black and soaked in what I guessed was blood. Sergeant Simon Alexander, who'd arrived at the scene soon after the attack, walked towards us. I tried to think of something to say but as we'd only just met I decided to keep quiet. None of the Grenadiers around me said anything either. Simon could see we were all uncomfortable and he reassured us. 'Don't worry, boys, everything's normal, we're fine', he said. And walked into the Naafi to buy a cup of coffee.

The burnt-out skeleton of the WMIK jeep didn't look that different to a brand-new one. WMIKs are old, roofless Land Rovers with machine-guns attached. Their only armour is a patchwork of small bomb-proof mats spread across the floor and seats. The bodies and heads of those inside are totally exposed. Tony Blair described them as 'the army that gets whatever it wants and needs' but I watched soldiers laying Kevlar plates from their body armour on to the floor of their WMIKs for a little extra protection. The Americans, whose smallest vehicles were heavily-armoured Humvees (and even these were soon to be restricted to bases or given to the ANA, because they weren't considered safe enough) think the Brits are insane for going out in vehicles that belong on small English farms. As the suicide bomber had shown, if you aren't killed in a WMIK, you will almost certainly be maimed.

One of the soldiers looked at the burnt-out WMIK. 'I wish everyone could form a line', he said, 'and march through the Green Zone annihilating everything in sight and burning down entire sympathiser villages, Vietnam style.'

Later that day, we drove in convoy along the same stretch of road, past the black patch left by the suicide bomber. Nobody spoke. In every vehicle, a soldier on a raised passenger seat held a rifle. Behind them stood gunners controlling fifty cal machine-guns. All scanned the locals as we passed, as if any one could be one of the remaining four suicide bombers. Company Sergeant Major Glenn Snazle, the gunner in the jeep behind mine, also carried a pistol in his right hand, which he pointed outwards as he swivelled around in the gun turret. Oncoming cars were waved to the side of the road with an aggressiveness I hadn't seen before. It was easy to see how a few deaths on both sides could destroy any chance of the counter-insurgency policy succeeding and turn the campaign into a fight for survival and revenge. It may well already have reached that point. It was certainly hard to see how to win hearts and minds when anyone who got too close was shot.

After fifteen minutes the tension eased slightly as the convoy pulled off the main road and drove across the desert back towards the base. I heard Michael Jackson's *Billie Jean* playing from the driver's iPod speakers. As we pulled up to the ANA checkpoint, Michael Jackson was drowned out by the trance music blaring from their stereo. As we entered the base, the soldiers un-cocked their weapons. The ANA's music faded away and the driver's iPod, now playing *Show Me Heaven* by Maria McKee, came back.

*   *   *   *   *

That night, there was a final briefing in the dining tent about the operation to clear and hold a stretch of the Green Zone. No soldiers from the ANA were invited and no paperwork was allowed to leave the tent. The t-shirt of the soldier in front of me read, 'God may forgive the Taliban. Mortars will make the appointment'.

Lieutenant Colonel Westley reminded everyone what they were supposed to be doing. 'In its wider context, this is about setting enhanced security. We need to go in and defeat the enemy in the upper Gereshk valley, so that the townspeople's confidence is bolstered and we can get on with our core job; development, reconstruction and reassuring the people that the government of Afghanistan is the way ahead and it is their future.'

The ANA weren't briefed about the operation until the day before it was launched. Even then, they were only told to be ready to leave the base at 4 p.m., in the hope that they might be ready by five. They weren't told where they were going. 'Otherwise they'll get on the phone and tell everyone they know', said Company Sergeant Major Glenn Snazle. I asked if that might include the Taliban. 'Some of their loyalties are in the wrong place. We just have to keep an eye on it', he replied. I asked if they'd shared information with the Taliban before. Snazle smiled. 'They have. They've been disciplined, kicked out and probably then gone and joined the Taliban.'

Snazle had given the ANA Sergeant Major a list of things he needed to do, including bringing water and a fuel truck. As four o' clock approached, it was clear the list had been ignored. 'As long as they've got ammunition that's all they give a shit about', he said.

'We try to make them feel like they have an input', said Sergeant Simon Alexander, 'and one day they'll come up with a plan themselves.' I looked at him quizzically. 'One day it might happen, we'll have to wait and see', he said, laughing. 'Do you think that will happen in your tour?' I asked. He laughed some more. 'No', he said firmly.

'They're very bright and colourful; it's a wonderful sight. They're a very visual army', said Major David. 'Today is the first time in weeks they've been on time because they're know they're going for a scrap.' He was also optimistic about the operation. 'With this amount of manpower we aim to destroy the enemy and take the ground this time, not cede it like before. This will be the first time for two months that we're actually going in to take and hold ground.'

Sergeant Alexander, like most of the NCOs, was unable to lie about the way things were. 'When the ANA are excited, they're very brave. But it only lasts about two days and then they get bored. They're like children – their attention doesn't last long.'

As the ANA were ordered into formation, someone started blowing a whistle. 'It's the easiest way to control them. It's like being at school', said Alexander.

I said it looked like a chaotic start.

'This is good!' he said, lighting another cigarette. 'This is fucking squared away, they've got vehicles and everything. We're happy.'

The ANA had been issued with helmets and body armour but only a few wore either. They preferred baseball caps, brightly-coloured bandanas hanging down to their hips, sunglasses, and orange and pink tie-dyed t-shirts. They drove unarmoured pick-up trucks with fifty cal machine-guns on the back and dozens of rockets jutting from every available space like golf clubs. Huge photos and murals were taped to the middle of their windscreens, often portraits of dead colleagues or idyllic mountain scenes. More than anything else, they displayed huge portraits of Massoud, the 'Lion of Panjshir'. Massoud is a hero to many around the world for his for his brilliance as a guerrilla commander during the Soviet invasion. But within Afghanistan he is hated as much as he is loved, especially by those who lived through the indiscriminate shelling of Kabul in the early nineties.

Afghanistan has been in various states of civil war for over thirty years. Although the sides and alliances have changed more times than it is possible for outsiders to comprehend, the fighting mostly has been between the ethnic groups of the north – the Northern Alliance – led by Massoud, and the Pashtuns of the south. Not all Pashtuns are Taliban but most of the Taliban are Pashtun. When the Taliban first swept to power, largely because they seemed to be an answer to the barbarism of the civil war and the corruption of the warlords, only Massoud resisted. Just a few years later, after September 11th, 2001, the Northern Alliance swept the Taliban from power, aided by American airpower. Massoud had been assassinated by Al-Qaeda two days earlier, on September 9th. There was no reconciliation after the fall of the Taliban. The southern Pashtuns watched aghast as the same old warlords and corrupt officials appeared again. There had been great hope that the outside world would deliver something much better.

So an army carrying Massoud's image everywhere didn't look anything like the national army it was supposed to be; more like the *Shura-i-Nazar* (Massoud's band); the Northern Alliance back in power and looking for vengeance. The vast majority of the ANA soldiers came from northern Afghanistan and spoke Dari rather than Pashtu. Its leadership was dominated by the northern ethnic groups, particularly Tajiks. Pashtuns from elsewhere in Afghanistan sometimes joined up but estimates of the numbers of southern Pashtuns hovered between two and three per cent. Even then, they often left, after their families were threatened.

Early on, there was a realistic hope that our intervention would put an end to the civil war. Instead, desperate for their support, we handed control of the police, army and intelligence services to the Northern Alliance. I suspect our efforts were doomed from that point. The very people we were trying to win over and persuade to pick sides would think that the civil war was very much an ongoing event and that we were fighting on behalf of the other side.

* * * * *

For the unit of the Grenadier Guards I was accompanying. the aim of the operation was to clear and hold the village of Kakaran. The area had been fought for three times but never held; there had never been enough manpower. At the same time, the Worcestershire and Sherwood Foresters were to clear and hold Rahim Kalay, to the north-east of Kakaran, overlooking the Green Zone. The two forces would then work together to clear the ground between them, moving the front line forward by about six kilometres. Other British forces would do the same from Sangin, about twenty miles up the Green Zone, and everyone would meet somewhere in between, flushing the Taliban out completely. This was the planned strategy across Helmand: clear, hold and build. But so far, it had never got much beyond clearing and holding; and rarely beyond clearing.

The Grenadier Guards drove in a huge arc across the Helmand desert, hoping to get into position without being seen, or blown up. We entered the Green Zone as the sun was setting, driving down a straight road that ran alongside a canal on our way to a small forward operating base. We passed a truck full of young men and several groups of children, who shouted 'hello, hello, hello', as we went by. On the other side of the canal, men on motorbikes drove slowly by. There was no chance our arrival hadn't been noticed.

At the patrol base, we were told to get a few hours' sleep, resting on the sand and gravel outside. At 2 a.m., we got up, crammed what we could into backpacks and walked into the Green Zone. Within minutes, we heard an explosion. A mine had struck one of the Worcester and Sherwood Foresters's vehicles but no one had been hurt. It was still dark as the Grenadier Guards crept through the fields that surrounded Kakaran, talking little, and then only in whispers. As we entered the village at dawn, it was clear that every compound had been abandoned, very recently. Piles of dried poppies lay all around, their bulbs marked with the rows of diagonal incisions that allowed the opium to ooze out and be scraped off.

'By and large, because this area has seen a lot of fighting, many families have moved out', said Major David. 'This is bad news, because it means we're not achieving the effect we're hoping for, which is to bring security. But hopefully after a few days we'll have taken this area properly and sent a message that people can move back.'

It seemed to be assumed that the owners of the houses had fled a long time ago and that anyone who'd been there recently was squatting. I didn't know if this was true or if it just made the soldiers feel better about rifling through abandoned homes. 'Either they're brilliant liars or the whole compound ownership thing is a very fluid concept', said Captain Paddy Hennessey. 'Because whenever you go into a compound, the people there never own that one; they're always friends of the owners.' Denial of ownership, he said, usually comes after weapons, mines or opium have been found. 'Of course, then, if you say "so you won't mind if I take this?", a different story emerges.'

I asked Sergeant Alexander what he thought the Taliban were doing. 'They saw us arrive last night, they've watched us all morning. They'll pull back to a line and if they're determined, they'll spank us there.' I asked him if he thought the Taliban could ever be made to give up. 'No, they won't, 'cause that's not in their nature. That's Islamic extremists for you. They'll switch to an Iraq situation, using IEDs. Obviously, the advantage we've got at the moment is that it's a stand-up fight, which we'll win every time. We're better-trained, better-equipped and we've got more fire-power. When they start getting the IED technology from Iraq, then you're digging in, you're entrenched.'

As I sat, leaning up against a mud wall, it was easy to forget that the Taliban were probably watching us and getting ready to attack. Water trickled past in sparkling streams, birds sang, houses shone in the dawn sun and perfectly-ripe bunches of grapes hung from verandahs. Gereshk and the Green Zone were once part of the hippy trail; I could easily imagine Dennis Hopper lookalikes laughing, smoking weed and listening to Jimi Hendrix on portable cassettes. 'It's paradise-like. Lush green vegetation, vegetables and fruit growing in abundance, idyllic little compounds. It's lovely', said Major David.

It was eight o'clock by the time we reached the other side of the village and nothing had happened. The sun wasn't yet scorching and I was enjoying a ludicrously false sense of security. Suddenly, a single shot was fired, close by. An interpreter raised his radio in the air. 'They are about to attack. They are getting ready for attack.'

'To attack us, here?' I asked. He nodded. 'Do you know where they are?'

'No, their location is not known.'

'Are they close?'

'Yes', he said.

The ANA spotted some Taliban fighters and called for their rocket man; every Afghan unit has a rocket man. This one emerged from the trees and jogged towards us, his rocket launcher slung over his shoulder in a bright pink sheet. This meant most of the right side of his body was also bright pink. This seemed to strike no one but me as odd, even though he was about to step into the open and fire a rocket at Taliban fighters thought to be fewer than a hundred metres away.

I followed Captain Patrick Hennessey as one of the ANA led him to the end of a long wall, with piles of harvested poppies stacked against it. The ANA soldier pointed to two men he had spotted carrying weapons. The rocket man loaded his weapon and got down on one knee. Captain Hennessey told him to wait. From behind the wall, he spoke into his radio.

'Possible positive identification of two times Taliban. Am preparing to engage with RPG. Can you confirm they are not the friendly forces mentioned earlier? Over.' He listened. 'Roger. We're going to engage with RPG, see if it provokes a response and if so assault that enemy position, over.'

Rocket man walked forward, knelt, and fired. We looked for any signs of movement. A few ANA soldiers were ordered to run beyond the wall, into the trees, to provide cover for an assault on the Taliban position. The terp heard a Taliban commander telling his men to stay in position and wait for the advance. '*Glea*-ming', said Captain Hennessey, as he was given permission to call an air strike on to the fighters. Rocket man reloaded his launcher, eager to fire again.

The Taliban were in a ditch, in front of a building about sixty metres to our right. Captain Hennessey struggled to identify the building on his map. 'See this tree? Taliban is behind', said Sergeant Syed Meeraj, a small, lean man with slightly oriental features, a moustache and a sparkling skullcap. Even when he smiled and joked he had an unmistakable seriousness; he was easily the most capable Afghan soldier I'd seen.

The ANA were brilliant at spotting anything slightly strange: an odd movement, a displaced piece of earth, or a suspicious piece of cloth hanging from a window. The Brits couldn't see what he was pointing at and still weren't sure which building they wanted to call the air strike on.

We heard two massive explosions on the far side of the field, nowhere near the Taliban position. Then a bullet crackled past. 'OK, that's us, that's contact', said Captain Hennessey. The explosions were RPGs, set to explode in the air above us. Soon, more bullets rattled towards us, in an accelerating rhythm, as if someone were winding a machine into life. The bullets weren't coming from the men we'd spotted but from directly ahead, making the wall we'd ducked behind useless.

'RPG fire?' asked rocket man, pointing to the gap at the end of the wall. Someone nodded. He almost skipped forwards, knelt and fired. Straightaway, he got up and ran back, only to fall to his knees, holding his ears in pain.

Sergeant Syed knelt just beyond the wall, firing single shots at a ditch, almost ninety degrees to the left of where rocket man was aiming. Captain Hennessey spoke into his radio: 'That's us now being engaged by RPG and small arms. If you could put air on it that would be lovely. Over.' He sounded as if he were about to invite the pilot over for tea and biscuits. The pilot said he could see four men in the building, identified on everyone's maps as Kilo. Rocket man slapped his ears, shaking his head to show that he was now deaf, which seemed to make him very happy.

'Five hundred pounder inbound now, everyone get their heads down', shouted Captain Hennessey.

Beyond the wall, Sergeant Syed knelt and fired a few more shots, trying to keep the Taliban where they were until the bomb landed. But the bomb wasn't dropped. 'Some muppet has decided we're too close', said Captain Hennessey.

The muppet, it transpired, albeit for the wrong reasons, had actually made the best decision of the day. Everyone had forgotten that less than two weeks earlier, twenty-five civilians had been killed when a bomb had been dropped on a compound that the Taliban were firing from. They hadn't checked then if civilians were inside the compound, because they couldn't. Just as they couldn't check now.

Sergeant Syed fired more shots, now aiming directly ahead. He stopped firing, saw movement; everyone pressed closer to the ground. The Taliban had moved into the building in front of us. We were totally exposed.

Rocket man was ordered to fire but, still deaf, didn't skip forward until Sergeant Syed pointed to the next field and the building the Taliban had moved into. Rocket man knelt to fire, forgetting we were standing behind him and would be burnt by the back-blast. Luckily, the abuse screamed by the British soldiers was so loud even he could hear it; he moved a little further away.

The soldiers were ordered to use mortars. Then a helicopter was supposed to be doing a gun run. So they were told they couldn't use mortars because they might hit the helicopter. Then they were told to use mortars first and the helicopter would follow. It seemed as though every request was denied or changed as more senior officers, further away and thinking of the bigger picture, intervened.

An explosion came from just beyond the trees in front of us. The soldiers thought it was an incoming grenade or rocket but it was actually their own mortars. Rocket man fired again, sideways. Another mortar landed uncomfortably close.

Over the terp's radio, I could hear the Taliban commander screaming. Two of the Taliban fighters had been hurt. They seemed to be still in the ditch they'd been in when we first spotted them. The mortars, fired from four kilometres away, were adjusted. They started landing closer to the injured Taliban. 'If it's within fifty metres it will pretty much rip them to pieces', someone said. They weren't landing much further than fifty metres from us.

We were ordered to get low, as another air strike had been called. Again, there was nothing. Captain Hennessey spoke into his radio, saying there was a compound south-east of our position that wasn't on his map; he thought the five Taliban were there. Four or five bullets whistled past. Sergeant Syed jerked his head backwards and to the side, like a boxer slipping a punch. 'Whoooah, where the fuck are they coming from?' said Hennessey. They certainly weren't coming from anywhere the Taliban were supposed to be. Two soldiers fired at random into the trees.

Captain Hennessey wanted two squads to charge the tree line and another two to attack the compound to our right.

'Lloydy, are you happy with the plan?' Behind us, Ryan Lloyd had arrived with two squads of British and Afghan soldiers.

'No', said Lloyd, who hadn't heard a word Captain Hennessey had said. The plan was explained again.

One group of Brits and Afghans ran forward. Another ran around the end of the wall and towards the compound on our right. There was a furious exchange of gunfire. Eventually, the sounds changed to regular bursts, coming only from the British. Then a few bullets zinged over our heads. The soldier manning the radio said there was now a third Taliban firing position, to the left of the trees.

We looked at the building from where a new group of Taliban

fighters seemed to be firing. A series of rapid thuds came from the field directly to our left, nowhere near any of the suspected firing positions. 'What the fucking hell was that?' said one of the soldiers, as a large chunk of twisted metal hit a British soldier's hand. An Apache helicopter had strafed the field next to us, nowhere near any of the possible Taliban positions. If anything, the Apache made me more nervous than the Taliban. The ANA in the trees ahead took it in turns to run out and fire. They seemed to be posing for each other as they fired, rather than actually aiming at anything.

The Taliban fire kept coming back.

I looked around the edge of the wall, to see what the Brits who had run to my right were doing. They were crouched against the outside wall of a compound, trying to call an air strike on to the Taliban position. The Apache came closer. I heard the whoosh and bang of a Hellfire missile. But nothing happened to any of the Taliban positions. I looked around the wall again. The British soldiers were staggering in different directions, almost completely obscured by dust. The compound they were leaning against had been hit, right where they were.

I heard shouting from up ahead, where the ANA were attacking the hedge. Angrily gesticulating towards the compound, they walked towards us. 'Do you speak Farsi? Tell the pilots not to bomb here. The Taliban are over there. What are the fucking British doing? They are giving me a headache. They are killing my guys', screamed Rocky, the ANA Captain, into his radio. He thought six of his men, those who had followed the Brits to the compound wall, had been killed.

I decided to join the soldiers who were about to run across the field and see what had happened.

I squatted in a ditch until there was enough covering fire to make me fairly confident the Taliban would be ducking, not shooting. But as soon as I climbed out and started running, I heard the fire-cracker sound of bullets breaking the sound barrier. Something chopped into the mud and grass around my feet. My leg disappeared into another ditch and I fell, face first, on the ground. I bounced back to my feet and ran, focusing on the compound walls ahead and the ANA soldiers behind them, waving me in, screaming: 'Come, come, come. Fast, fast, fast.' I ran as quickly as I could, imagining the impact of bullets hitting me, knocking me sideways.

I made it safely across the field. The entrance to the compound led into a small, walled garden, shaded by vines. The floor was carpeted with harvested opium poppies, in piles several feet high. Then I saw something that made my heart sink and my throat tighten. The compounds in Kakaran were supposed to be abandoned. Next to me, I saw a family of seven crouched up against the wall: an old man and six children. Three of the kids were toddlers and one was just a baby. The man seemed to be begging for mercy but no one paid him any attention. The kids were covered in dust, apart from wet patches around their mouths and eyes and tear tracks running down their cheeks. They must have been right next to the explosion when the Hellfire missile hit. It didn't matter that it could have been worse; things could always be worse. One of the interpreters did his best to calm them and tell them they were now safe. They got no reassurance from the ANA soldiers, who helped themselves to the family's grapes and lit up spliffs.

There were no ANA casualties. A single wall had separated them, and the British, from the missile strike. Close enough to make the ANA think that their colleagues had been killed.

'The tendency the ANA have is ... it's all a bit "white man magic". They absolutely love it when it's working well but when they see the other side, they get a bit shaky', said Captain Hennessey. He thought that if the Hellfire had landed just outside the compound or slightly further inside, his section or the family would have been killed. He wrote later that he was haunted by the thought of what could have been. I imagined what would have happened if the 500lb bomb he'd requested hadn't been denied.

The fighting continued for hours. Bullets bounced off the walls above our heads, seeming constantly to come from new directions. Nobody knew where to shoot, although that didn't stop the ANA, who fired wild bursts into the air. The Brits screamed at them to stop, to conserve their ammunition. 'Are they shooting *at* anything?' was the frequent question. The answer was always no.

Rocket man fired a few more RPGs at something and walked back inside. 'Taliban finish. One RPG, three Talib finished. Good', he said, re-tying his bandana and giving me the thumbs-up. But the Taliban were far from finished, spraying the building with bullets from what felt like 360 degrees.

Some soldiers shouted, 'Enemy mortars incoming'. We were ordered to spread out. But no mortars hit the compound. Most reports were wrong, or had passed through so many soldiers that they had lost all meaning. Major David asked the same question into his radio five times, seeking confirmation that the aircraft above us had been replaced and wouldn't be disappearing to refuel. Eventually, he was told that new planes would be arriving in half an hour. The forward air controller, who was speaking to somebody else on his radio, said an F15 would arrive in ten minutes. The person on the Major's radio said that was 'Bollocks'. It was chaos.

Inside the compound, the ANA lay on the opium poppies, passing another spliff. 'I don't know how they smoke it in the middle of a battle', said Lance Corporal Jack Mizon, 'but as soon as they get a few minutes, they start passing it around, laughing and joking. Then a minute later they're running towards bullets.'

'I thought it might make them more cautious', I said.

'It would make me more cautious!' he said, laughing. 'They love it. Smoke a spliff and run at the bullets. The senior ones [British officers] try and stop it but you can't. It's their country; if they want to smoke, let them smoke. They're never gonna be a British-style army; they're their own army, so if they're gonna smoke they're gonna smoke. You just have to learn to work with them while they're doing it.' Jack was the Grenadiers's bruiser, both in Helmand and in the pubs near their barracks back at home. He spoke in a strong North London accent and often described himself as thick and uneducated. But he understood exactly what was going on around him and often articulated it perfectly, in a few pithy sentences.

One of the ANA soldiers came outside and pointed his gun into the air, holding it almost above his head. It was struck by a Taliban bullet. A piece of metal, the top cover, went spinning into the air with a twang. When it landed, the Afghan soldier picked it and walked back inside, laughing.

The temperature had topped fifty degrees and we'd been on the move for almost nine hours. Six soldiers, including the medic, had collapsed with heat exhaustion. One had a temperature of forty-one degrees. Ammunition, water and radio batteries were all running low.

Major David ordered a 500lb bomb to be dropped into a compound beyond the trees, where he was 'confident' the largest group of Taliban was hiding. A helicopter would immediately follow the bomb, to evacuate the heatstroke casualties.

Bullets were still hitting the building. One came right through the door and disappeared into the wall above our heads. Before long, we heard an F16. 'Thirty seconds until impact', said Major David. 'Charlie Charlie One (all stations) stay in hard cover … the bomb has been dropped. Out.'

There was silence. Major David smiled for the first time that day. Then there was more silence. 'Thirty seconds until impact', said the forward air controller. 'Please don't land on here', said Snazle, echoing my thoughts exactly. 'Twice in one day would surely be too much', said Captain Hennessey.

Through the terp's radio, we heard the Taliban Commander shouting instructions to his men. Suddenly, the jet was on top of us and everyone curled forwards as the huge bomb exploded. The compound shook. What was left of the grapes fell to the floor. The terp's radio went silent. 'He's not fucking talking now, is he?' said Snazle, laughing again.

I looked out of the doorway. A mushroom of huge grey cloud billowed, not a hundred metres away but outside the compound it was aimed at.

Bullets sank into the walls around us again. Another air strike was called. As the plane circled, preparing to drop another bomb, the Brits and Afghans showered the compound with a horrendous rattle of constant fire to stop the Taliban escaping.

As ever, there was no way to check for the presence of civilians. 'Heads down, twenty seconds', said Major David. The explosion rocked our compound. This time, the silence lasted; it looked like the fight was finally over. 'Hopefully that's given them enough of a headache to stop', said Major David. According to the pilots, the forward air controller reported, fifteen Taliban had been killed. But through the terp's radio, we could still hear someone talking.

We were hit by more fire from more angles than any time that day. The pattern was depressingly familiar: millions of pounds' worth of the latest weaponry was dropped, a silence of perhaps twenty seconds followed, and then the Taliban popped straight back up and started firing again.

Another soldier – the biggest in the squad – collapsed from heat exhaustion, slumping back against the wall and sliding down until he was in a deep crouch, trembling and mumbling deliriously. The sight of this huge man collapsing so completely made me think he must be suffering from some kind of shell shock. The soldiers around him were shocked too. For a few seconds they froze, watching him. Then they ran over, tore off his clothes and poured water down his back and into his mouth.

More bullets hit the compound, this time from a direction exactly opposite to where we thought most of the Taliban were. We were surrounded, with no way of escaping. Hedgerows they might have been behind were strafed from the air. Ditches were sprayed with heavy machine-gun fire from the roof. Mortars were fired. The soldiers tried anything that might discourage them.

I heard a strange but vicious chopping sound in front of us. It sounded like a thousand tiny zips being pulled closed all at once. 'Flechettes', said the soldier next to me. Also called 'shipyard confetti', flechettes are nail-filled rockets that shower thousands of small steel darts across a wide area. 'You wouldn't want to be the poor fucker under that', said another soldier, in tones of pity, rather than glee.

Suddenly, and for no obvious reason, the attack stopped. Perhaps the Taliban, who'd probably only been three or four groups of four or five fighters each, had run out of ammunition.

At about 4 p.m., the huge soldier I'd watched collapse was loaded on to a makeshift stretcher and carried by six struggling soldiers. We walked wearily back to the patrol base. Almost thirteen hours had passed since the Grenadiers had entered the Green Zone; eight since they had first come under attack. The depressingly familiar trend had continued. An area had been cleared but couldn't be held. It would have to be fought for again, another day. As the sun started to sink away and stop punishing us for a few hours, the news came in over the radios. The Taliban had retaken the compounds.

On the way back, I rested against a wall, next to Lance Corporal Mizon, for whom this was the latest of many bad days. Two weeks earlier, his platoon commander, Second Lieutenant Falorin Kuku, had been blown up right behind him. A week after that, he'd been in the front of the jeep hit by the suicide bomber. One of his friends had been killed and four others wounded.

'I expected it to be bad but these last two weeks have been fucking … … really bad.' I said it was a lot for someone to take. 'I suppose it is but I try not to think about it.' He wetted his lips and shrugged slightly: 'I'll be alright.'

It didn't help they found it hard even to see the Taliban. 'They're up for it, as you've seen today. We've gone two kilometres in about seven hours, which is fuck all. They're hard to fight. It's rare you even see them. Most people here haven't ever seen them. And as soon as it's getting a bit rough and they look like they're gonna get it, they drop their weapon, pick up a pitchfork and they're Farmer Joe for the day.'

'Does that make you suspicious of everyone?'

'Yeah, especially after that suicide bomber. I don't trust anyone. I don't let no one near me any more. If someone's coming towards me on the same path, I cross the path.' He looked down; suddenly, you could see the impact of it all. 'I just want to go home', he said.

A lost little boy, not the GPMG-carrying bruiser who was always first into the fight that everyone else saw.

He found it hard to understand the Taliban. 'They fight as if they want to die. They're the kind of people that believe when they die they're going to wake up with twenty-seven [sic] virgins. How can you fight against someone like that? Someone who doesn't give a shit. If as soon as I died I'd go back to Tottenham, I'd be running at the bullets.

'The ANA aren't much different', he said. 'As soon as the bullets go down they get stuck in but they don't put no flank protection down, they don't bring no water or food and as soon as they're hungry they come to us. "I want water, I want food." Well, I haven't got no water meself. If we wasn't here, they wouldn't get no water. If we wasn't here they wouldn't give themselves flank protection or rear protection. If a mine goes off, we get down, stand still and poke our way out, carefully. It takes hours and hours. They get in a straight line and just walk through it. They're all gonna get blown up. But that's their way of thinking.'

I asked how many times he'd fought for ground and then had to give it up again. 'It always happens, you take ground then you lose it. There's no one to hold the ground.' In the past, they had established small patrol bases, supposed to be taken over by the Afghan police. But the police hadn't turned up.

When we finally got back to the base, most of the soldiers collapsed on the floor. They struggled to string sentences together, if they tried to speak at all. Most stared straight ahead, so exhausted they appeared to be in shock. How could they have been through all that only to end up handing the ground back to the Taliban?

The next day, I asked Major David what had happened. 'The resistance was so fierce and it very soon became apparent that without a considerably larger force it would have been extremely difficult to hold there.' I asked if it was pure chance that the family – indeed, a section of his men – hadn't been killed by the Hellfire missile. Major David was admirably honest. 'I was fortunate that none of them were injured. I directed that attack. I gave clearance for it to fire and the responsibility lies on my shoulders. In this instance, I'm extremely lucky that there were no casualties, either friendly or civilian. But that is combat. In the confusion that follows an engagement like that it's extremely difficult sometimes. Yesterday was probably the hardest day I've had in seventeen years of service and I think all the others who fought in it would agree. It was eight hours of unrelenting combat against a canny, wily and determined enemy who was prepared to fight to the death to defend the ground that they held.'

I asked if so much damage and trauma – five compounds bombed and one flattened – wouldn't lose the support of the local people or even make them turn to the Taliban, if they hadn't already. 'It's a fine line', he said. 'I think if we were completely indiscriminate in our fire then yes, we could lose support quite quickly. But we always try to minimise collateral damage. Yesterday, I agree we were reasonably lucky that the family weren't injured but these are the risks in this kind of combat. When the ANA spoke to that family afterwards, they said the Taliban had forced them to stay in that compound. They are very canny. They understand, probably more than our public at home, that any collateral damage plays directly into their hands. The civilians yesterday said that the Taliban said "we won't kill you, we're just here to protect you", but they also made them stay in the compound, knowing that they would probably be killed or injured by the coalition air strike.'

Major David thought that seven Taliban had been killed and six injured, out of probably fifty fighters. I asked how fifty fighters with old AK47s had managed to cause 160 British and 130 ANA soldiers, with air support, so much difficulty. 'I'd have had an easier time if I'd had only had British troops under my command. The ANA have come on leaps and bounds but their command and control isn't quite as advanced as ours. My men took significant risks yesterday to push them forward. Or should I say pull them forward? As such, it's a significantly harder battle to wage.' While their job was supposed to be to act as mentors for the Afghan Army, they were still commanding them. When I asked what had happened to the ANA's company commander, Major David couldn't quite stop himself from breaking into a huge smile. He was a bit more diplomatic than most of his men: 'He manages to locate himself in the safer rear areas on most occasions. Yesterday, he was not present and I had to command his companies.'

I followed the Grenadiers as they cleared the abandoned village of Rahim Kholay. We walked into a small valley filled with walls, buildings and caves, hiding perfect bunkers, trenches and firing holes; invisible until you were so close you'd be dead. They were deserted, but there was no relief, no joy at this lucky break. Their exhaustion was so complete it was impossible to care. Even when mortar fire sent the ANA, who were ahead of us, sprawling, there was no reaction. No one had enough energy or strength left for fear, anger or the desire to fight back. Only when the ANA started moving dangerously close to another British position did Hennessey, Mizon and a few others send jeeps to cut them off and direct them back into the village, where they were less likely to get into trouble. 'It's like herding cats', said Hennessey. 'Cats with guns.'

Rocky, the ANA Captain, didn't want to clear Rahim Kalay, because he thought the Taliban had just moved into some nearby trees, and were waiting to attack. 'These poor soldiers have not come here to die in vain. War has its own tactics and I am not going to be in the front. I'm not a boy of fear, I wouldn't go back to the womb of my mother from where I have come. I would obey you and go to anywhere you send me, even unarmed, because you are my boss. If I don't go you can shoot me but please let us fight this war with our own tactics. The enemy has entered those orchards. If I move forward I will be destroyed.'

Major David, one of the most thoughtful and considered soldiers I'd ever met, lost his patience. He interrupted this speech, snapping: 'The best thing is just to do what you're told' and walked away.

That was translated as 'Yes, that's fine, do whatever you want to do.'

*　*　*　*　*

I left the Grenadier Guards. They'd been told they were to rest, as they had been out on operations for seventy-four days. I was persuaded to believe in the ridiculous idea that I could get a helicopter ride back to Bastion, go out on operation with the Light Dragoons and return to the Grenadiers before they headed back into the Green Zone. Instead I spent three days in a tent, waiting for a seat on a chopper that never materialised. In the meantime, the Grenadier Guards were told that rather than heading back to camp for showers and some good nights' sleep in an air-conditioned tent, they would be taking the town of Adin Zai.

While I was desperately trying to get back to them, the Guards had walked towards the town and had immediately come under fire. By the end of the first day, they had dropped twelve 500lb bombs, lost one soldier and had two seriously injured. They thought they'd killed around eighty Taliban fighters. I regularly heard such assertions but the overall numbers of Taliban never seemed to drop. I never saw anywhere near enough bodies or blood to back up the claims of enemy casualties. The Taliban were very good at evacuating their dead and injured, but not that good. I assumed they exaggerated their losses on the radio, perhaps to ease their escape or possibly to keep the British focused on buildings that had long been abandoned.

By the time I reached them, the Grenadiers had taken Adin Zai and the Taliban were about to start their counter-attack. The first thing I saw as I ran from the Chinook helicopter was Company Sergeant Major Snazle on his quad bike, towing what looked like two bodies in a trailer. As he came closer, I saw that they were Afghan soldiers, apparently close to death. I solemnly asked what had happened: 'One shot a dog. The bullet went through the dog and bounced off the floor and the wall. The fragments hit one in the leg and the other in the belly. They'll be fine', he said, with equal measures of annoyance and amusement. The rest of the Grenadier Guards told me it was even worse than Snazle had described: the ANA had missed the dog.

I walked with Major David through destroyed compounds.

Most seemed to have taken direct hits. Within what remained of the outer walls, everything was reduced to rubble. We stopped at one of the first they had assaulted when they entered Adin Zai. It was possible to see where the rooms had been but the walls, roofs, supporting beams and even a tree now lay in a mangled heap, spilling on to the path where we stood. 'This one had a large enemy position in it. Actually, coming back here now you can smell the bodies, so probably some enemy dead are still lying under the rubble.'

'I don't feel bad', said Major David, 'because we had to do what we did. There's always going to be a slight tinge of sadness that human conflict leads to this and that there's no way of dealing with it other than fighting.'

I followed Sergeant Major Snazle to a large house on the edge of Adin Zai: the soldiers' base for a few days. Everyone was relaxed; most didn't bother to wear helmets or body armour. An ANA jeep was parked outside, with a DShKa ('dushker') gun mounted on the back. A small crowd gathered to watch an ANA soldier fire it. Every time he fired, he lost control and bullets shot high into the air. Others ricocheted off the ground, far away from the Taliban positions. The gun was too powerful, even when the soldier grabbed it with both hands and sat back, trying to use his weight to keep it steady. His British mentors screamed at him to shoot *down*. Others shouted the now familiar question: 'Are they shooting *at* anything?' The answer was still 'no'.

A young soldier was delighted to be given permission to fire a Javelin missile. (Each rocket costs about £65,000, three times the soldier's annual salary.) Javelins are designed to destroy tanks but in Afghanistan they are regularly used to attack Taliban fighters. The missiles come in huge shoulder-mounted tubes, each with an infra-red monitor attached. A target is selected on the monitor and the rocket is fired, high into the air. You think it must land miles beyond its target. But just before it's too late, it turns, moving almost vertically down. It's as if it had forgotten where it was going, then remembered at the last minute. Then, it accelerates furiously towards its target. The missiles plop absurdly out of their tubes, falling towards the ground briefly, before roaring up and away. This always looked like a mistake, no matter how many times I saw them fired.

The Taliban fired back. Although they weren't getting anywhere near us, they were very hard to kill or even see. Air support was called in and I saw a shiny white missile skim through the air over my left shoulder, landing just in front of us. A huge piece of hot metal fell at our feet. I thought I'd seen another mistake; the missile had come down barely a hundred metres in front of us. But it was perfectly accurate. It had landed exactly where the Taliban were. I put on my helmet and body armour.

The battle lasted into the night, more like an air show than a war. The range and power of the weapons dropped on the Taliban made the Brits cheer and the Afghans whoop and giggle, as if they were at a karaoke party. The climax came when a jet flew over and fired a Gatling gun at the trees in front of us, turning them into a row of fireballs whose black smoke rose high into the air. We saw the flash of the explosion, then its sound rolled slowly towards us across the field; one of the most evil noises I've ever heard. A deep and powerful roar (this version, the Vulcan, could fire up to six thousand rounds a minute) that made my internal organs quiver. The Taliban must have thought the foreigners had Satan on their side, burping fire from above.

There was a brief silence. Then the sound of small arms fire came back. Pathetic-sounding after the air show but impressive in its defiance. I wondered if maybe the air support wasn't as accurate as was claimed. Or perhaps the Taliban were so used to the planes and helicopters that they simply dived into ditches whenever they appeared, making anything short of a direct hit a waste of effort. A few soldiers admitted to admiring the Taliban, some for their tactical ability but mostly for their bravery. 'Even when they're on to a complete loser, they insist on pushing forward', said Major David. 'On the one hand, you have to admire that determination. On the other hand, you just feel rather sad. It's just a shame that they don't seem to be able to surrender, which would save us a lot of pain and hurt.'

I asked him how much he thought this engagement had cost. The overall British effort in Afghanistan had just topped a billion pounds. 'Um, I wouldn't really want to hazard a guess', he said, laughing. 'But, um … a lot.' His radio operator appeared, smiling. 'I-comm indicates at least forty enemy dead, sir.'

The Taliban were so persistent, without any hope of assaulting the compound, that I eventually grew tired and went inside to sleep, bedding down on a pile of ration boxes in the back of an ANA pick-up truck. About 2 a.m., the sound of another 500lb bomb exploding woke me up. But once I realised it had landed outside the compound, I fell asleep again.

The Grenadiers moved into a recently-abandoned small compound not far away. Jack Mizon had been on the roof when the neighbouring compound, fewer than fifty metres away, had been destroyed by a 500lb bomb, again by mistake. The ANA found a girl's bike, which they rode around inside the building's walls. Major David moved into a tiny watchtower on the roof, where he finally got some time to himself.

The Taliban had faded away, so everyone had a few days off to sleep, eat, clean their weapons and play with the ANA. Ryan Lloyd taught them Monty Python-style drills and a young, boyish-looking Grenadier got a few excited by spending all day with his shirt off. Some of the other Brits played along, pointing at him, saying, 'hey … jiggy jiggy?' He got very uncomfortable when the Afghans started touching his nipples, looking like they were about to lunge.

Major David sat on the roof, outside his little room, taking in the scenery and sudden peace. His hair had grown long and blew in the wind, and he had a thick salt-and-pepper beard. 'Down here in the Green Zone it's pretty spectacular, with the fauna and flora. It's quite easy to forget where you are at times and that there's some bunch of lunatics out there that want to kill you. It's easy to transport yourself away from what's going on here, just because of the natural beauty of it all.'

The Grenadiers were relieved by the Worcestershire and Sherwood Foresters and drove back to Camp Bastion for some rest.

They had been out in the field for eighty-two days. Captain Hennessey was first out, as he was due two weeks' leave. 'In seventy-two hours I'll be in Chelsea', he said, climbing on the back of a quad bike, wearing a bandana and sporting a recently-grown moustache, '...in the bath, with a glass of champagne.' Lance Corporal Mizon was also heading home on leave, back to Tottenham. In Britain, their lives were as different as their accents.

Back at Bastion, everyone attended the repatriation ceremony for Guardsman Daryl Hickey, the soldier who'd been killed as they had entered Adin Zai. His coffin, draped in a Union Jack, was loaded on a Hercules plane to be flown home. 'I was looking forward to coming back', said Mizon, 'but I didn't want to come back to my friend's funeral.'

As the plane took off, everyone saluted. In return, it too saluted, dipping its right wing before climbing into the clear blue sky.

CHAPTER 4

After four weeks at home, I was back at Camp Bastion. This camp was designed to accommodate 2,300 soldiers; it now held four thousand and the number continued to rise. Building was happening everywhere, as the army struggled to house the expanding population of soldiers. Other than the major bases in Kabul and Kandahar, which have airstrips, cafés, showers, beds and complete networks of perfectly smooth roads, this was the only place I ever saw serious construction in Afghanistan.

On the military flight in, we'd been handed a plastic bag containing a Yorkie bar, two Tracker bars, a tube of Polos, some Starburst chews, a bag of KP nuts and a small carton of syrupy orange drink. English MREs ('Meals Ready to Eat') were the same, with the addition of a packet of biscuits and a vacuum-packed main course and desert. The food was designed for English winters; in the Afghan summer it took ten minutes to wipe melted Yorkie off everything else before we could eat.

I waited with the soldiers for ninety minutes, until a battered coach arrived to take us across the base to the huge warehouse, RSOI-5, where soldiers in transit slept. It looked like a factory farm. Hundreds of neatly-arranged and tightly-packed old metal bunk beds, holding two dirty mattresses each, were lined in rows under bright, naked lightbulbs. The bunks squeaked so loudly and disproportionately that calling it a 'dormitory' seemed a cruel joke. Soldiers arrived, left, or fidgeted in the heat, creating a constant chorus of frog-like croaks and squeaks that made it impossible to sleep unless you were exhausted, which most were.

The next day, as I queued for food outside one of the three huge 'scoff tents', a soldier told me that we were achieving nothing, it was not our fight, just Blair sucking up to Bush. He claimed this was the majority view. He said he spent every day and every night counting down the time until he went home. Most of the soldiers deployed to Afghanistan never leave the safety of bases like Camp Bastion.

It was my third stay in Bastion and I was beginning to understand how the soldiers felt. I needed a ride to Sangin, to rejoin the Grenadier Guards but there were so few transport helicopters that it took five days to complete a journey that could be driven in forty minutes. The road to Sangin couldn't be used because it had been dotted with IEDs. It was no different for the soldiers, unless they were wounded. Even those going home on leave had to wait for days on end and those days weren't added to their time.

There was nothing to do while I waited except try to avoid the heat. This was almost impossible, because the air-conditioning in the tents didn't work. One Naafi, with a dry bar and a small supermarket, served the entire base. Its generator could only power half of the building so the bar never opened. In the supermarket, drinks didn't stay in the fridge long enough to get cool. The only magazines on sale were lads' mags, the gossip weekly *Heat* and for some reason, *Bizarre*, which is an odd mix of porn and gore, mostly real. There was lots of excitement when a double-decker *Pizza Hut* bus arrived one day. When it eventually opened, some soldiers came down with salmonella poisoning and it was immediately closed.

When I finally got a seat to Sangin, I found myself next to a military policeman, there to train the ANP. He had just sacked two men who had been caught smoking opium once too often and was on his way from a base he'd found being guarded by a twelve-year-old, in uniform, with a machine gun. I told him I was filming with the OMLT and he asked how long the soldiers thought it would take to train the ANA. Ten years, I replied. How long it would take to train the police, I asked? 'Double that, at least', he replied, seriously.

I was dropped at the Sangin District Centre, the base that had been used by the Paras and Royal Marines when they first arrived. They had suffered almost constant attack and had barely been able to leave the base. Instead, they had spent their time on the roof of the Centre's highest building, firing everything they had. The view from that roof suggested that winning the people over would be impossible. Barely a single building stood. The few walls that remained upright were pocked with bullet-holes and bombed-out metal containers littered the floor of the wadi.

Destruction, I said to Major David, still seemed to be happening far more than reconstruction. 'It's a long process', he replied. 'It's going to take years. But we've got the will and the locals seem to have the patience, so it should be a success.' Everyone said the Taliban had been routed from Sangin. I asked if they could come back. 'I don't think so; they are reeling from the operations we've conducted against them and they're low on morale.'

I followed Major David to a *shura*, where a young and nervous soldier from the Royal Engineers gave a presentation to a hundred or so local elders. She started by announcing that the rubbish had been cleared from the bazaar. To be fair, in her photograph, Sangin's dusty bazaar did look to be free of litter. She then said that funds had been approved for a tractor to keep clearing the bazaar, that the Americans had put up street lights, that irrigation ditches had been dug, two electricity transformers had been provided, a school would soon be refurbished and funds had been approved for ten more wells, in addition to the ten that had already been dug. 'All this in the last three months', she said to the elders, expecting a reaction. They looked at her blankly, nonplussed. Even with the massively inflated prices the contractors would have charged for these projects, they were nowhere near the cost of a Javelin missile or two.

When the locals got their chance to speak one man said this was the eighteenth *shura* he'd been to. He'd heard it all before and nothing ever appeared. 'The promises made by the government have not been met. First we need water, then schools, then clinics. The government needs to help us. We are hungry and our land is drying up.' Others complained that their homes were being damaged during fighting, which the rich could flee but the poor couldn't. They also said the reconstruction projects only benefited the few who heard about them. Ninety per cent of funds were spent in district centres, leaving the countryside, where eighty per cent of Afghans live, free for the Taliban. They found it easy to convince the local people that the Afghan Government and the foreign troops had done nothing for them.

A group raised their arms and complained that their opium had been seized. Major David stood up to speak. 'The Governor of Helmand's policy is that significantly large amounts of drugs will be confiscated by the counter-narcotics police. He understands that in some compounds there will be one or two bags. Those will probably be ignored. But in this case there was over half a tonne of opium in one compound.' He looked at the men in front of him, naturally expecting to see some guilt on their faces. Instead, their expressions of outrage became more pronounced, as if to say, 'Exactly – half a tonne! How dare you take so much?' Major David continued: 'All inquiries about this must be addressed to the counter-narcotics police in Lashkar Gar. We have the phone numbers for them. This is a subject that is completely beyond the control of any of the people here today.' As Major David wrote down the number, the men leapt up and scrambled towards the front table. It was the first time I'd seen enthusiasm from the crowd and the first time I'd seen drug producers chasing the authorities they were supposed to be running from.

The soldier standing next to me whispered in my ear: 'They'll probably get it all back too, we can't piss the drug lords off; they aren't against us yet.' Others told me they were under orders to ignore opium finds of fewer than sixty kilograms; some said all opium finds. There were many stories about people with government connections being left well alone.

The Taliban had successfully banned opium-farming when they were in power, yet now earned significant amounts from it. They curried favour with the local people by protecting their crops, help-ing smugglers and offering poor farmers loans against the following year's harvest; thus establishing exactly the kind of long-term rela-tionship the British sought.

Helmand's 2006 harvest was forty-nine per cent up on the previ-ous year. That had beaten the previous year's record, making Helmand the world's biggest single producer of illicit drugs, outdoing entire countries like Colombia and Burma. There was supposed to be an alternative crops policy but other than a lone mint farmer who lived just outside Lashkar Gar – journalists were often taken to see him – fields of opium and stacks of harvested poppy were everywhere.

As the *shura* ended an Afghan policeman handed out leaflets with pictures of a dirty-looking Taliban fighter on one side and a handsome Afghan soldier on the other. 'I'm telling them to help these guys', he said, pointing to the soldier, 'and FUCK these guys.' He pointed to the Taliban and burst out laughing.

After the *shura*, I caught up with Jack Mizon and Ryan Lloyd and followed them to Tangiers, a patrol base that used to be a *madrasah*. There, they discovered the ANA had been through their rooms, stealing nine dollars and their favourite porn magazine. They'd also pulled all their favourite porn pictures off the 'morale wall' and put them in the bin. After a blazing row, the ANA apologised profusely, promising it would never happen again. They spent the next hour building a pathetic wire gate across the corridor that separated their sleeping quarters from the Brits.

That night, as we finished some Afghan bread and a can of fizzy orange drink that an Afghan soldier had bought for us from the bazaar, an RPG exploded against the outside wall of the room we were sitting in, knocking us off our seats. It was followed by two or three more, then long bursts of gunfire from several different positions.

I ran outside behind Jack Mizon as he sprinted to one side of the base with a mortar. No enemy firing positions had been identified – it still seemed to be coming from all round – but Jack fired a few mortars over the wall anyway. Then he was ordered to get up on the roof and fire in exactly the opposite direction. The Taliban were firing from a hill-top house, which allowed them to shoot over the base's high walls. Jack ran up on to the roof and was soon angrily firing an over-sized machine gun, pausing only to scream, 'FUCK OFF', at the house. By then, there didn't seem to be much incoming fire. Whoever had fired had emptied whatever they had and disappeared. I could tell the ANA were also firing, because much of the tracer fire was going high into the air, over the top of the house. But the Brits also fired an awful lot, often not at a specific target.

I was left with the feeling I'd had in the Green Zone; much of Helmand was being used as a giant sports field, on which two groups of consenting adults fought. It was football hooliganism with guns. What everyone seemed to forget, despite the talk, was that Sangin was home to thousands of families.

* * * * *

After Sangin, I spent ten days in Lashkar Gar, with the Provincial Reconstruction Team (PRT) whose mission was to 'facilitate reconstruction and development'. Their work was supposed to be a major plank of British policy but spending time with the PRT had also been a condition of my getting access to British troops.

After Sangin, it was surreal. Soldiers were allowed to wear flip-flops to 'air their feet' if they had been 'in theatre' but not otherwise. Certainly never in the scoff tent; a sign inside declared footwear offenders would be removed. Three more signs were stuck above three sinks, with eleven separate instructions on how to wash our hands. A special toilet was set aside for vomit and diarrhoea. Even when you found an ordinary cubicle and sat down for some peace and quiet, an entire page from Kellog, Brown and Root told you how to pull the chain and make sure it went all the way back up, to avoid flooding. Any civil servants leaving the base went under the protection of heavily-muscled private security guards from Armor-Group, whose weapons and armoured jeeps put the British Army's wrecks to shame.

A big operation started the next night. British forces suffered an attack that went on into the following day. I was supposed to be going with the head of the PRT to a meeting with the provincial council but it was cancelled; the medical evacuation helicopters were too busy to collect us if we got blown up. A trip to a *shura* in Rahim Khalay, the first since the town had been taken from the Taliban, was cancelled because the helicopter had broken down. More than five hundred local elders had turned up for it. There was a chance the chopper could be repaired and we'd only be a few hours late but the *shura* was mortared and everyone told to go back to their offices.

David Slynn, the head of the PRT, managed to get to a provincial council meeting where elected local councillors told him the Taliban were hated and it was the perfect time to hit them. But, they said, local institutions were so corrupt that people still chose to side with the Taliban. They complained that development, human rights and democracy remained a dream. Beyond Gereshk, Lashkar Gar and Sangin, they said, nothing was done. There was no communication with local people and no aid had arrived. The provisional council, which was supposed to include at least one woman, appeared to be all-male. In fact, there was a woman member, who sat at the far end of a long table and wasn't acknowledged. When she saw the surprise on my face when I spotted her, she smiled knowingly and nodded, as if to thank me for noticing but also to tell me there was nothing anyone could do.

Back at the base, as we sat down to dinner, news spread of a double suicide bombing in Gereshk. The bombers' target was a high-ranking local official, probably the Mayor, but instead they had killed twenty people: six policemen and fourteen civilians.

Nine of the eleven PRT events I should have covered were cancelled for security reasons. The only other trip out of the Lashkar Gar base was a helicopter ride to the Sangin base, for a meeting with Major Martin David, another British officer, and the district governor, who soon left.

I walked across a small footbridge to the house occupied by the Grenadier Guards. A few men were washing in the river. They seemed glum, which surprised me, because their six-month tour had just a week to run. They asked me if I'd heard about Goolie, Lance Sergeant Adam Ball, a soldier I'd met briefly during my first trip. The Taliban had placed two IEDs behind a wall, then ambushed a patrol at the perfect point where they'd use the wall for cover. Goolie lost a leg, an ANA soldier lost both legs and an interpreter was killed, probably because he was crouching when the IEDs went off.

The soldiers were already more nervous than usual, so close to the end of their tour. Some were annoyed they had to go out at all. I asked Major David why they weren't allowed to relax and see out their last few days in Helmand in safety. He said if he allowed them to do that, the enemy would take advantage of the freedom of movement that gave, and make life much more difficult for the soldiers who were about to take over. In the event, the last seven days of their tour passed without incident. But the Grenadier Guards paid a high price overall: two of Queen's Company were killed and fifteen seriously injured.

I walked back across the bridge. The PRT meeting was still going on. Even without the security situation limiting their movement so much, I wondered how successful they could really be. Few members engaged with Afghans, spoke Pashtu or ever left the base. Their budget was about £25 million for the whole year, an amount the military often got through in a day. And they numbered just thirty people, including administrative staff, compared with almost eight thousand soldiers. There were rumours that Foreign Office staff had threatened not to renew their contracts in protest over the inadequate funding.

After the meeting, we visited a building site next to the Sangin District Centre, which would one day be a school. I asked if it would be mixed or just for boys. 'There are small girls coming to this school', said one of the Afghan officials. 'But the older girls are scared of the Taliban … when there is security every girl will come to this school.' Inside, he explained why progress had been slow: 'The Taliban threaten to kill contractors. When the security improves the contractors will be back.'

Despite everything, the British mission was still officially described as facilitating development and reconstruction, extending the authority of the Afghan Government and building security. It should have been described as struggling to stay alive. In 2007, the UN reported there had been a thirty per cent increase in violent incidents over the last year; averaging 550 a month. Suicide attacks had risen sevenfold. So it was no surprise that many local contractors were too scared to work on the few building projects that were under way. The Taliban permitted local NGOs to work if it was in 'the national interest', which begged the question of why the British soldiers were there at all. There hadn't been an insurgency until they arrived. I asked Major David why there were foreign fighters in Helmand. 'To fight us', he said. So what would they do if you left? 'They would probably leave too', he replied.

For the soldiers, a six-month tour was hard enough, without wondering what impact they had had on the country. 'There are parts of it that have been exhilarating in the extreme', said Major David, who was later to receive the Military Cross. 'There have been parts of it that have been terrifying. I think everyone has grown up. I've seen a lot of the lads mature out here.' I asked what the tour had cost him personally. 'The strains on our families have been extreme and I'm grateful to my wife, to my children ...' He couldn't finish the sentence. His cheeks tightened above the corners of his mouth. After months of juggling too many responsibilities and emotions, he couldn't do it any more. His head fell forward into his hands and he wept.

A few years later, I was able to ask him what he thought the British had achieved in Helmand. 'We increased the secure zones in which the Afghan government could operate', he told me. 'We set the conditions for the spread of governance and redevelopment.' But everything that was supposed to happen next hadn't. The Afghan Government weren't willing, able or even there to govern. And with the few experts and civil servants holed up in Lashkar Gar, governance and reconstruction was left to already over-stretched soldiers. 'While the military forces achieved commendable results, it was all very amateur and slow. Too slow. As a result, we started not to garner support from the population. The local communities were pragmatic; they weren't going to blindly back the new horse. They needed convincing but our words spoke louder than our actions.' He was nervous about the future. 'For the sake of those who have sacrificed life and limb I pray that the international community have the perseverance and courage to see it through to an appropriate conclusion. But time and the global financial crisis will not allow this to sit comfortably.'

PART II

US MARINE CORPS
JULY TO AUGUST, 2009
2ND BATTALION
8TH MARINES

Since the British had first entered Helmand in 2006, every year had been bloodier, and by every available indicator worse, than the previous. The British Army was at breaking point, regularly describing its experience in Helmand as being the most intense fighting it had seen since the Korean War.

Barack Obama had been the only presidential candidate to say that Afghanistan was in danger of being lost because essential resources had been diverted to the wrong war, in Iraq. Now, he'd been elected President and seemed determined to turn things around. He'd authorised seventeen thousand additional troops, most of which would go to Helmand. He also began a major policy review.

Most of those troops were to be US Marines. I'd once spent time with the Marines: three weeks with the US Navy's Fifth Fleet, in the Persian Gulf. Despite being stuck on an aircraft carrier, they ran six miles a day wearing heavy backpacks, regularly practised hand-to-hand combat in large groups and spent hours playing Iraq War games on X-boxes, actively encouraged by their commanding officers. In a refreshing contrast to the uptight sailors I'd filmed, the

Marines were instantly and completely honest and didn't seem to care what I, or anyone else, thought of them.

They talked about Fallujah, where they had been involved in the most brutal fighting of the Iraq War, in the same way that I talk about Rio; that is, they loved and missed it. They appeared to be a guerrilla army within the American military, whose lack of restraint no one dared criticise. When I asked what part of the navy they were – and they are part of the navy, although they operate autonomously – I received a disdainful snigger: 'We're the *men's* department.' I instantly warmed to them and knew that if I got the chance to film them in action, I'd jump at it.

In the early hours of July 2nd, 2009, approximately four thousand US Marines, the first of the seventeen thousand additional troops, landed in southern Helmand province. They were there for Operation Khanjar, 'Sword strike', a dress rehearsal for the policy that Obama would later decide on. Finally, it was thought, there was enough manpower, equipment and will to defeat the Taliban, offer good governance and win over the war-weary Afghans. Finally, somewhere would be cleared, held and developed. This would be replicated elsewhere and the war could be won.

The British Army had shown incredible bravery and suffered horrendous losses, yet it was impossible not to see the US Marines, with their billions of dollars' worth of new equipment, unlimited support, aggressive ambition and unapologetic bluster, as the big boys coming to take charge. Roger Moore was charming but the fighting had spiralled out of control and John Wayne, Ted Nugent and Ice-T had been sent in to finish things off.

'It's time to change the game in Afghanistan', said the Marines' commanding officer before they took off. 'To force the Taliban to react to us, instead of us reacting to them. We are attacking to seize control of the population from the Taliban, because once we've secured the population, they no longer have a sea to swim in. The insurgents are going to die on the vine. We are experts in the application of violence. The world will remember what we do here and believe me, Echo Company is going to change history.'

CHAPTER 5

The first convoy I joined was hit by an IED. I heard the boom and looked through one of the tiny bullet-proof windows to see the lead vehicle crumpled forwards, as if beaten to its knees. The front left tyre had been blown about eighty metres into a nearby field but the main body of the truck, like the seven marines inside, survived intact. Even Blue, the explosives-sniffing dog, jumped out wagging his tail.

If British soldiers, in roofless old Land Rovers, had driven over the same bomb, everyone would have been killed. The US soldiers already had about twelve thousand bomb-proof trucks but would soon order over four thousand more, because the design had been improved. The Americans, and certainly the Marines, seemed to take war much more seriously than the British.

The crippled MRAP (Mine Resistant Ambush Protected) was dragged to a nearby base. I followed the marines on their foot patrol to recover parts of the IED and truck from the site. We passed one crater ('No, this is the one from three days ago') and came to two craters, one right in the middle of the road, the second a little beyond it, at exactly the spot a vehicle would pass to avoid the first. Barely thirty minutes had passed since the explosion but every scrap of metal had been cleared.

'There are fresh motorcycle tracks here', said a marine on the other side of the crater.

'Motherfuckers', said another.

A canal ran parallel to the road. On the far side, two men on a motorcycle rode past, staring at us coldly. Another motorbike, carrying a man and his wife, came towards us on our side. The marines studied the couple through their rifle sights before ordering them to stop and get off the bike. The man looked only mildly inconvenienced as he lifted up his shirt and walked toward the marines. They kept their sights trained on him. He said didn't have any information about the Taliban.

'If you've finished with him, let him go', shouted someone behind us. 'Just because we have to get blown up doesn't mean he has to as well.'

'You think he'd be standing there if there were more explosives, you fucking idiot?' shouted Lance Corporal Gomez, crouched next to me. 'He knows where everything is. They all know.'

We walked back to the base. The convoy was ordered back to FOB Delhi, the marines' main base, close to the Helmand Green Zone but far south of anywhere I'd been with the British. We'd been trying to get to Echo Company, who had pushed further south than anybody so far, into the small village of Mian Poshteh.

Soon, so many convoys had been hit that the two roads from FOB Delhi to Mian Poshteh were closed. The second convoy I joined had to drive through the desert. Two of the massive MRAP trucks, which weigh over thirty tonnes, sank into the thin, powdery sand. We had to wait for lorries to come and tow them out; a journey of sixteen kilometres took us thirteen hours.

I was ordered to switch vehicles. When I climbed into the back of the second truck I was surprised to see two Special Forces soldiers. There was an awkward moment as they eyed my camera and I looked at their elaborate weapons and long beards. They eventually spoke but batted away my questions about what they were on their way to do.

The driver, excited to have such exalted company in his truck, told them a house in front of us had been used by a sniper a few days earlier. 'I hope he shoots at us again, then we can set you guys on him.' He turned around and smiled hopefully. The Special Forces soldiers looked away.

I was later told that the sniper was a sixteen-year-old Chechen girl. I remembered I'd been told exactly the same thing by the British, two years earlier. They had described her as if she were an evil super-hero from a comic. I had no idea she was so good she didn't age.

It was dusk on July 4th when I finally made it to Mian Poshteh. Echo Company had already been involved in a seven-hour gunfight. One marine had been killed, the first American to die on an operation approved by President Obama.

Described by Lieutenant Colonel Christian Cabaniss, the commanding officer of 2/8 Marines, the mission sounded simple. As the sun rose, the Taliban would 'wake up to find marines everywhere'. They would call for reinforcements, only to be told that they too, saw marines everywhere. The Taliban would have 'no stomach to stand and fight, and would disappear', enabling the marines to 'target the population, not the enemy'. Sadly, it's necessary to point out that in this case 'targeting' means 'winning over'. The thinking, based on the counter-insurgency books that are the bibles of ambitious American officers, was that if you won over the local population they would reject the enemy, who would then become 'irrelevant'. It sounded remarkably similar to the comprehensive approach the Brits had been trying for the last two years. I lost count of how many times I was told that the Taliban were about to become irrelevant. In that time, the Taliban, rather than becoming irrelevant, had become increasingly successful and audacious in their attacks against foreign and Afghan forces.

Main Poshteh is a small market town straddling a canal. Its two rows of shops, merely tiny storage rooms with mud walls and small, shaded, outside trading areas, had been abandoned hastily. Goods were on the shelves, scales and weights were neatly piled on the floor and vegetables were on display outside, rotting in the sun. The marines helped themselves to cigarettes and sweets, leaving behind generous amounts of dollar bills.

The marines slept on the concrete floor of a long, thin building that was once a school. I was told to sleep with the medics, who had one room to treat casualties, one room for the doctor and a mud courtyard that I shared with about fifteen others. My bed was a stretcher, unless the medics needed it.

'Have you seen what's next door?' said a marine. 'A gynaecologist's bench with a dustbin at the end. How apt for this country.'

There was one casualty at the medical centre. He was a local boy, a paraplegic who, despite being 'somewhere between sixteen and thirty', couldn't have weighed more than six stone. He'd been discovered in a nearby house, on fire after being hit by a Hellfire missile. His family had fled, together with everyone else, when the marines landed. Unable to move and barely able to talk, the boy had almost starved to death. He told the interpreter that he'd been injured in a farming accident, which none of the marines believed. They assumed anyone with such injuries had sustained them fighting or making IEDs.

I couldn't sleep that night. When I heard the medics asking for a fourth man to help carry the boy out to a chopper that would take him to the hospital in Kandahar City, I got up and grabbed one corner of the stretcher. After my delay in getting there, I was anxious to see as much as possible.

We jogged to the end of the government building, treading on marines trying to sleep on the dusty ground. 'Is that the cripple?' 'Is he even alive?' 'Is it true his family just fucking left him there?' 'He probably crippled himself making bombs.' Dust and dirt blown by the chopper's blades whipped our faces as we carried the boy into the helicopter's huge belly. The staff at Kandahar hospital would have to try and locate his family.

That afternoon, four Special Forces soldiers who everyone knew had been on operation the night before, appeared, covered in mud and dripping with sweat. Marines shouted out compliments as they went by. The two men I'd met in the truck walked past me without making eye contact. The rumour went round that they had twelve confirmed kills and many more unconfirmed. But the

awe they inspired wasn't shared by all the marines: 'They're nothing but Rangers with a few skill sets and some extra assets, they
ain't special', said one.

Some of that resentment could have been because the Special
Forces went out and killed people within hours of arriving, whereas
Echo now rarely saw the enemy. Local people were returning to
their homes; the marines were sure Taliban were among them,
studying Echo's movements.

The men in this tricky position were often no more than nine-
teen or twenty years old. Mostly from Florida, North Carolina or
South Carolina, (their base is Camp Lejeune, NC), many had never
before left their home state. They'd been trained to kill; some openly
fantasised about 'dropping' people. But now, they were under orders
to hold back and concentrate on building relationships with the
local community.

I joined Lance Corporal Brady Bunch, a chubby-faced, frustrated young marine, and Second Platoon, as they went on patrol to
a compound from where they'd been attacked several times. As we
prepared to leave, Bunch stroked his favourite weapon. 'Big Tom –
the best weapon in the Marine Corps. I'm gonna drop a raghead at
eight hundred feet with this', he said. Then he looked away, laughing: 'Probably not.'

As we approached the compound, a man dressed in black, carrying a bag on his back, ran away. Bunch got down on his belly and
got the man in his sights. After a few tense moments, the platoon
leader decided they would approach the house slowly and try to
talk to whoever was inside. So Bunch wasn't allowed to take a shot.
The man crossed a footbridge and disappeared into another compound.

'Fuck. Every fucking open shot I get. Fuck', said Bunch as he
stomped towards the house. He turned, grinning: 'I could have
waxed his ass.'

A small boy, about twelve years old, came out of the house. 'No,
I don't want a kid. Where is his father?' asked Bunch. The boy said
he was alone. He and the interpreter carried on talking, without

translating. Bunch became more and more frustrated. A young girl appeared. 'OK, this is a bullshit story, there's another kid here. We're going in this house.' Three men gathered on the other side of the canal. The boy kept changing his story. 'This kid's about to cry and all these people are trying to talk to him. Something's definitely going on', said Bunch.

I followed him up to the entrance to the house. As he walked in, a sudden violent movement sent everyone darting backwards. Another small girl had appeared, startling Bunch into a firing position. 'That little girl almost got blasted', he said. More girls appeared, then a woman who seemed to be their mother.

'Now there's a woman in the house. What the fuck is going on? There wasn't supposed to be anybody here, now there's a whole family. Tell the kid to stop lying and tell us the truth', said Bunch. 'Ask him why he's so nervous.'

Eventually, the boy said there were three women in the house, that his brother had 'escaped the Taliban' and that his father was ill in hospital.

Before they searched the building, the marines told the boy to get all the women into one room. We were ordered to turn our backs as they were ushered past. Any Taliban fighters could easily have escaped or sprayed the whole platoon with bullets. It was odd to see one of the world's most lethal fighting forces offering such a gift to the enemy. They had to be ready to blow people's heads off or walk into booby-trapped buildings, but they also had to be culturally sensitive. When all the women were in one room, the marines searched the rest, telling the boy to go in first because 'they won't shoot if he goes in'.

The last place left to search was a side passage where animals were kept. The boy tried to block the entrance. 'What's he so worried about?' demanded Bunch. Marines pushed past. One shone a light into the chicken coop. He found a rifle, wrapped up.

'You're fucked, kid', said Bunch. Everyone gathered at the doorway but no one was allowed in; the gun might have been booby-trapped.

'What is this? What is this? Why is there a rifle in here? There's probably a shitload buried in there.'

The boy was ordered to go in and pick up the rifle, which he was reluctant to do. 'Right there! I know you see the rifle, kid.' Eventually he picked it up. 'Don't fucking touch it, put it down, put it down. Get away from the rifle.'

The interpreter picked it up, carried it outside and unwrapped it. Bunch opened it to check for ammunition. His shoulders dropped. 'Are you kidding me? It's a fucking BB gun.'

'Why was it covered up?' he asked the boy.

'I use it to kill some birds. I can't kill somebody with it', said the boy.

They told the boy not to cover things up, because it causes suspicion. 'Tell him thank you for his time, we're going to leave now, sorry.'

Outside, the three men still watched. Bunch asked the interpreter why they were so concerned with this house but he didn't get an answer. Then, the man dressed in black, who we'd seen running away earlier, joined them. One of the marines spat on the ground. They asked who the local elder was and were given a name they hadn't heard before. Bunch went down on one knee: 'They give a completely different answer every time you ask them.' The boy had followed and was standing behind Bunch. Bunch turned towards him, discreetly pointing at the men across the canal. 'Talib? Talib? Taliban?' he asked in a whisper. But the boy just stared.

'He ain't telling me shit', said Bunch, after a few more attempts. He turned back to the men, who were being asked for help by the platoon commander. 'If we help you the Taliban will kill us', they said.

Bunch was sure the man in black was Taliban, 'eye-fucking' the others into not talking. He sighed. 'I wish the bad guys had uniforms.'

It was almost dark, so the men were told that if they did have any information, they should come and see the Marines at their patrol base. Then we started the long walk back.

Later, I approached the adjutant. 'Is Brady Bunch his real name? Did his mother actually call him that?'

'Yep. He gets a lot of shit for it.'

The next day, I joined First Platoon on another patrol. As one of the marines attempted to talk to an old man using a Pashtu phrase book, a few rounds from an AK47 popped over our heads. We moved in the direction the bullets seemed to be coming from. Leaning against a low wall, we peeked over but no one could see anything. Staff Sergeant Funke, a recent divorcé, permanently disgusted but with a sense of humour that made him instantly likeable, studied his map, simultaneously listening to his radio. The person at the other end identified two men with RPGs and AK47s. Funke worked out where they were and laughed. 'They're right fucking there, gentleman. Right there', he pointed. 'They're about … … Ha! Less than a hundred metres from us.'

We heard the harmless-sounding whoosh of an RPG over our heads and everyone dropped to the ground. Everyone except the old man, who stayed upright, looking down at the marines. Then he turned and slowly walked inside. The rocket didn't explode but everyone stayed down, giving Funke something else to get annoyed about: 'Can we fucking move on these people, goddamnit?'

'Does anyone see anything?' shouted another marine. A heavy and constant burst of gunfire came from very close by. Everyone seemed to have someone ranked below them to shout at. Funke yelled at one marine, who yelled at the marine next to me: 'Get your fucking goddamn fucking muzzle up, pay fucking attention. See that window? Watch it.'

The marines ran into the next compound, kicking open doors and searching rooms as they went. AK47 rounds popped over our heads but never seemed to hit anything. We all ran, crouched, at the same time; all except Funke, who stood straight, looking down at us impatiently. 'The rounds are going over your heads. Let's go.'

Everyone jogged towards the next compound. Funke strolled casually behind, until we started going in the wrong direction. 'Gentlemen, the enemy is to the south. We are to the north. We need to get through this', pointing to a compound to the south. 'They are there, we need to kill them. Let's go.'

Someone shouted, 'Incoming'. We all fell on one knee and put our chins on our chests. But whatever it was didn't explode. We ran to the last compound, which had much higher walls than the others. A rickety-looking ladder stood against one wall and a door led in to a field, beyond which were the trees from where we were being attacked. Everyone looked confused. No one wanted to be the first through the door, because they would be an easy target for the as-yet-unseen enemy.

Funke marched to the middle of the courtyard. 'Gents, listen up. They are waiting for us to expose ourselves in front of this tree-line. I need a three-man position on the outside of this corner. I need a three-man position on the outside of that corner. I need two marines at the door and one person doing over-watch on this fucking ladder. It does you no good being inside. This is what you wanted. You fucking got it. Now go get it.'

Lance Corporal Gomez, a dark-skinned Ecuadorian, was ordered up the ladder first, because he was carrying a SAW (Squad Automatic Weapon), a bigger machine gun than everyone else's. He climbed the ladder very slowly, fully expecting it to collapse under his weight. Carefully, he eased his head above the wall. I asked him if he could see anything.

'I see weed, man.' There was a huge field of marijuana on the other side of the wall. 'I want to jump in. But I see nothing else.'

Suddenly, he did see something. He started firing, showering me with dozens of hot bullet cases. Three or four other marines started firing, although asked for an exact location, all they could say was 'on the tree-line', which we had known from the beginning.

Gomez fired a grenade. 'Come on baby, hit, hit.' He stared at the trees, so desperate to be on target that it looked like he'd be in physical pain him if he weren't. I heard the grenade explode on the far side of the field. He fired another but the grenade launcher came away from his gun: 'Motherfucker'. The marines around us kept firing. Funke ordered some through the door and into a ditch in the field. I ran after them, not realising until I jumped to the ground that it was just ploughed earth, not a ditch. A small bird could have pushed the furrows aside to get a worm. It certainly wouldn't stop bullets. The mud was so hot it burnt my elbows. Either side of me, marines looked through their sights at the trees hiding our attackers. They couldn't see any movement. Neither could I.

'They're in that tree line next to the building just in front of us?' I asked the marine to my left.

'Are you asking me or telling me?'

'Asking', I said, startled that he might actually listen to what I had to say. I ran back inside.

Gomez, drinking water, wiped sweat from his face. 'I love this shit, this is what I re-enlisted for. Four deployments now, you can't keep me down.'

A few marines sheltered in the narrow slice of shade offered by the wall of the compound's one room. 'If I move I'm gonna pass out', said Staff Sergeant Paz, wobbling. Some marines went inside and sat down. One, with a startled look on his face, started vomiting. It looked like his stomach was being pumped but nothing but pasty water came out. He vomited three times, took a deep breath, and jumped to his feet, strapping on his helmet. 'Let's go, y'all. Let's go, Bravo, GET ON YOUR FEET, LET'S GO.'

'You sure?' his platoon commander asked.

'I got it.' The two men bumped fists and marched outside. 'Let's go, gentlemen. ON YOUR FEET. FUCK THESE BITCHES.'

But the battle was over. Our attackers had either been killed – at least three marines claimed to have hit them – or fired everything they had and vanished. The marines searched the trees but found neither blood nor bodies.

*　*　*　*　*

The marines continued to patrol daily but the Taliban remained invisible. 'This is some Vietnam shit', said Bunch. 'Most of the time it's like we're getting shot at by bushes.'

In the middle of another patrol, everyone settled down for a quick nap in a house they had just cleared. On the walls, children's drawings showed fighters firing AK47s.

'A fucking little kid drew a picture of his dad shooting down a fucking helicopter. These people are amazing. This country never ceases to amaze me. I drew pictures of my dad driving his truck to work, not shooting a fucking helicopter', said one marine.

'This one got shot down', said another, laughing. He'd found a drawing of a grounded helicopter lying on its side. 'Sick bastards, man. Dude, have you even seen anyone that lives here? They're like hippies, because of all the pot. Except they're not liberalish, they're like, extremist. But they smoke a lot of weed. They should relax and be like the hippies. No war! Just peace!' He let his head drop, leaving his fingers in a V-sign in the air.

On another patrol, I was with PFC Janos Lutz when we found a huge field of weed. 'Wow! That is by far the biggest pot field I've seen.' Lutz was just twenty-one but already, he'd done a tour of Iraq and time in prison for assault. Lutz was downbeat when I spoke to him. He'd been allowed to use the company sat-phone to call home. During the pep talk before the operation, Echo Company had been told that 'the world is watching' but the people on the other end of the phone didn't know there had been any fighting.

'Our families know what's going on. People in the military know, but the general population doesn't. America's not at war, America's at the mall', Lutz said, visibly angry. 'No one fucking cares. It's "what's up with Paris Hilton now? Britney Spears fucking this …" The average American doesn't fucking know when people die over here.'

Bunch agreed. 'There's no way people back home could understand what this country is like. It's like every day, we get shot at. I finally got to make a phone call today, expecting it to be like "Oh, I miss you so much" and all kinds of stuff. No. I call home and it's "everything's fine, I'm partying, having a good life down here". Doesn't even ask me how I'm doing. That's when I realised that people don't give a shit about what we're doing here. No one even really mentions 9/11 any more. To me, that's the whole reason I'm over here, that's why I went to Iraq, why I joined the Marine Corps. Now we're here and I really don't know why.'

A marine stroked a small bush with his gloved hand. 'Look at this fucking thing, it's nothing but thorns. It's just angry. It literally has no function except to cause pain. Everything in this country is just so fucking angry.'

I asked if this still felt like the 'War on Terror', even though the phrase was no longer used. Some of the marines were just eleven or twelve years old on 9/11. Some said it did. 'There are three thousand reasons why, three thousand names who aren't with us any more. And the fucks who did that are here.' But the younger they were, the less clear they became. One private, who had signed up exactly a year before, five days after his eighteenth birthday, said, 'I guess … I don't know. Where I was, the economy wasn't good, you couldn't get a job, my stepdad was suffering, had a hard time finding a job. I knew this was a good organisation, regular pay check, they take care of you. Sitting here now, I'm helping my parents out a lot.' His pay was just over twenty thousand dollars a year.

One of Echo Company's captains, Eric Meador, believed he was still fighting Al-Qaeda but more important, 'we abandoned these people after the Russians pulled out, just like we abandoned the Iraqis after we kicked Saddam out of Kuwait. So we owe it to them to help now.' He told me about an Iraqi woman who had approached him a few tours ago, holding a child who had Down's Syndrome. She screamed at him, saying he had let Saddam gas the Shiites after the uprising of 1991 and now her baby was like this. He said he'd never forget her; he'd never seen anyone so angry and he understood why.

There were marines who genuinely wanted to help the Afghans but even the strongest sense of moral obligation couldn't make someone do more than they are capable of. I didn't understand how the policy could succeed. Of the twenty-one thousand extra men Obama had sent into Afghanistan, only four thousand were actually fighting to provide security. The rest were in secluded and isolated bases, in supporting roles. Even in Mian Poshteh, the latest focus for massive resources and manpower, control and reach was extremely limited. As one senior marine confided, 'we only control as far as we see'.

Before I left Echo Company, I sat with the Commanding Officer, Lieutenant Colonel Christian Cabaniss, and asked what he thought his marines could achieve.

Killing the Taliban, he said, was 'almost irrelevant'. What I'd seen in Mian Poshteh may have been the 'end of the beginning but it wasn't actually that decisive'. What would be decisive was good counter-insurgency, which Cabaniss was evangelical about. While I was waiting for the convoy to Mian Poshteh, he'd gone out of his way to discuss it with me, before one of his men politely told him he had more important business to attend to. Counter-insurgency – COIN – as it was known in Helmand, had become a verb. 'I'm gonna coin the shit out of these people', said one engineer, heading out to work on an irrigation project.

Cabaniss thought that only now were there enough troops on the ground to apply it properly. 'Some places here, they had seen brief periods where the British had come into their villages and left. Where we went, we were going to stay. And that's where we start to gain some trust from the local population. They'll start talking to us and telling us about things that are going on in their community. I think in the past they have not wanted to say anything to anybody, out of fear.

'I don't like the term "hearts and minds", because most people don't understand it but their heart is ... they have to believe it's in their best interests to be on the side of the government of Afghanistan. Their mind is ... they know we're going to win. They can't sit on the fence any more. We're not going to build Jacksonville, North Carolina in the next six months but I think we can expect to have sustainable progress. The people connected to the government, the government connected to the people, they work together in common cause to bring tangible progress. Not shove the Taliban out completely but marginalise them. Where most of the locals look at them as common criminals, people that are just disturbing the peace.' During an earlier conversation, he had described this as 'armed social work'.

I said that over two years ago British officials had said exactly the same things, and yet the Brits had just suffered their worst month so far and the Taliban were stronger than they had been since being overthrown.

'The Brits had a good understanding of what was going on down here but they never had enough combat power to do what they would like to do and sustain it over time. My battalion taking over, we're obviously just a little bit larger, we've been able to position forces all over the central Helmand river valley and really get out among the people. They just didn't have the capability to do it right.'

I said that while it was obvious the Taliban couldn't win a military victory, why couldn't they keep laying ever-more-sophisticated IEDs and taking pot-shots for years to come, costing lives, billions of dollars and eventually bleeding all the foreign forces dry?

'If we can take a deep hold, in the areas that we're in, by wintertime the Taliban are going to be on their heels, sitting in Pakistan, wondering what to do next. And we'll have the people.' He smiled as if this had already been achieved. 'Once the people decide they won't tolerate the Taliban's presence, there's no way they can stay.'

I asked if this was the new way America fought wars.

'Not tooting the Marine Corps horn but before General Petreaus went to Iraq, the Marine battalions in Al Anbar [a province in Iraq, where many marines believe COIN was first successfully applied] had already come to the conclusion that working closely with the local population, building relationships with them, had a greater impact on security than going street to street and shooting did. We learnt that the hard way in Iraq and we're starting the right way in Afghanistan.'

These levels of faith in COIN were new in Afghanistan. Many Americans had become converts in Iraq, where they thought it had worked. One of the COIN bibles was David Kilcullen's *The Accidental Guerrilla*, which I read at FOB Delhi, frequently interrupted by officers telling me what an amazing book it was. The rise to prominence of the 'COINistas' – now shaping Afghan policy – was no less momentous than the rise of the neo-cons ten years earlier.

I waited two days for a helicopter ride to Camp Bastion, which had expanded to include Bastion 2 and Camp Leatherneck, the Marine Corps base. One soldier had been told the camp would eventually include Bastions 15 and 16. I had another three-day wait before I could fly to Kabul and I bumped into some Afghan interpreters I'd met on the way out. Many had become American citizens when their families had fled either the Russian invasion or the Taliban. When I told one Hazara man, paid just $700 a month, what I'd seen, he said: 'Man, the Americans are being too soft down there. They need to go into the villages and say "if we see one Taliban here or if you help them once, we'll flatten every building". The problems would end that day.'

PART III

US MARINE CORPS
FEBRUARY TO MARCH, 2010
1ST BATTALION
6TH MARINES

The operation by four thousand US Marines in southern Helmand had proved that a small area can be made relatively secure when flooded with troops. The numbers needed to apply the same tactics across the country were far beyond what was available.

Things continued to get worse; October 2009 was the deadliest month of the war yet. Even General McChrystal said that there would be complete failure unless the 'serious and deteriorating' conditions were not changed. He referred to the current policy as 'Chaos-istan', which would leave the country as a 'Somalia-like haven of chaos that we simply manage from the outside'.

His solution was more troops. President Obama was lobbied hard to approve a 'surge', to replicate what had happened in Iraq. After a lengthy review, the President agreed on a new policy, and thirty-three thousand additional troops, for Afghanistan.

Talk of liberating the women of Afghanistan and creating a democracy had evaporated. The new policy had three, far more modest, objectives: deny Al-Qaeda a safe haven; reverse the Taliban's momentum and deny it the ability to overthrow the government; and strengthen the capacity of Afghanistan's security forces and government, so that they could take the responsibility for the country's future.

I learned that when the first of the new troops arrived, 'the big one' was going to happen. 'The big one' was a long-rumoured assault on Marjah, a farming district in Helmand that had become a Taliban stronghold. The assault would be led by the US Marines, the first of the additional troops to arrive. The world – and America's enemies – were to be shown that the new policy could work; the Taliban could be removed, the population could be won over, the Afghans could secure their country themselves and we could leave.

Because I worked alone, was able to keep up, stuck around for longer than a day or two and carried everything I needed on my back, the Marines asked if I wanted to join them. This was the biggest military operation since the war had begun; one of the biggest stories of my career. I thought I'd be rewarded for my persistence and bombarded with offers. I contacted all the BBC executives I knew but was completely ignored. BBC America showed some interest but at the last minute, someone I'd never heard of went out of his way to prevent me from going. No one was willing to tell me why or even to talk to me. I simply heard a rumour that my trip had been 'red-carded' and that was that.

During my best friend's stag weekend in Copenhagen, I got a phone call from the Marines: the invasion of Marjah had been brought forward. I needed to get there immediately. I had no chance of getting a commission at such short notice. I either had to pass up this chance, wasting months of work, or go out there on my own, without backing, insurance or funding.

I might have been making the biggest mistake of my life but I couldn't say no. I said an awful goodbye to my friends, got the next plane back to London, borrowed or hired everything I needed and headed back to Afghanistan. There was every chance I could come back in debt, without a film, without legs, or worse. But I had to see America's latest – and probably last – attempt to win the war in Afghanistan.

CHAPTER 6

For me, Operation Mushtaraq began with a bus ride to a giant sandpit. A model of Marjah had been created, with little piles of bricks for the landmarks. Marines moved around the model holding flags representing the different companies that would soon be invading. This was an ROC (Rehearsal of Concept) drill.

We began with recitations of verses from the Qur'an by Lieutenant Colonel Awal Abdul Salaam, of the Afghan National Army. Salaam, we were told, was a former Mujahadeen; 'our secret weapon', according to General Larry Nicholson, the Marines' commander in Helmand. Salaam had a magnificent (dyed) black beard that reached almost to his belly button and his eyes were rimmed with thick black kohl eyeliner. 'Trust me', said General Nicholson. 'You don't wanna mess with this guy.' Later that night, in the tent we shared, I caught him going through someone's backpack. I didn't tell anyone about his pilfering but he soon vanished. He'd either been exposed as a fraud or fled as soon as he heard what was happening. Several marines said he'd begged them for a seat on the next helicopter out as soon as the ROC drill was finished. That ought to have been a sign.

The recital finished, General Nicholson took over. His boxer's face was craggy and lived-in; he'd been badly injured in a rocket attack in Iraq in 2004, losing a large chunk of muscle from his back. A marine sitting at his desk, to repair his computer, had been killed. I didn't know whether the general had been happy since surviving that attack, whether he was always happy or if he was just happy leading marines into battle. But on that day he looked ecstatically happy. The certainty with which he spoke clearly delighted him.

'Just fifteen kilometres behind me you would be in the centre of Nad Ali. Just a few more and you would be in the centre of Marjah. We have people in this camp who run further than that every day. So it's no great step to imagine that we are on the doorstep of the objectives that we're about to face. For several years now Marjah has been under the control of the Taliban. It's been no-go terrain to us and to our Afghan security partners.

'The purpose of this mission is to return Marjah to the lawful government of Afghanistan and to rescue the people from many years of Taliban rule. They are waiting for the Afghan security forces, partnered with coalition forces, to come in and lift that burden, lift that yoke of Taliban rule off them.

'The D-Day force will go sure, big, strong and fast. We will place the enemy on the horns of a dilemma. They will have three choices: number one, stay and fight; number two, make peace with this government; number three, try to flee. If he tries to flee we certainly will have folks around waiting for him. And if he tries to blend, the importance of the Afghan security forces is that they will help us separate him when he tries to hide in plain sight.

'The goal of this operation is the people. It always has been and it will continue to be. In Marjah, the people are the prize. The Taliban is what separates the people from their government.

'This may be the largest IED threat and largest minefield that NATO has faced', Nicholson continued. 'We will breach and continue to move without losing momentum. There will be no opportunity for time out, no opportunity to take a knee, no intervention at any level that will stop us from achieving our D-Day objectives. We will immediately, upon achieving those objectives, engage with the local population. Every Company Commander will hold a *shura* on D-Day. This will be continuous. We will work closely with the Provisional Reconstruction Teams to be able to show an immediate improvement in the people's lives. You get one chance to make a first impression with the local population. We understand that, we get it and we'll pursue it with great vigour.' Speaking elsewhere, General McChrystal, leader of NATO and American forces in Afghanistan went further, promising a 'government in a box, ready to roll' within days. He said the Marjah operation was 'a model for the future: an Afghan-led operation, supported by the coalition, deeply engaged with the people'.

'You will hear noise in the background', Nicholson continued. 'You will hear gunfire on the ranges. That is ANCOP (Afghan National Civil Order Police) training. We have three hundred ANCOP here today on this base; we'll have them for about eight days training then we'll get more ANCOP and we will continue to help prepare the Afghan Security Forces for the challenges ahead.'

Standing next to the lectern as General Nicholson spoke was Captain Saed of the Afghan National Army. In a few days' time, the racket he'd make beating the shit out of one of his men for smoking weed on watch would wake me in the middle of the night.

General Nicholson handed over to General Mahayadin, an incredibly handsome Afghan man, whose face could have been carved from stone. He had a thick black moustache and a head as bald and shiny as a bowling ball.

'Marjah is a place of fear, panic and terrorism', he began, 'and the people are tired of those controlling Marjah. The Afghan government and its partners, the army and ISAF decided to terminate the concerns of Marjah people. We have planned, and decided to do our best to free these people from these terrorists and the landmines they are losing their kids and families to. The ANA, ANP, Marines and other forces will attack Marjah and take it over from the enemy. We will raise the Afghan flag again and bring back the people to their normal lives.' He then repeated almost exactly what General Nicholson had said: 'The enemy has three choices: one, fight or die; second, surrender to the government; third, run away. Wherever the enemy goes we follow them. Kill them. Be sure that we will bring peace in Marjah and we will terminate and destroy the enemy. Thank you.'

Nicholson and General Carter, the British head of Regional Command South, chatted with the reporters, telling anecdotes that made everyone laugh. Beside him, General Carter's assistant smoked his pipe and carried an umbrella. There was a sense of unreality. The atmosphere was jolly, as if everyone were setting off for a game of golf, not about to invade a town the Taliban had spent months seeding with booby-traps, sniper holes, trenches and bunkers.

General Carter spoke. 'From the perspective of the Afghan people, what will happen is that they will see their government is genuinely committed to making life better for them. That effect will start in Marjah; it will spread to Nad Ali, to Helmand and through-out Afghanistan. And you, as the key participants in this operation, will be those who will achieve that effect. But you should also be clear that the outside world will wish to see a successful operation. And what they will see is an increasingly capable Afghan Security Force at the helm of what will be a combined operation.' He emphasised 'helm', just as McChrystal had emphasised 'Afghan-led'. Even the name of the operation – *Mushtaraq* – meant 'together'. I could see why they were all making the point: *the Afghans are as good as us now, so we can soon leave!* But they actually seemed to believe it.

General Nicholson took the mike again. 'I cannot recall an opera-tion, anywhere, where we will have had such multinational, joint, combined talent leading it. This is a magnificent force that's been assembled for a specific reason. We have confidence in a lot of things: our mission, our ability to accomplish the mission, the inevitability of this mission. But most of all we have confidence in our team.' He motioned with his hand to the two Afghans next to him; unfortu-nately, they weren't getting a translation. 'And wherever you see a marine, you'll see the Afghan army or police with them. No one is going to be able to do this alone. I know that we're ready. I think his-tory will judge us favorably on our efforts and our resolve. So thank you all for coming. We are ready. *Semper Fidelis*. Have a great day.'

Everyone posed for a photograph. General Nicholson shouted 'Team Marjah!', adding, 'That will be in the history books some-where.'

Later, General Nicholson held an impromptu press conference with General Mahayadin by his side. 'I don't know that anyone is closer-embedded. We don't just talk it, we live it. Story after story: Christmas Day, Afghan soldiers coming in with turkeys; Ramadan, marines buying goats. A brotherhood that has evolved over ten months of great trust and co-operation. This isn't fluff, this isn't talk, this is the real deal. The Marines have great respect for the Afghan Army and I think that's reciprocated.'

One of General Carter's assistants complained light-heartedly to the American reporters that there were no Brits. When they pointed to me, he asked who I was going in with. When I told him, his face dropped: 'Be careful, old boy. It's going to get fruity in there.'

A few nights later, I got a chopper ride to Camp Dwyer, the staging post for the operation. I felt no excitement. Just a grim and draining foreboding that I might badly regret my decision to come here.

* * * * *

The atmosphere at Dwyer was entirely different and matched my feelings about the operation. Here were the people who would be fighting their way into Marjah.

During the ROC drill I'd paid attention to what 'my' marines – 3/6 – were planning to do. Their aim was to approach Marjah slowly over three to four days, clearing all the IEDs along the way. I'd been switched to 1/6 Marines at the last minute but assumed that everyone had roughly the same plan, except they'd all be approaching from different directions.

Bravo's commanding officer, Captain Ryan Sparks, didn't seem pleased to see me. He was very serious, even among other serious men I'd met, about to go into one of the biggest battles of their lives. Captain Sparks looked like a Pixar version of the perfect marine. Chisel-jawed, with light blue eyes, he was an absolutely efficient machine. Nothing in his speech or appearance was unnecessary. Not a hair out of place, not an ounce of fat on his body. No tattoos and didn't do small talk. Originally from Kansas City, Missouri, he held a first degree in Political Science. Sparks was in 'Force Recon', the closest thing that the Marines then had to Special Forces, on September 11th. He'd been on his way to Afghanistan that day, originally to set up a few airfields and later to kill or capture Mullah Omar. After tours in Fallujah and Haditha and another in Afghanistan, he had been made CO of Bravo Company. In between all that, he'd managed to get married, have a baby and complete a masters degree in global leadership. He also loved surfing, which, he said, had 'some sort of mystical hold on my soul'.

Sparks took me to one side and asked how much risk I was willing to take. I told him I wanted to be with the guys who'd be right in the thick of it, at the front. He nodded slightly and told me the plan. Several waves of helicopters would drop Bravo Company into central Marjah at 4 a.m. on day one. For the first few days they would carry only their rifles and a few rockets, have no outside support, no electricity and no vehicles of any kind. I was stunned. It had to be a joke. My mind started racing: IEDs, anti-aircraft guns, trenches, bunkers, a thousand Taliban fighters, perhaps two. I wanted to ask Captain Sparks how he intended to deal with all of this when he landed, in the dark, on day one, without support. Instead I just made a crappy joke about the mission being insane and suicidal.

'Yes. We were surprised too', said Captain Sparks, without laughing.

Jesus, I thought, you could tell this guy to walk into Marjah alone with nothing but a Stanley knife and he'd do it without blinking. I'm dead.

When we'd finished, one of the other officers asked me for details of my next of kin and my blood group. This was called my 'kill data'.

*　*　*　*　*

I joined Captain Sparks the next day as he gathered all his men together for their final pep talk before the operation began. The marines were assembled in a tight circle, some sitting, some squatting and the rest standing, so that they formed a perfect little human ampitheatre.

As Captain Sparks walked past me into the centre of the circle he said: 'I don't know what I'm going to say yet.'

'What's going on Bravo?' he said, pacing back and forth.

The marines responded with their traditional chant. 'Ooh-Rah.'

I'd been told his pep talks were emotional affairs that built up to a crescendo until he – and sometimes the whole company – were screaming and ready to rip off heads with their bare hands. But everywhere I looked, there was a sense of doom, although no one would openly express it. This was a company of men about to suffer. Some would undoubtedly die; others lose limbs. As I scanned the faces, waiting for Captain Sparks to speak, I wondered which ones it would be.

'You guys ready to go?', he asked.

'Ooh-Rah.'

'Long road to get here right?' He paced some more. 'Hey! Who can tell me what the point of this operation is? Or the point of our deployment in general … or even this war?' There was silence. 'Anybody got a stab? Corporal Hernandez?'

'To help out the Afghan people and remove the Taliban', said Hernandez.

'Corporal Hernandez is absolutely right. This whole war, at the strategic, operational, tactical level, it's all about the people. At the strategic level, September 11th 2001. Fundamentalist Islamic extremists attacked New York City and killed three thousand people. Civilians. Since that time the Taliban have been here, controlling the people of Afghanistan. Islamic fundamentalism has caused problems all over the world. At the operational level, for us, the Taliban have their fist in the mix here in Afghanistan. They're controlling the people, destroying their freedom, imposing a way of life that is not comfortable. They are not free. At the tactical level this operation is about the people. The people of Marjah every day live under the iron fist of Taliban law.'

In the build up to Operation Mushtaraq there had been a lot of talk about life in Marjah under the Taliban. Tales of brutality carried out in the name of *sharia,* stories about the opium trade, heroin-processing labs, Taliban prisons and IED factories.

Sparks went on. 'Our new motto: "no better friend, no worse enemy". No better friend is first for a reason. There are eighty thousand people in this city; there's maybe a thousand enemy. These people are pretty callous to being around violence. It's entirely likely that a couple of days into this fight they'll be going to the bazaar and they'll be walking right through the middle of your firefight. It's more important not to hurt the civilians than it is to kill the enemy. Most importantly, what you have to remember as we go out there is that what happens over the next five months, and probably even more over the next five days, will be a cornerstone of your memory for the rest of your life. One way or another, good or bad, those memories will either give you strength or haunt you for the rest of your life. Most importantly, what it comes down to is: we're the good guys. We're here to spread freedom throughout the world. We're here to ensure our way of life at home and give everyone else in the world a chance at democracy.'

The marines were transfixed. I couldn't see the faintest hint of scepticism on anyone's face. They were all absolutely committed and determined. The Captain moved on to the plan.

'I've talked to you before about the gift of aggression. You're here for a reason. That's an important concept, because trust me, this is going to be chaotic. This plan, that we've drilled over and over, as soon as you get off the bird it's not worth anything. Every single one of you, from me down to Ward, who's probably our newest guy, every day are going to have to make a hundred decisions that there is no right answer to. You're not going to have all the information. You're not really going to know what's going on. But guess what? You have to act. None of us will be perfect but have faith in your training and make sure that every day you're looking out for those guys to your left and your right.

'The guy that wrote *On Combat,* one of my favourite books, Lieutenant Colonel Dave Grossman, refers to us as modern day

Paladins. The knights of old, the old Paladins, put on their body armour every day, their steel suit, got on their horse, went through their little area of operations and made sure everything was safe for the people they were in charge of. We're about to put on our armour and go out and free these people from an oppressive fist that they've been dealing with for a long time. Victory is inevitable. When the enemy chooses to fight us on the battlefield, we'll win the direct firefight right now with overwhelming surgical firepower. Destroy him, immediately, so that he doesn't come back tomorrow and get in the way with the civilians. Air is there but it takes a long time to get approved. But I'm telling you, look to your left and your right. You're carrying what you need right now to win this fight. What do we need? We don't need anything. There's a bunch of idiots out there with AK47s and explosives made out of two by fours. You're carrying right now what you need to win this fight.'

When he told the marines to look to their left and right, he was telling them to look at the M16 rifles they were carrying; that they always carried. It seemed odd in this age of laser-guided missiles, remote-controlled predator drones, bomb-proof trucks and Apache Helicopters, that these marines would walk into battle with nothing but a rifle first used in Vietnam in 1963. I thought modern warfare was supposed to be like a computer game – fought from a distance, sometimes from twenty thousand feet. In comparison, this felt gladiatorial.

'Alright gentlemen. I'm not gonna make this long-winded, I'll sum it up with this. It's killed me every day since I've been here, fulfilling my duty, because I'm away from the most important things in my life: my daughter and my wife. But every decision when I'm out there, for a split second it's going to flash into my head that when I go home to them, I want them to be proud of what I did over here. I don't want them to feel ashamed because I'm the new Haditha story [in Haditha, in Iraq, US Marines killed twenty-four people, including at least fifteen civilians, in retaliation for an IED attack]. I don't want problems sleeping at night because I'm not sure that I did the right thing. I'm a hundred per cent confident in each and every one of you. I couldn't be more proud of you guys. I love you to death. Do yourselves proud. Do all the marines that came before us proud. We have centuries of ethos built on marines doing the right thing when it mattered, so do them proud. Most importantly, take care of the marine on your left and right because three days from now that's really all that's going to matter. Alright gentlemen, that's all I got.'

There was another 'Ooh-Rah', but it was subdued. They were sure they would take Marjah but they were also sure that everything else Captain Sparks had talked about was bound to happen. Someone would die. Someone would step on an IED. Someone would kill civilians by mistake. The rules and restrictions of counter-insurgency would make them so frustrated they'd question the point of being there in the first place.

The Captain took the squad leaders to one side for another talk. 'I've done all I can to help you out and I'll be at the friction points to give you what you need. But this is your fight. This is the best crew of NCOs I've ever seen, you guys are phenomenal. Just understand that you have all my trust and confidence. If the enemy manoeuvre on us: let them. Do not get sucked in to one of their ambushes. If this thing goes kinetic, I guarantee you we will lose marines. Even if it doesn't, based on the IED threat, it is very likely that we will lose marines. It is up to you guys to honour the marines we lose by maintaining the focus in the right direction. Don't let emotions control you. The fight is still there to be won. We have to win the people. Trying to take somebody out for revenge, complaining about the ROEs or letting your marines go feral and crazy: that will significantly deteriorate the combat effectiveness of this company. You are the barrier, you are the ones that will make or break us there. Treat these people like you would the victims of Hurricane Katrina or down in Haiti; just another bunch of people that need our help. Then you'll come out on top, I guarantee it. Let your guys relax but don't let anybody go off on their own and worry about this too much. At this point, it is what it is. The beautiful thing about being in our situation is, there's no decision to make. There's only one way out and that's through it.'

A chaplain and two female marines arrived, carrying a guitar. Seventeen marines joined them in a corner, next to a metal container. In high tones, they sang 'Shining in the light of your glory'. 'Pour out your power of love, as we sing holy, holy, holy. Holy, holy, holy, I want to see-ee you.' It was surreal, although probably only to my godless English eyes. The song was upbeat and full of joy, the kind you hear on American tele-evangelist shows where the people raise their hands in the air and collapse in tears of happiness. This happy-clappy music was completely at odds with the grim task ahead. The deathly, dour hymns I might hear if I ever went into an English church felt more apt. The chaplain led a prayer: 'Lord, we thank you for the beauty of this day. We thank you for every day of life that you give to us. We thank you that we have bright sunshine and warm temperatures. Lord, we thank you for the chance to step aside from all the preparation and all the busy-ness so we can focus on you for a minute just to listen to your voice and just to feel your presence. So Lord, I pray that you'll come to us in this time.' The prayer was followed by a reading from Joshua, on being strong and courageous not because 'we are anything special' but because 'our Father is there, he's holding on to us and he's never going to let go'.

'Isn't that good news?' he asked the marines rhetorically, then led another prayer.

'Lord, whatever it is that we face in life, whether we're trying to help a buddy or whether we're trying to kill an evil person. Lord, I pray that we would know your presence is with us through all of those things and all of those struggles that we face. Lord, I pray that you would fill us with your strength and courage so that we can fulfil the work that you've set out for us. We just trust these things and we pray in your name. Amen.'

CHAPTER 7

About midnight, we assembled at the spot where Captain Sparks had given his pep talk. There was no moon, so even when our eyes had adjusted to the dark, it was impossible to make out faces. Most people hadn't slept. The marines were tense, fuelled by caffeinated drinks, cigarettes, chewing tobacco and most of all, fear and excitement.

An hour or so later, in the freezing cold, we lifted our bags and marched in single file to the huge landing strip where CH 53E Sea Stallion helicopters waited to take us into Marjah. The roaring sounds of the machines' twin blades and engines made conversation impossible, so as we climbed on board and the helicopters took off, we had half an hour alone with our thoughts. I pictured the morbidly determined faces around me wailing in pain from gunshot wounds or looking down in horror and suddenly realizing that the future without legs that they'd imagined was now real. Everyone had visualised that life. I'd joked about it with my football team the week before, asking to play up front so that I might score a goal in my last game with legs.

The Taliban were rumoured to have three anti-aircraft guns in Marjah, so simply landing was a relief. As I walked down the ramp, the deafening blast of the engine was quickly swallowed by the ferocious whipping sound of the rotating blades. Dust and heat hit my face as I staggered under the helicopter's exhaust, then the freezing night air bit every piece of flesh that wasn't under several layers of clothing.

There were so many different sensations, sounds and forces that it was impossible to tell which way you were being pushed and whether the pain was burning or freezing. I waded forwards, half-blind. Through one barely-open eye I caught glimpses of camouflage uniforms, hands gripping rifles, shuttered eyes, straining legs and arched backs, sharply-drawn muscles where clothes were blown tight against skin. Over it all, debris and dirt whipped up from the ground lashed against our faces and bodies. It was a relief to have landed without setting off any IEDs. But it was a struggle to stay upright, let alone tread carefully; every step was filled with dread.

Marines shouted each other's names or grabbed limbs blindly, shouting: 'who's this?' Then I was suddenly aware of marines falling around me. They fell sharply, sideways and backwards. They didn't get up but writhed around on the ground, like flipped woodlice. Suddenly, the choppers were gone and I could hear again. The falling marines had slipped in the mud and because they were carrying so much on their backs, they couldn't get up without help. There had been no shots and no IEDs. There was only silence, freezing wind and an impenetrable blanket of darkness.

After unfolding a temporary bridge and crossing a canal, everything calmed down. The squad leaders got their men together and by about 4.30 a.m., everyone had started moving in the same direction. Then, the buildings around us suddenly awoke. Cockerels started crowing and dogs barked. Was this when they normally started? Or had we set them off early? Did everyone in Marjah now know exactly where we were? Were they watching us? I could hear every noise the marines made: boots being pulled from the icy mud, rifle metal hitting the equipment attached to almost every part of their bodies, deep breathing and whispered radio conversations. Then, in concert, a mad, rhythmic chant, fast, repetitive and threatening, blared from the speakers of the local mosque. It was a disturbing sound, nothing like the call to prayer. The speaker seemed to be working himself up into a frenzy. I was later told the message was: 'The Infidels have landed, get your guns'.

As the light strengthened, I saw marine snipers climbing on to a nearby roof, looking through the sights of their rifles. There was an almost constant metallic hum from jets high overhead. I found myself kneeling next to Wesley Hillis, a lean, skull-faced young corporal with a cold, quiet authority.

'Right now we're sweeping for IEDs, hoping we don't step on anything', he said quietly. 'It's a very slow process with this many guys. Everyone's aggressive and wanting to move fast, so they're forgetting the basics. But everything will straighten itself out. The light's coming up and we'll get more comfortable and this terrain won't be whipping us so bad. We just sit and wait.'

He took off his anti-ballistic visor, wiped it clean and seemed to think, I'll be honest with the reporter. 'This is really fucked up right now. I wish the sun would come up, people would start shooting and then we'd fix ourselves. Most fucking grunts don't understand slow and methodical. That's what these IEDs do, they take us away from our game plan. We have to swap up our tactics and play a chess game. It's not chequers now.' He stood up and walked off.

In the gathering light, I saw we were spread across an open field. If Taliban fighters were waiting, we were completely exposed. Some squads went down on one knee while others moved slowly forwards. If they had radios, they talked to each other constantly. If they only had rifles, they constantly looked through their sights, scanning every inch of ground for movement.

'Hey, Morrison. You see that bright flashing light at your two o'clock?' whispered Corporal Hillis. We could see a long straight road ahead, lined by trees on one side. Hillis could see two men moving along the road. 'They definitely know we're here now. They're just walking around watching us, like we're the zoo. But they know where the bombs are and we don't, so we still have to take our time.' He looked again. 'I don't know if the people are going to help us or if they're still on the side of the Taliban. They could be onlookers, they could be forward observers for mortars. It's an uncomfortable situation.'

I asked him what kind of reaction he was expecting. 'From what I've got it's kind of mixed. The people don't know any better, so they've been on the side of the Taliban, under that iron fist. We're just trying to show them the right way and hopefully they'll choose sides. But we can't have this being a safe haven for any type of fighters or terrorists.'

Most of the marines' legs, arms and backpacks were soaked through with the cold dark mud we'd lain in. As everyone started to spread out, I followed Hillis, who'd become a reassuring presence. Hillis was in charge of a four-man machine-gun team, following 1st Squad, led by Sergeant Matthew Black, one of the few marines who didn't look at all nervous, didn't try to look tough, but wore an almost cheeky grin. Soon it was just me and about twenty marines, walking to the long straight road up ahead.

Hillis said he saw two more men at one end of the road, which had a huge ditch, about twenty feet wide and twelve feet deep, running alongside. The ditch would have been a perfect trench if there hadn't been a filthy stream running along the bottom. The marines struggled to jump the stream, climbed up the other side, then lay down and scanned the horizon through their sights. 'Where are these motherfuckers at, man?' said one.

We had two Afghan soldiers with us. One, nicknamed Rambo, had the Afghan flag draped over his shoulders, with the bright red part covering his left arm. 'Look at the fucking asshole', said one of the marines. They told Rambo to lie down, like they were doing. The ANA had issued green camouflage, rather than desert, so the red flag only made him stand out a little more than he would have anyway. The other Afghan soldier was digging into the road with a knife, at what looked like an IED.

The road and ditch were perfectly straight. In one direction was a petrol station, in another, several compounds surrounded by high walls. The marines saw men moving around outside. Lying side by side and looking through their rifle sights, they described what they could see.

'There's a possible IED up there.'

'Who's this guy on the right?'

'See the one closer to us on the right?'

'He's got something on his side, like something slung.'

'A rifle?'

'I don't know, he's leaving.'

'There's three people now.'

'Man this sucks.'

Another group of marines looked in the opposite direction. 'He's looking awfully suspicious, just standing there looking at us.' The men they were talking about were fewer than two hundred metres away. They took a few steps towards us, then turned back and walked quickly away.

'If they pop up and start firing, lay into 'em.'

I sat next to Doc Morrison, one of the corpsmen, or medics. He lay on his stomach with the men in his sights. He was chewing such a big lump of tobacco that his jaw looked broken. He spat out some tobacco juice, looked at me and back at the men. In the distance we heard the dull thuds of exploding IEDs.

'That's three in the last ten minutes', said one, 'and it's still early.'

Sergeant Black stood up to point out another group of men he'd seen moving around behind a wall. 'They're just doing their thing, you know? Being shit-heads. See where that black cloud is at? There's a wall. I guess one of them is just chilling behind the wall. Then there's that tree line and they keep moving back and forth between there and that wall.'

There were at least four groups of about five men each: one at either end of the road and two on the other side of the field in front. A few men drove around on scooters, some with passengers, some carrying long objects wrapped in blankets. Another explosion sounded in the distance.

The rules of engagement meant the marines couldn't fire on anyone unless they saw an undeniably hostile act being committed. General McChrystal had made the prevention of civilian casualties the top priority, even if it meant the marines took more casualties themselves. He called it 'courageous restraint'. The Taliban had already worked out how to use it to their advantage, moving around without revealing weapons, mobile phones or radios. They knew that as long as it stayed that way, they wouldn't be shot at. The marines knew they were watching a perfect ambush being set and there was nothing they could do about it.

Hillis walked over to Sergeant Black. 'You can see a lot of people over here.'

'All they're doing is probing our lines without shooting, to see how far we're stretched out.'

A man on a scooter, carrying a propane tank, drove slowly towards us, then turned around.

'They're just trying to see how we'll react to a suspicious vehicle. Who straps a fucking oxygen tank to a moped?' asked Sergeant Black.

'Someone that wants to go scuba diving, probably', said Hillis.

Hillis and Black shared some chewing tobacco and made jokes about what the Taliban might be saying to each other, giving them redneck accents. I wondered what kind of a person thought this was a situation normal enough to make jokes about. 'I'm really not too thrilled about my feet', said Sergeant Black, looking at his boots, which were just lumps of wet mud at the bottom of his legs. Then he saw that mine weren't as high as the marines' and laughed. 'Look at yours, you must be soaked.'

Hillis thought we were almost surrounded by at least forty Taliban fighters. Unless we walked back in the direction from which we had come, we would walk right into them whichever way we went. Sergeant Black decided to take his men across the field. There, they'd have no cover at all, and would be completely surrounded.

'Do you want some ass?' said Hillis, offering some of his machine-gunners. Black said no, he wanted to leave them in the ditch.

Walking behind five other marines, I followed Doc Morrison into the field. I asked him what had happened to the advice we'd been given about not walking anywhere that hadn't been swept for IEDs. 'I guess that don't fly here', he replied.

We weren't fifty metres into the field when a burst of three shots crackled over our heads. Everyone fell to their knees and tried to work out where it had come from. Then came a much longer burst of fire. We ran back to the ditch. Suddenly, dozens of bullets fizzed past us. I scrambled into the ditch and tumbled down towards the putrid stream; Doc Morrison screamed at the last man left in the field to 'get back'.

Bursts of gunfire came from all sides. Some bullets passed so close over Doc Morrison's head that he ducked and slipped down into the ditch for a second. The firing filled the air above us. Bullets hit the mud where we lay, so close that some marines flinched as they felt them. But they got straight back into position, trying to find something they could shoot at. I caught glimpses of facial expressions, sometimes from great distances and only for fractions of a second. They were as vivid and readable as a photograph: terrified and confused, panicked and lost, making me realise how bad the situation was.

For the first time in Afghanistan, I felt I was not on the strongest side and I'd finally pushed my luck too far. The feeling of fragility you get from so many bullets passing so close is almost impossible to describe. Imagine a snowman in the rain, a spider in a toilet or a piece of bread floating along a river that has miles of falls and rocks ahead. I thought that there was nothing I could do except lie down and wait for the bullets to enter my body. It seemed inevitable, and the way I accepted it made me wonder if I'd discovered I was a coward, after all. I remember hoping meekly that I might wake up in a few days and see doctors. Then I imagined waking and looking at the feet of our attackers. A rocket whooshed over my shoulder and exploded against the small wall that ran alongside the ditch, filling the air with dust and shrapnel.

'AW FUCK, I'M HIT, I'M HIT', screamed Morrison, next to me in the ditch. His right leg was covered in bright red blood that gushed from beneath his knee.

'WHAT THE FUCK', he moaned.

'I'm hit too', screamed the marine on the other side of me, holding the back of his left leg.

'Am I bleeding?' he asked, moving his hand away briefly.

'No, you're good', I said, sounding calm for a second. I rolled on to my back, expecting to feel pain or a warm wet patch somewhere. The bullets clattered above us and the screams around me seemed to be saying the same thing. *We don't know where it's coming from and we're all going to die.*

Sergeant Black ran along the bottom of the ditch towards Morrison.

'Come here, come here, GET DOWN', screamed Black. Morrison sat upright, groaning in pain.

'Where you hit at?'

'In my fucking leg, dude.' He looked down at his right leg, still gushing bright red blood. He rolled backwards. 'AAAAGH I'm hit, what the fuck?'

Someone else screamed he'd seen one of our attackers. 'I GOT EYES ON, I GOT EYES ON.'

Sergeant Black got out a tourniquet and screamed at the other marines. 'HEY WE NEED TO GET EYES UP AND START CLEARING THIS SHIT', pointing to the top of the ditch. Bullets cracked over our heads from all directions and another awful clatter broke right above us.

'WHERE THE FUCK IS THAT COMING FROM?' screamed a marine, just in front of me. They still weren't shooting back, still didn't know where the fire was coming from. One of Hillis's machine-gunners started firing but that only seemed to encourage the enemy. More bullets fizzed over us.

Sergeant Black put two tourniquets on Doc Morrison's leg. 'I got you bud, I got you', he said, looking up to see what his men were doing. Morrison apologised. Black told him he had nothing to apologise for. Bullets kept landing on the mud, chopping through the dry grass at the top of the ditch. Occasionally, one zipped past so crisply I was sure it was just inches away. I imagined the first one entering me, then the second, then slowly fading away as the third, fourth and fifth sank in. Someone screamed at everyone to get their heads up and start firing back.

Slowly, the frantic movements and flinches, the panic and the confusion ebbed away. Marines started to fire steady bursts down the ditch or across the field. The marine next to me shouted instructions and started firing single shots, slowly and methodically, just like Hillis had said grunts couldn't do when things weren't going to plan.

Soon, more fire came from the marines than from the Taliban. I thought I was witnessing a miracle; survival suddenly seemed possible. I swore that if I did survive, I'd never go out with these guys again, and never come back to Helmand.

Three or four men ran across the road and hid in the buildings near us.

'SHOOT 'EM' screamed Black, still looking after Morrison.

'START SHOOTING, MOTHERFUCKER', yelled someone else. 'We're still taking fire from left and right.'

'It's from every direction, Staff Sergeant, every direction', pleaded one marine.

Doc Morrison sat up and looked more annoyed than in pain. 'Hey, call in some fucking air, man', he shouted. Another burst cracked over the ditch.

Suddenly, a steady stream of bullets came right at us in the ditch. At least fifteen, each closer than the last. Next to me, Black and Morrison ducked. I pressed myself to the ground. 'WHERE THE FUCK IS THAT COMING FROM?' screamed Black.

'CALL IN SOME FUCKING AIR', screamed Morrison.

Everything went quiet. I heard someone shout: 'I got his ass, he was right there on the fucking corner.'

Staff Sergeant Young, a short and stocky marine, walked towards us. He stopped to shout to some other marines that they still needed positive ID before they could shoot. He didn't walk in the stagnant water at the bottom of the ditch. He didn't walk along the inside of the bank. He walked right along the top, in full view of whoever was shooting at us.

'Have we stopped the bleeding yet?' he asked, as he climbed down the ditch towards us, out of breath.

'You need to get down bro, we're taking fire from fucking three goddamn positions', said Sergeant Black, smiling.

'We'll be alright', said Staff Sergeant Young, still standing. He jumped over the stream and got down on one knee. He said that most of the fire was coming from the direction he'd come from. Then a burst of fire from exactly the opposite direction almost hit us. Staff Sergeant Young stood up again.

'Hey listen', Black yelled, 'get down there. The next time those fuckers open up, I want you to unload some rounds on them.'

Young, still standing, ordered some of his men to follow. He waved his right hand in the air so they could see where he was. The Taliban must have thought it was a trick; I can't think of any other reason why they didn't shoot him.

Bullets came into the ditch, right next to where the four of us sat. The bursts of fire from the marines had no impact.

'Come on guys, get a better view somehow', shouted Young, assuming the other marines cared as little about the incoming bullets as he did.

Jets roared overhead but did nothing. Usually, by this stage, the horizon would be exploding, as millions of dollars' worth of bombs and missiles were dropped on to every building from where the Taliban had attacked. In the past, the mere presence of aircraft – the show of force – was enough to discourage the Taliban. Now, they didn't seem to be the slightest bit concerned about the incredible technology high above.

Another burst of gunfire slammed into the ditch. 'GET TO THE TOP OF THE FUCKING BERM', screamed Young, 'I WANT A 203 [air grenade] LOBBED OUT ON THE NEXT ONE YOU FUCKING SEE. YOU HEAR ME? GET A FUCKING SHOT OFF.' He turned back to Morrison: 'you'll be alright.' Young stood and looked through his rifle sights, then lifted Morrison and carried him along the bottom of the ditch to an easier crossing point. Young jumped into the water and put his rifle on the bank, ready to lift Morrison across. Morrison, still apologising for being hit, wanted to make his own way across the water, with his weapon. His bandaged right leg was soaked in blood and his trousers, rolled above the knee, were dark red. 'I'm worried about you getting an infection. Come on, this could be very serious here', said Young. He and Black lifted Morrison over the water. MEDEVAC helicopters were on their way.

I looked around. Blood, leafless trees, a bumpy dirt road, dark brown mud and stagnant water at the bottom of a ditch. It could have been 1916.

Sergeant Black sat down to get his breath back. 'Fucking bastards, man.' I asked if the buildings nearest to us, not a hundred and fifty metres away from where the helicopters would land, were clear. He laughed. 'No.'

Hillis ran back. 'Fuck me', he said. He and Black exchanged glances. 'Fuck me is right', said Black. 'You can't fucking see dick, dude.'

Another marine said he saw someone's head appearing over a wall. 'Then shoot his ass', shouted Hillis.

'If he pops his head up, you rip one off', said Black.

'There's one down over there', said Hillis.

'Dead?' asked Black. He giggled when Hillis nodded yes.

'I got him and the other guy that was running to the left. They started firing from that compound over there.' He pointed across the field. 'There was eight of them and they were effective. There was no pangs or claps, it was all TSINNNGGGGG! TSINNNGGGGG!' he said, imitating the sound of bullets fizzing past your ear.

Black and Hillis planned the defence of the MEDEVAC helicopters that would soon be landing to pick up Morrison. 'That compound's live as fuck right there Black, we need air on that motherfucker right there', said Hillis, pointing the building where he'd seen eight men. 'Every time that moped stopped at the other end, he was dropping guys off and they ran in there, that's where they were flooded. There's at least ten to twelve now. Altogether I've seen about forty.'

He pointed at buildings all around as he spoke. 'It's not just one guy spraying, like we're used to. These guys actually know what they're doing. They're probably foreign fighters.'

Hillis was frustrated that air strikes hadn't been called. 'They're worried about collateral damage affecting the people. You don't want to take out innocent people but it's a ghost town. You got just a few guys in one compound where you've been taking fire. Even if they're not holding weapons that should be enough. Alleviate the problem. What's more important: your marines or the guys shooting at you and then laying a weapon down?'

Purple smoke spewed out of a grenade thrown in the field behind us as the two MEDEVAC helicopters approached. One flew just above the ground in erratic arcs, like a wasp in a greenhouse, while the other landed so Morrison could be carried on board. As the second helicopter briefly touched down, the Taliban fired, but they both took off without being hit. That had been Doc Morrison's first-ever day of combat. Shrapnel had torn out eight centimetres of nerve and he would later have a tendon transplant, be unable to walk without a splint and be deemed 'combat ineffective'.

In the ditch, another marine casually described the day's events, pointing in every possible direction as he talked about bullets that hit the ground next to him and two fighters he'd seen killed. As he spoke, I heard a gun being fired, then the bullet zipping above us. Apart from being amazed about how much ammunition the man had, the marine was totally unconcerned. He laughed, 'that's coming awfully close to us.' I wanted to inject a little more urgency, so I asked if the whistling sound really was the noise of the bullets.

'Yup', he said, still smiling, then went on talking about his day. 'They use really good tactics. They hide an AK47 in one spot, then move to another that's a good hiding place and where they have another AK47 and they shoot off all those rounds. Then they move, doing the same thing over again. Then they blend with the population.'

The marines were ordered to get out of the ditch, run across the road and back to a building we'd passed on our way in; moving in the opposite direction to Bravo's objective. As we approached, someone shouted, 'Women and children in the building.' An Afghan family, a couple and their six children, including three toddlers, were being pushed out by one of the terps. A tiny girl tried to jump over the muddy ditch outside the house but fell short. She landed on all fours but got straight up and moved away. A slightly bigger girl, the mother and the father all carried babies. The father stopped and held his hands out towards his house.

'Don't worry about your house', shouted the terp. 'Go quickly, go to that house.' He pointed to a building about two hundred metres away.

'I understand', the father shouted over his shoulder, terrified.

Inside the house, the marines poured water from a well over their heads and climbed on to the roof. Others took it in turns to use an old shovel and an axe to smash firing holes through the thick mud walls.

Hillis slumped on the ground, lost in thought, when one of the ANA soldiers suddenly appeared in a hole that led to a small storage room. 'RPG!' he said, beckoning someone to climb through the hole with him. He gave me the thumbs up. Hillis was startled from his thoughts.

'You can't shoot an RPG from in there. Are you fucking stupid?'

The Afghan soldier nodded his head. 'Nice.'

Hillis was flabbergasted. 'Not in here, you'll kill everybody!'

'No good?' said the Afghan, as someone handed him his RPG.

'You can give it to him, just don't shoot', said Hillis, stunned. 'NO SHOOT!'

'No shoot', agreed the Afghan soldier and disappeared back into the hole.

'I'm just waiting on the mortars to start', said Hillis. 'I don't like being here. It's too fucking small, close to a fucking attack position, perfect range for rockets and mortars, an easy distance to judge.' He paused, staring intently at nothing in particular in front of him. 'I'm pooped.'

Hillis was one of those men who looked serious and ready to fight all the time, no matter what they were doing. You couldn't even attack him in his sleep, because he'd still be ready. He was twenty-six years old, from Corinth, Mississippi. He'd been an all-star baseball player, scouted by many professional teams, until he picked up an elbow injury that took too long to heal. He had a few odd jobs, got bored and joined the Marine Corps. 'I joined to fight', he told me, 'that's all I thought the Marines did. When the recruiter told me I could be in an office or shop, I said fuck that, I want to kick in doors and shoot bad guys.' So he went to boot camp, then the school of infantry and became a machine-gunner. This was his second tour in Afghanistan.

I asked how the events of the morning had made him feel about taking Marjah. 'Oh, we'll be fine, we just got started. Everybody will be on their toes now, if they weren't already. It's a kind of a wake up.' He laughed. 'But it's a long time before we go home.'

The gunfight continued. We were being shot at from several different positions by people no one could see. Second Lieutenant Rich Janofsky, who was just twenty-four years old, with a pleasantly surprised look on his face as if he'd just found a fifty-dollar bill, spoke to Captain Sparks over the radio and announced a new plan. Everyone would run four to five hundred metres back towards the objective. At the same time, rockets would be fired into the building next to the petrol station, where Taliban fighters were believed to be. Six minutes' worth of smoke would be provided as cover from the fighters across the fields.

Marines use 'fucking' more often than most people say 'very' but Janofsky was going for a record. 'First is going to fire a fucking Jav into Building 20. Be prepared for fucking volley fire and LAWs [Light Anti-tank Weapons] into the fucking side of 20. And also be fucking prepared to fire fucking LAWs and 203s into Building 19. That door.' He pointed to a doorway on his map. 'I ain't about going through it because they could probably fucking run back and forth. Not kosher. Fucking throw some shit up, punch through, hold security. Then fire another fucking damn bitch into fucking Building 19. If they fucking drop smoke, it's going to be stupid danger close to fucking those guys.' What he had just said was a mystery to me but everyone understood and nodded. 'Alright, what formation you guys want to roll out in?'

Before Bravo could move forwards to their objective, they had to take care of the other fighters, still shooting from the building behind us. Three marines crouched down behind a huge pile of harvested opium poppies and fired air grenades. Then a Harrier flew low and did a few gun runs but everything landed outside the walls surrounding the building. The fighters inside went quiet and were soon forgotten. There had only ever been a handful of them and they were no longer shooting. I don't remember a decision actually being made but the marines walked out and started bounding towards their objective.

Suddenly, we were sprayed with bullets again. And no one had a clue where the fire was coming from. I followed a few marines into a ditch no deeper than a kitchen sink. The others ran into a field whose short grass offered no cover at all.

'We're getting shot at from behind', one shouted. The men in the building hadn't been killed or scared away. They'd just stopped firing and waited for another chance. The explosives one of the marines carried on his back stuck out high above the grass; he wrestled them off as quickly as he could.

I was next to Hillis. He let go of his weapon for a second and lurched towards me as a bullet cracked past. 'Whoooooah, it's coming from that exact same building', he said. A machine-gunner from another squad fired, but not at the building we were looking at. 'What the fuck did he just shoot?' asked Hillis. No one knew. The firefight was going in three different directions; the bullets that were almost hitting us came from more than one position. I lay flat on my back but Hillis and another marine, also called Black, sat up, trying to see who was shooting at us. 'You recognise that zinging by now?' he asked.

'That means it's within a few feet, right?' I asked.

'I believe so, yes', said Black calmly. Marines had a habit of suddenly becoming exquisitely polite and eloquent in the worst of situations, as if it made them feel more at home in a situation that would make most people cry for their mothers.

We were told to get up and sprint towards the objective. 'Go, go, go', shouted Hillis. 'Haul ass, haul fucking ass.' The thick mud and the kit we carried on our backs meant we could sprint only about fifty metres before our legs burned. Slowing to a quick walk, we made it to a collection of strange, U-shaped buildings, like stables without doors, that the marines called 'the Chicken Shack'. I collapsed into the first building. Alongside me, eight marines were trying to work out how much ammunition they had left. 'Conserve', said Hillis, 'short fucking bursts, accurate fire.' Most of the marines were puffing so hard they couldn't talk. One asked the others how many kills they'd had. One held up a single finger, another held up two. 'We got three between us', said a third, smiling.

'Dude, you gotta drop bombs, bombs don't miss', said Hillis. He undid his boots so he could remove the thermal underwear most of us still wore from the night before. 'We ain't had no problems out of Hiroshima and Nagasaki.'

'They wouldn't even fight us for this long last year', said a marine called Carver, as he re-arranged his bandana. 'They wouldn't get closer than six hundred metres. These guys are a hundred and fifty metres away, if not closer. And they've got effective fire. Last year it was just sporadic, never hitting anything really.'

Lance Corporal Godwin took off his helmet. Inside was a picture of his baby boy, five months old that day. 'I miss him', said Godwin, who'd been deployed when his son was just two months old. 'I'll be home to him soon. He's gonna be big. I can't wait.'

Within a few minutes everyone was asleep. They flopped to the ground or slumped against the walls as if they'd been gassed, in what looked to be hugely uncomfortable positions. The fighting had lasted six hours and we'd been awake for at least thirty.

I woke to find that Captain Sparks had arrived. He sat alone, without moving, outside the buildings, where anyone could see him. He looked at a group of marines, 2nd Platoon, who lay on the other side of the field. I didn't know it then but one was dead. A white smoke grenade had been set off; 2nd Platoon was waiting for the MEDEVAC helicopters.

'We lost an engineer who was trying to bring up some breaching equipment', Captain Sparks told me later. 'And I'm the one that called back and told them, get the A-POBs [route-clearing explosives] up here and somebody, I can't remember who it was, was arguing with me about how heavy the fire was. I told them "I don't care, get the A-POBs up here, we gotta get into the objective". And about a half hour after the incident I found out that doing that, one of the marines had been killed. He'd been shot in the back as he was moving out to get that piece of gear. We always go into these fights and I know that in a fight like this I'm going to lose marines but this guy was doing exactly a task that I told him we needed to do and … you know… he got killed doing it.' Captain Sparks swallowed and looked at the ground. 'That was definitely the lowest point I've had so far. That took me a while to reconcile in my head.'

As the MEDEVAC helicopters landed and the stretcher was loaded on board, a loud bang sounded right behind me. I jolted forwards, as if someone had slapped me on the back of the head. The Taliban had fired a rocket at the helicopters as they took off but missed, hitting the outside wall of the buildings where we'd slept. Sergeant Black had been urinating against the wall that the rocket hit. He'd been knocked to the ground; the other marines quickly dusted him off to check for bleeding.

'That scared the fuck out of me', he said.

'No cuts, baby, no cuts', said Staff Sergeant Young as Black got up and started laughing again.

'Motherfuckers. Man, I'm telling you. I'd just put my dick back in my pants. I was pissing. That fucker hit right above my head.' What was left of the rocket, the central pin, splintered at one end, lay on the floor next to him. The sturdy walls, baked hard by so many merciless summers and cursed by so many marines and soldiers, were suddenly a blessing.

The A-POB explosives that Captain Sparks had ordered arrived. Marines prepared to fire them from the other side of the Chicken Shack. A-POBs are designed to clear a path through minefields. Imagine a small rocket dragging a huge football sock behind it, stuffed with grenades every foot or so; when the rocket lands, the sock lands behind it, in a perfectly straight line. The grenades explode, detonating any close-by IEDs and creating a safe path. The A-POBs were aimed to blast a path right up to the building that was Bravo's objective for day one; an old police station that had been used by the Taliban. As the first sock flew out of its case every-one put their fingers in their ears. 'These things are fucking great', said Black. Fifteen seconds later, the A-POB exploded, followed by another. Black roared with laughter. 'Fuck you, cocksuckers.'

'They were probably like "Ah, look at our RPGs!" They friggin' rattled the wall! Well, imagine how *that* felt', said Young.

The marines blew a hole in the wall at the end of the path they'd just made. From there, it was just over a hundred metres to the old police station. Some marines dived to the ground, into firing posi-tions, while the rest ran towards the building.

'Qadeer, Qadeer, you gotta be the first one going in', Young shouted to one of the Afghan soldiers. For the first time – and for this one miserable task only – the Afghans were in the lead. It was their job to be the first to enter the old Taliban building, which was highly likely to be booby-trapped. They were also there to talk to any civilians who might be inside. General McChrystal's claim that Operation Mushtaraq would be 'Afghan-led' looked like a sick joke. Qadeer, who had a thick black beard and was a good foot shorter than most of the marines, jogged awkwardly to the front of the line making its way towards the old police station, carrying his rifle in one arm and holding the other outstretched to keep him upright in the wet mud. Following him was an even shorter Afghan soldier, Romo, whom the marines described as 'actually, slightly retarded'. They approached the door to the building. A marine with a metal detector swept the ground leading to it.

'Hey! Kick the door and go in, OK?' one of the marines shouted to Qadeer. He called to the other Afghan soldier, 'Romo, up here, get up here', gesturing for Romo to go behind Qadeeer. 'Little pussy ass! Romo, kick the door in, then move out the way, then you're gonna go in, ok? Kick the door and then you're gonna move.'

The Afghans were nervous. Qadeer first froze, then kicked the door in and ran back a few steps. The others moved towards the door, fidgeted nervously in front of it but wouldn't go in. It was pitiful to watch. 'Go, Go', screamed the marines, 'GET THE FUCK IN THERE.' One looked through the door and edged in, the others stood still. 'Go, go', screamed another marine. Several marines charged up to the Afghans and shoved them through the door: 'Get the fuck in.' Five Afghans and five marines burst into the building almost as one. If the door had been booby-trapped, they would have all been hit. The marines charged round inside the compound, looking though their rifle sights as they went from room to room, shouting that they saw movement. But the building had been abandoned. The compound was linked to a second. Qadeer and Romo, now being called Qadaad, were ordered to clear those rooms too. They tried and failed to kick in a door, then looked through the windows. 'Good. Talib no. Yes sir.'

'No Taliban, good, let's go to the next one', said a Marine.

Bravo Company now held two large compounds, surrounded by high thick walls. The larger of the two, the old police station, would become their Combat Operation Centre (COC), their base and home for the next four months. Most of the building's six rooms were empty but one was piled high with sacks, yellow jugs and wooden boxes. Qadeer showed me one box holding a Qur'an, which he saluted, then carefully closed.

Tim Coderre, former army sniper, now Law Enforcement Advisor, searched the bags. He showed me some brown, sticky opium. Then opened a bigger bag, saying, 'which is then processed into that', lifting a sealed plastic bag full of heroin. There were eight identical bags, each worth about $60,000. He laid them on the ground. 'That's pretty much half a million dollars' worth of heroin', he said, sucking a lollipop.

'And this', he said, taking the lollipop out of his mouth and pointing to some yellow sacks in the corner, 'is ammonium nitrate. And there's some aluminum powder over there and a sifter. They mix the two ingredients to make ammonium nitrate and aluminum – ANAL. This is IED-making material.' In total, he found IED precursor chemicals weighing almost ten thousand pounds.

He also showed me a ledger, compiled by a Taliban mullah, listing taxes paid.

Veterans of Fallujah (scene of some of the most vicious fighting in Iraq) said this had been the most intense day of combat they'd ever experienced. But Bravo controlled only two buildings. The marines were completely cut off from the other invading forces, had no electricity, no vehicles and no chance of being re-supplied soon. And the surrounding Taliban still had freedom of movement. Their wider objective, of taking the bazaar and the village of Karu Charai, which included the densely populated 'Pork Chop' (so called because on the map, it looked just like a pork chop), remained to be met. It felt like they'd barely started.

As the light began to fade, the marines did whatever they could to keep warm; sharing thin camouflage sheets, wrapping scarves around their heads and smoking the last of their cigarettes. Our beds were cold cement, damp mud and broken glass, which I was too tired to sweep away.

CHAPTER 8

At 3 a.m. on the first night in Marjah, a series of explosions woke the few marines who had managed to fall asleep. Someone shouted that mortars were being 'walked' on to the base. It felt as if a giant animal were approaching, its huge feet crushing everything in its path as it stomped slowly towards us. Whoever was firing the rockets probably had a spotter watching from a distance, radioing in changes to the range, aiming for a direct hit. 'Holy fuck, that's right there', screamed a marine, as explosions rocked the building, each closer than the one before.

'It's in the bazaar; it's blowing up the bazaar.'

'It's that mortar position we were talking about.'

'So they're hitting short. Means they're gonna be adjusting on us.'

'KEEP DOWN.'

'Holy fuck, there's a bunch of propane tanks on fire.'

'The gas station's about to fucking blow up.'

Barely thirty metres away, flames climbed high in the air. The propane tanks could have exploded, flying in all directions like missiles.

Three men were reported to have stormed one of the small look-out posts at the edge of the compound. They'd been repelled by a hand grenade and pistol shots. The marines who fought them off swore they were suicide bombers but no bodies were ever recovered.

The fire in the gas station eventually died down. The propane tanks, remarkably, had safety valves that prevented them becoming rockets. No one ever knew if the explosions had been mortars or if the men that had approached the base had been suicide bombers. Both felt perfectly plausible.

When daylight came, the Afghans attached to Bravo Company appeared in the courtyard in front of the base. They intended to ceremonially raise the flag that the Afghan soldier the marines called 'Rambo' had worn over his shoulders. Captain Sparks's Afghan Army counterpart, Captain Saed, a short, proud-looking man with a wiry black beard and a mischievous grin ordered his men into two lines of about fifteen soldiers each. Three soldiers attempted to thread a stick through one end of the flag, so that it could be attached to a pole on the wall and flown over Marjah, in defiance to the Taliban, who still controlled most of the district.

Captain Saed changed his mind and ordered his men into a single line. I recognised Qadeer, whose white teeth appeared in the middle of his thick black beard as he grinned at me. 'Morning how are you good?', he asked. He had a wonderfully expressive face that ran through three states: deep concentration, unbridled joy and heavy sadness. Behind Captain Saed, Rambo finally got the flag up, to applause and cheers. From the middle of the courtyard, Captain Saed turned and shouted at him to take it down again; he had a speech to make before the flag was raised. The Afghans were in full combat gear, wearing flak jackets and helmets, with rifles held in front of their chests, pointing to the ground. I'd never seen them look so good.

One Afghan soldier put his RPG on his shoulder. 'Whoa, whoa, put that down', shouted one of the marines. The marines watched from the verandah at the front of the base, with patronising but benevolent pride, like parents watching their children's first school play. This was a shambles but at least it wouldn't get any marines killed. As soon as anything important happened, the marines' feelings toward the Afghans would go straight back to frustration and contempt.

'AT THE READY!' shouted Captain Saed. The Afghan soldiers hit their heels together and stamped their feet in unison. 'Nobody move until the flag is raised! Even if a snake bites you or a bee stings you. This is our national flag, we must respect it. It is for this that we have fought and sacrificed ourselves. We did it for the people of Afghanistan and to be able to fly our flag here in Marjah.' 'Allah Akbar [God is great]!' the soldiers chanted.

The flag was raised. Everyone applauded. As they dispersed, a few Afghans hugged the watching marines. 'Good day, good day', one said to me. A bullet zipped overhead, presumably aimed at the Afghan flag, but only a couple of people noticed.

On the other side of the compound was a small outbuilding, being used as a toilet. Or rather, it was a room full of rubble where the marines went to shit into plastic bags, which were then burned. The toilet had a small flat roof, of no more than ten square feet, which three marines were turning into another look-out post. Sandbags were handed up to them, which they assembled around themselves for protection. They had piled only eight bags together when a few bullets fizzed over their heads and bounced off the wall beside them. 'Keep those sandbags coming faster, we're pretty exposed up here', said one, nervously. Another fired a few shots back. Behind them Captain Saed stood, oblivious, trying to get the flagpole to stay upright.

'It's coming from that compound six hundred metres out, to my direct front', shouted the marine who'd fired. His direct front was one of the sides that didn't yet have any sandbags. Captain Saed finished tying the flagpole and climbed down.

A few hours later, one of the marines, still taking fire on the roof, approached Captain Sparks. 'If we may, can we take the flag down? It's an excellent wind indicator for their snipers, Sir.'

'The fucking flag stays up', said Sparks. 'It's like a lot of things right now, I don't care. I like the flag, it's like saying fuck you constantly.'

* * * * *

Bravo needed to extend their area of control. Two squads of marines, a handful of ANA and the EOD (Explosive Ordnance Disposal) team set out to clear five buildings to the north of their base.

Every step had to be taken carefully; every bag, bump or pile of dirt treated with suspicion. This created an awful amount of work and required an exhausting level of concentration. IEDs are often made from the yellow plastic jugs that Afghans use to carry water; they're scattered all over the place in every home. Here, every jug had to be approached carefully and checked before anyone could walk past it. It was like walking across New York knowing that every takeaway coffee cup could be booby-trapped.

The first compound we entered contained a small two-roomed house. On one side, two cows were tied to a wall, on the other was a tiny garden. The door at the far side of the compound was closed but a marine was sure it had been open when we first walked in. Everyone went down on one knee and pointed their guns at the door. The explosives-sniffing dog ran around, followed by a marine with a metal detector. 'Hey – let the ANA go first', said a marine behind me. 'Get the fuck out, back the fuck up.' Four Afghan soldiers shuffled nervously through the door, followed by the marines shouting 'going in the next building'.

Beyond the door was a huge well, twenty feet wide and twelve feet deep. In a crescent shape, covering half the surface of the water, floated what must have been a month's worth of human shit. The marines gagged at the smell. In shock, one pointed to a bucket and pulley. You could see them thinking: *these people actually use this water?* Every new building and new contact brought more evidence that the people they'd come to liberate were, to put it politely, not at all like them. Sometimes, I saw the moments of revelatory shock on their faces: 'They're not like Americans; what kind of a person does that; how can they allow themselves to be beaten down like that; how can they lie like that?' were questions I heard often.

Next to the well was a mosque, which the ANA had already entered. Beyond the mosque, they found a 'line', trailing over the far wall: a suspicious-looking white wire. The EOD team – Tom Williams and Rich Stachurski ('Ski') – were called forward. 'They say they got one, they can see the line', said Staff Sergeant Young, as Tom turned on his Vallon metal detector. Crouching, he walked across the mosque's courtyard and looked over the far wall.

'Hey. Listen up, how far to the right have we got guys?' shouted Tom.

'We've got guys in the far corner here', said Young, referring to the marines who had stayed by the shitty well.

'There's a fucking IED over there', said Williams.

'PUSH BACK AWAY FROM THAT WALL, PUSH BACK INTO THIS AREA', screamed Young. The wall was all that separated his men from the IED.

I followed Young across the courtyard.

'It's fucking huge', said Tom as we approached him. 'I don't know what it is; it looks like maybe a fifty-pound bag or something. It's big as fuck and it's electric, it's running into the other compound.'

'And there's a kid over the wall', said another marine.

The IED was a white parcel, held together with black tape, which sat on the ground, just around the corner of the wall surrounding the well. It looked like a large bag of laundry, or a giant rolled-up sleeping bag. No effort had been made to hide it, so it had probably been placed there just before we appeared. The white wire ran from the IED along a ditch beside the mosque, over the wall and into a neighbouring compound. Someone would be at the other end, wire in one hand and a power source, probably a battery, in the other, waiting to make the connection as soon as the marines walked around the corner. Fifty pounds of explosives is easily enough to blow several marines to pieces. If they'd continued straight from the well, rather than clearing the mosque first, they would have walked right on to it.

Tom climbed over the far wall and walked slowly towards the wire. He cut it and pulled it away from the IED, then came back over the wall and said he was going to place a charge next to the IED to set it off. Ski asked where they could run after the charge had been set. The marines' rules didn't allow them to enter the mosque, so they would have to run around to the other side before the IED blew. Tom asked for cover while he approached the IED.

He was worried that whoever had been on the other side of the far wall, ready to detonate the bomb, might pop up and shoot him from close range. He walked towards the IED, sweeping every inch of ground in front of him.

Staff Sergeant Young spoke to the terp. 'There's a kid on the other side of the wall but that's exactly where the wire was leading, so we don't know if he's the one that was going to set off the bomb. In any case, when the EOD runs back, you're gonna yell across and tell them that the explosion's about to happen.' The terp nodded. 'They got two minutes and they need to run away, OK?' The terp nodded again. 'Yell as loud as you can so they can hear you.'

Slowly, Tom walked along the ditch. Young shouted that over the wall, smoke was burning; probably some kind of signal. Tom nodded and continued. When he was close enough, he put his metal detector on the ground, took out a block of C4 explosive, ignited it, placed it right under the bomb, picked up his metal detector and ran back towards us.

'Everybody back, behind here', shouted Young.

'Yell across the courtyard. Yell, tell the kid to run', he said to the terp, who didn't yell anything. 'YELL ACROSS, QUICKLY, YOU AIN'T GOT A MINUTE, YELL, JOHN!' The terp stared at him. 'OK, just stand there, then. Get out. Get over here, get down, behind this wall.' Tom, Ski and two ANA soldiers made their way around the mosque. 'You were supposed to yell at the kid in the courtyard, John. That was the whole thing you came over for.' The terp said nothing.

'After it goes off, listen for frag, so everybody be quiet', said Tom, visibly frayed and struggling for breath.

I asked him if he'd volunteered for this job. 'Yes, I did', he said, laughing slightly.

We braced ourselves. The explosion smashed the mosque's windows and made us all wobble, even though most of us were crouched on one knee.

Tom looked at the crater the explosion had made. 'It was probably about a hundred pounds.'

An old man with a thick white beard suddenly appeared on top of the wall, right where the wire lay. He threw it towards us. 'No, no, no, tell him to stop, tell him to leave it', shouted the marines. The old man was terrified; his eyebrows arched up into the thick curved lines that ran across his forehead. He held the palms of his trembling hands towards us. 'There is no Taliban', he said, 'come in, come in. Don't worry, just come.'

'I got two men', shouted a marine.

'Two men?' shouted Young.

'They just went down behind a berm or something. You see 'em? You see their heads?'

'Keep an eye on 'em, see if you can spot a weapon.'

We heard a few bursts of gunfire. 'Is that shooting at us?' asked Young.

'No', someone replied.

The old man went back behind the wall. The next burst of gunfire definitely was aimed at us. Some of the marines collapsed on the ground, others ran back behind the cover of the mosque.

'Hey, let's go, where's the fucking target at?' screamed Young. More shots came into the compound. 'Get a fucking shot off.' While everyone else ducked behind a wall or ran behind the mosque, Young stayed standing. 'Give me a goddamn 203 shot, for Christ's sake.' More bullets came right into the courtyard where he stood. The marines fired back. 'You see a guy out there, you fucking hit him!' screamed Young.

'There's two guys on the roof', shouted a marine, as he pumped shots at them. 'See the brown top? He's firing from there. I fucking saw it. They're right there, twelve o'clock.' He fired single shots at the men on the roof. Other marines hit the building with air grenades and bursts from their machine-guns. Someone screamed for a LAW rocket to be brought forward.

'Taking effective fire from Building 89 and Kilo 22', said Young into his radio. 'One shooter on top of the roof, we spotted him, we're gonna take a LAW shot and knock him out.'

I ran behind the short wall surrounding the mosque. Three marines fired at the brown rooftop; one was ready to fire the LAW rockets. Occasionally they stopped, and ducked behind the wall as bullets cracked through the air around them. As one of the marines got ready to fire the rocket, another screamed: 'DO NOT FIRE THE LAW! NAZIR, COME HERE!' Nazir, one of the Afghan soldiers, was sitting cross-legged alongside the wall, right behind the rocket. He'd have been badly burned, at the very least, if he stayed there. Nazir got up and ran towards me. The marine got ready to fire the rocket again and the others ducked down and put their fingers in their ears. Suddenly, we were covered in dust and the air was sucked from around us. Everyone looked over the wall. 'We got a hit, that's a confirmation hit.' Then another bullet cracked over our heads and we ducked again. One of the marines who'd been next to the firing rocket ran back towards the mosque. 'I can't hear anything', he said, holding his ears and keeling over.

'Keep eyes out in that direction', screamed Young, 'a group is moving and we're taking sporadic shots from that direction. Get out of the mosque. If you can't get cover, back out.' In the middle of a battle, they remembered their cultural sensitivity training. I thought having gunfights in people's gardens was probably more offensive than entering mosques but didn't think it was a good time to raise the point.

The battle died down inconclusively. The Taliban had probably run out of ammunition, dropped their weapons and retreated. They could have walked right past the marines a few minutes later and not been touched.

We lined up to climb over the wall into the compound from where the old man had appeared. An Afghan soldier stood right next to a marine who was lifting people up and over the wall but didn't want any help. The marine looked at him: 'Get out of my way or I'm gonna punch you in the face.'

I looked over and saw ANA soldiers were searching the old man, yanking him roughly by his waistcoat. I also saw the kid they'd spotted earlier, complaining, shouting and gesticulating wildly. He was about three feet tall and looked about six years old but his hand gestures were those of a fully-grown man with attitude; a New Yorker arguing or an Italian football player protesting against a referee's decision. As the marines stabbed sacks with their knives, looking for ammonium nitrate, the terp asked the old man and the kid if the Taliban had forced themselves into their home.

'Yes, they did', said the old man.

'It's like with you', said the kid. 'If you slit our throats, what can we do about it?' He raised his right hand, twisted it clockwise and opened it, as if to say, 'Are you stupid?'

'What were they wearing?' asked the terp.

'I don't know. Something like this', said the kid, grabbing the old man's tattered green shirt. He looked disgusted at the level of questioning.

'Did they have Kalashnikovs?'

'Yes', said the old man, who still instinctively held his hands in the air.

'Come on, pops', said the kid, leading the old man away.

A few minutes later, a marine turned, in shock. 'He just called me a motherfucker', he said, laughing. 'The little son of a bitch.'

A large black dog approached, barking. The kid spun round and ran towards it, picking up a rock on the way. 'Go away, dog', he shouted, 'I'm going to kill you.' The dog cowered and the kid threw the rock, hitting the dog hard in the ribs. 'Take that.'

'He is twenty years old', said one of the terps.

'Is he a midget or something?' said one of the marines.

'Is he really twenty years old?' said another.

The kid, Mohammad, was actually a man and really was twenty years old. He was a dwarf and a heroin addict. He'd been a refugee in Iran for five years but had recently returned to Marjah; one of the approximately two million Afghans who'd fled from the Taliban but returned after their overthrow, expecting peace and prosperity.

'That's freaky', said one of the marines.

'The Taliban ran out of ammunition', said the old man. 'They threw down their guns and left.'

'We'll stay here', said Mohammad. 'I'm a tough guy. Fuck the Taliban! And fuck their mothers!'

'Why don't you seal off both sides and search in the middle?' asked the old man, demonstrating with his hands.

'Tell him we're going to find the Taliban', a marine said, 'and we're going to kill whoever needs to be killed.'

Mohammad walked up to Qadaat and another ANA soldier, who were keeping watch through a gate. They were on their knees, so as Mohammad berated them, they were face to face. 'I am a Baluch [the region of Baluchistan straddles the borders of Iran, Pakistan and Afghanistan]. It's five years since I've been back here. We came back for work', he said. 'I ask you for money but you do nothing to help, what can I do?'

Qadaat smiled. 'We're here to get rid of the Taliban, we're here to help you. Build schools and lots of other things.'

'Right', said Mohammad, disdainfully. 'Thanks a lot.'

He looked down the alley and stared up at the marines around him, one at a time, as if they were just the latest bunch of men who were going to make his life miserable.

Captain Sparks appeared. Mohammad's appearance threw him for the briefest of seconds, then he stepped around him. He joined Young, the terp and the old man at the end of the alley, next to a door that marked the edge of the cleared ground. The terp and the old man began an intense conversation both speaking at the same time.

'What's he saying?' asked Captain Sparks. The terp continued the conversation. 'Tell us what he is saying.' The terp went on speaking in Pashtu. 'NO, no, no. It's not for you to talk, you need to tell us what he's saying', demanded Sparks.

'We don't want to move, he says', said the terp.

'He doesn't have to move', said the captain.

'His family is over there and he wants to stay with them', said the terp, pointing through the door and along the path.

'He doesn't have to move', said the captain again.

'We want to know if it's safe to move out there. Are there any more Taliban bombs?' said Young.

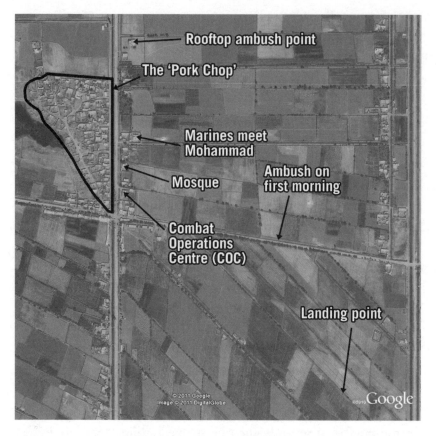

Figure 2 Operation Mushtaraq (© Google 2011; Image © Digital Globe 2011)

The old man had started explaining there were no bombs, when Mohammad, who had followed Captain Sparks up the alleyway, sprinted through the door. 'No, no, no, don't go, don't go', yelled the terp, trying to grab him. But Mohammad was too quick. He made it to the other side, turned and ran back. 'There's nothing, no mines', he said, talking as if everyone were stupid. The old man wanted to walk across too, to be with his family. 'He's free to go wherever he wants', said Captain Sparks. The old man and Mohammad walked through the door and across a small bridge before turning into the next compound, the last one that Bravo planned to clear that day. The ANA followed and then the marines ran out, darting in different directions, going down on one knee and looking through their rifle sights.

Inside the compound was a family of three men and over a dozen kids. One man, crouching in front of a huge pile of harvested opium poppies, held an enormous dog in a neck lock to stop it barking. Another carried a baby wearing an all-in-one suit; with the hood covering its head and a cone shape over its feet, the baby looked like a mermaid. The men were patted down as the marines walked around their home, checking for IEDs or weapons.

'Who's the elder? Who's the guy I want to talk to?' asked a marine. The terp pointed to an older man, who held the baby in the mermaid suit. Two boys and a young girl walked from the back of the building. The boys smiled as they were searched. The women were hidden somewhere.

'Have the Taliban been here?' asked the marine.

'Yesterday, they were in the yard around our house but they haven't been here today', said one of the elder's sons. The elder walked past me, still holding the baby, gesticulating towards a small room next to the gate. 'Look! This is where we make our bread.' He disappeared inside and came out with a piece of thick, round bread. He pretended to take a bite out of it, before offering it to me. He had one of the kindest smiles I've ever seen, so kind I was instantly convinced he'd offer the piece of bread if it were the last thing he had. He wore a beaten-up old purple jumper with holes over a tatty green jumper, followed by a dusty green waistcoat. His turban had once been white but was now the same colour as the mud walls.

He put both the baby and the bread on the ground and excitedly reached into his pocket. 'Card, card', he said. The baby started crying. A gorgeous little girl, with dark red hair and a bright green headscarf, walked over and picked it up. She was probably no more than eight years old but knew how to look after the baby on her own.

The old man pulled out a small bundle, unwrapped several layers of cloth and handed over a card bearing his photograph in the bottom right corner and the Afghan flag in the top left. 'This is an ID card', said the terp, 'a vote card.'

Outside the main building, one of the man's sons and Mohammad were talking to a terp and the marines' intelligence officer. 'Tell your jets no to bomb this place', Mohammad told them. The terp spoke over him. 'Hey, are you listening to me?' demanded Mohammad. The son smiled at him, bent down and gently pressed his hand against Mohammad's, urging him to be quiet.

'We've been stuck in the house', said the son. 'We listened to the radio and they said to stay indoors. We haven't been able to go and wash at the mosque. We've had to wash like women.' When they'd finished, I asked him what life in Marjah had been like under the Taliban. 'When the Taliban governed, there were no robberies. And they ran quick and fair tribunals to settle disputes. If you left them alone, they left you alone.' An Afghan soldier who understood Pashtu listened and didn't look the least bit surprised.

I'd heard so much about life in Marjah under the Taliban that I asked everyone I could what it had been like. They all said similar things. 'It was fine'; 'it was not like under the government'; 'there was no crime, no thieves and no robberies'. The only bad things I heard about the Taliban were that they smoked too much marijuana and didn't spend enough time with their families.

The sound of gunfire filled the air above us. The family ran inside.

Some marines ran outside to see where the firing was coming from. Others smashed firing holes through the compound walls. Everyone else went into the house, with the family. The son who'd told me about life under the Taliban sat on a sack of seeds. He asked Mohammad to join him: 'Come, come, have a cigarette', he said, patting the sack next to him.

'We've been living in constant anxiety', the elder told me. 'We thought the Taliban would beat us or the government would come and bomb us. We're stuck in the middle, so we hide indoors, worried about the bombings.'

Mohammad took a cigarette and asked the marines if he could smoke. They told him of course he could, appearing to think this was his first time. He lit up and started smoking like a trooper, making a show of it and enjoying being the centre of attention. Faces eased every time they looked at him. I could still hear marines whispering to each other that he was twenty years old. 'He's got a cigarette in his right hand, imagine a prison shank in his left', said one. Others joked that they wanted to put him in their backpacks and give him a pistol, so he could protect them. But their jokes were made discreetly and Mohammad didn't know about them. The ANA had no fears about political correctness. They picked him up and showed him around. At one point they put him in a kind of swinging basket that hung in the middle of the corridor, which infuriated him.

Four children stood in a corner, transfixed by everything the marines did and said. After months of rumours and fear, here they were, laughing, joking and handing out sweets in the children's very own home. Everyone had expected much worse. One man said he'd been told the marines would eat his children.

Janofsky took the elder to one side. He wanted to rent a room for himself and his squad for the night. The elder kept saying he was afraid of the helicopters.

'The helicopters are on our side and when you're in here, you're on our side too, so the helicopters are here for you too', said Janofsky.

The man bent down and touched his sacks of seeds, begging the marines not to take them. Janofsky assured him that no marines would take any of his food. 'We're here to provide security to you and the people of Marjah', he said.

'All we have here is tea and bread', the man replied. He couldn't grasp the idea that armed men had entered his home but wouldn't hurt him or steal his food.

Janofsky looked confused too. All he wanted was 'just to rent his place for the night'.

The interpreter wasn't helping: 'You should leave this house and go away', he told the old man, totally mistranslating what Janofsky had said.

The man's kind and pleading smile dropped into a look of absolute terror. He couldn't speak. He thought he and his whole family had been handed a death sentence.

'There is fighting so you shouldn't be here', added the terp non-chalantly.

'Where can I go? What if you bomb us?' asked the man, panicking.

Janofsky sensed the terror in the man's voice and asked what he was saying.

'Where should we move?' said the terp.

'Who should move? No, they'll be OK to stay here with us, for tonight', said Janofsky, confused.

'OK, you can stay here', said the terp, casually, as if he'd been abusing his power just for the fun of it. The old man had almost been reduced to tears.

More bullets cracked over the compound. One smashed through a window and sank into the high walls of the corridor above our heads.

We sat down and started talking. The sons made everyone glasses of tea. You could hear the deep piston thuds of guns being fired outside but everyone had stopped noticing. The family weren't going to be turfed out of their homes to face the bombs, their babies weren't going to be eaten and nothing would be taken. There was a delightful sense of relief throughout the room. For an hour or so, everyone enjoyed being in each other's company. Marjah seemed not such a difficult place to be.

On the marines' maps, the compound where we were was called La Mirage. It was one of several strange names I'd heard. Other houses were called Toby's, the Cave, Cherry's and Heroes. It wasn't until I was in North Carolina, some months later, on my way to Camp Lejuene, 1/6 Marines US base, that I realised where the names came from. I drove past a warehouse surrounded by cars; it looked like Tony Soprano's strip club. It actually was a strip club and I looked at the sign to see if it was named the Bada-Bing. But it was La Mirage. When I'd passed the Cave, and later Cherry's, I realised the Marines had named the landmark buildings of Kuru Charai after North Carolina's titty bars.

Janofsky and First Squad stayed in the house overnight. Everyone else had to make a mad dash back through the four buildings they'd fought their way through earlier on. The first two were easy; it was possible to go through them without ever leaving the protection of their high mud walls. But as soon as we entered the mosque compound, the crackle of machine-gun fire filled the courtyard and everyone darted under the covered porch. The fire was so great it felt like a giant was throwing huge fistfuls of stones against the mosque. Marines on either side of me fired into different parts of the pork chop, the densely-populated area the marines had still to clear, suggesting we were being attacked from two different positions.

Whenever anyone stepped into the courtyard, there came another ear-piercing crackle of shots. The four marines next to me lined up and took hand grenades out of their pockets. *Hand grenades?* I thought to myself. *They don't still throw hand grenades, do they? And anyway, the enemy can't be that close.* I thought they were over a hundred metres away. I'd been telling myself, as I always did when I heard that awful cracking sound, that the Taliban were terrible shots, that they didn't know how to use their sights and if they did, their guns were so old the sights would be no good anyway. But they were a hand grenade's throw away? A child could be on target at that distance. The four marines ran across the courtyard and threw their grenades over the wall in front, not behind, where most of the firing had been coming from. *They're over there as well? We're surrounded? Again?*

'Frag out!'

'FRAG OUT!'

'FRAG OUT!' The marines tossed their grenades, cackling with delight as they exploded.

The gunfire continued and soon, the courtyard was covered in broken glass and hot bullet cases. Every time the marines fired, someone replied with greater fire. Then it stopped. The Taliban seemed to have worked out that if they launched attacks from several positions at the same time, they had a good few minutes before they were in serious danger. One by one, we sprinted across the courtyard, over a wall, across a ditch, over another high wall and into the last compound before the base.

* * * * *

Back at the base, Captain Sparks wrestled with the biggest surprise of Marjah, the highly-skilled snipers. The tiny roof I'd seen being turned into a watchtower was now walled with sandbags but even so, a marine had been shot there. Two marines had been shot on the roof of the main building. The snipers were in well-concealed positions, roughly three hundred metres from the base. One sniper had fired just four bullets during those first two days and hit three marines. Locating someone so patient was hard enough but there were also marksmen nearby, who followed each sniper's shot with a few single shots from their AK47s, confusing anyone who thought they knew roughly where the first shot had come from.

Captain Sparks stood outside the base, trying to work out the sniper's positions. There was another crack. 'Did he just shoot the sandbag? It sure looked to me like he shot the sandbag', he said. 'He did', said a marine in front of him. Sparks had walked out of the big double doors that led into the courtyard and stood on the verandah, studying the watchtower. In front of him were a line of marines in full combat gear. It looked ceremonial; as if a king had come out of his palace to survey his land and the sentries had assembled to protect him.

Another crack filled the courtyard. Captain Sparks looked up. There was another crack. 'Is that Koenig firing?' he asked.

'It is, Sir.' Lance Corporal Koenig was one of the marines lying down behind the sandbags.

'There's no holes in the Afghan flag yet. *Semper Fi*', said Sparks as he walked inside. 'The sniper is the most psychologically effective weapon on the battlefield, because there's nothing you can do about it.'

'Stay low, keep your heads down', shouted one of the marines on the verandah. Their eyes were fixed grimly on the sandbags at the top of the watchtower. There were different theories about where the snipers were; Captain Sparks was sure they were two to three hundred metres north-west of the base, hiding somewhere in the pork chop. 'So there's nothing we can do about it until we clear it', he said.

Captain Sparks walked into his room and began putting on his helmet and his body armour, his chest rig, stuffed with sixteen magazines of ammunition. As he walked through the door, he passed a marine standing in the corridor looking lost. 'Bozman, stay motivated!' he said, like a gym instructor rallying a sagging spin class.

Above us, the cracks of the competition between marksmen continued. Its structure was polite, like a conversation between strangers; back and forth, back and forth, sometimes in single words, sometimes in sentences. Often, the participants waited minutes to take their turn. In between, there was an awful silence. It was careful, considered and cerebral. There seemed to be rules, tricks, feints and a mutual respect that suggested an etiquette. Occasionally, of course, someone at either end collapsed into a lifeless heap.

'It's not *Enemy at the Gate*', one of the marine snipers explained later, 'but you do try to get in the other guy's head.'

The first sergeant ran outside and told the men in the watchtower to get their heads down. One of the terps had heard the Taliban on their radios, saying they were trying to hit the tip of something, 'And it better not be a fucking Kevlar', he said. The panicked look I'd seen on the first morning appeared again on a few faces.

'Someone sticks their head up and you get a round which just misses, or hits, it will paralyse a unit', said Tim Coderre, the law enforcement advisor. He thought there were at least five snipers. 'There's probably nothing more lethal other than unmanned aerial stuff.'

The forward air controller, whose job it was to call in air strikes, asked Captain Sparks where he thought the snipers were. Sparks thought there were two positions he could be sure of. The forward air controller said he'd drop a Hellfire missile on them next time the marines took fire. 'It's friggin' counter-insurgency in a ghost town. There's nobody out there', he said, thinking all the civilians had fled.

'That's what I thought earlier', said Sparks, 'until I went into that compound and there were thirty women and children hunkered down inside, where third platoon's at.' Such brief exchanges were the difference between those thirty women and children living and dying.

The following day, one of the snipers fired again, hitting Lance Corporal Koenig in the head as he bobbed up over the top of the sandbags.

'I came up and turned around to get my rifle passed to me and as I turned around, I guess my head was just a little above the sand-bags and he shot and ended up hitting me directly in the head', said Koenig. He had an incredible glow about him for someone who'd just been shot in the head. Or maybe he glowed because he'd been shot in the head and was able to tell me about it. He glowed like a born-again Christian or a Hare Krishna. His whole face was smiling. 'It cracked me back and I was dazed and didn't really know what was going on. I was like, "I'm hit!"' He picked his helmet off the ground and showed me a huge dent in the front. 'This is where I was hit, about an inch above my eyes. And this is the mount where it hit. This is what they say stopped the round from going through the Kevlar.' He showed me a broken metal brace, for attaching night vision goggles, that had been on the front of his helmet. Con-trary to popular belief, even of the soldiers and marines who wear them, their helmets aren't actually bullet-proof, especially if they're hit square on. 'It hurt really, really bad. I thought I was dying. I thought I'd actually been hit, it scared me pretty bad.'

Four marines had been shot on the roof above us in the space of just two days. They had probably all been shot by one sniper, whose position was still unknown. This would be terrifying to most people but Captain Sparks was encouraged by it.

'He's not a real sniper', he said. 'If he was we'd have a lot more casualties. He's just very good with whatever he's got.' That was perhaps what separated Captain Sparks from everyone else and made him either a genuine warrior or a complete lunatic. He always worked out a way to be encouraged by everything and anything, no matter how discouraging things first appeared. Sometimes you could see it happening. He'd say something that sounded like an admission of failure or an acknowledgement of limitations. But then he'd say something to temper it and by the time the third sentence had left his mouth he'd created an argument to destroy the hopelessness of the first and was completely gung-ho again. I've met people who could pick themselves up and come back from things but never anyone who could do it in the space of three sentences.

To me – and I'm sure to many of the marines – it looked like there was still an awfully long way to go and a lot that could go badly wrong. Bravo Company had been in Marjah for two days; they'd lost one man, suffered four casualties, were surrounded and cut off from the other companies, who were still miles away. And they only controlled five buildings in Karu Charai village, a slither of Marjah.

CHAPTER 9

Day three in Marjah. The Forward Air Controller, Ben Willson, was almost having a nervous breakdown. I hadn't seen him sleep since we'd landed. I hadn't seen him anywhere other than the cold central corridor of the old police station, hunched over, fixated on the chunky laptop that showed him what the drones above us were filming. He was even there when I got up to go to the outside 'toilet' (just a plastic piss tube hammered into the ground) in the middle of the night. And although on day three he looked particularly obsessed with the tiny white figures on the little screen, it looked like he'd been building up to a nervous breakdown for some time.

Everyone called Ben 'Nascar' because in his normal job as a helicopter pilot he had a reputation for only ever turning left. (NASCAR is a massively popular American motor racing sport in which the drivers race anti-clockwise around an oval track, thus only ever turning left.) Tall and slim, with a closely-shaved head and good-looking enough to be in a Marines recruitment video doing push-ups, running and looking determined, Ben also defied the stereotype; he was a philosophy graduate who read Kierkegaard and William James.

What drove Ben to the verge of that nervous breakdown was that he requested up to forty air strikes a day but almost all were denied. The few approvals that came through took so long – one took two hours, by which time the planes had run out of fuel and flown away – that the little figures he saw on the laptop screen laying IEDs simply escaped. Nascar, like all the other forward air controllers in Afghanistan, had to go through five levels of approval for an air strike, including a lawyer and ending with the general and his staff.

That morning, Ben had received approval to bomb twenty-five to thirty Taliban fighters he'd seen getting out of a van and making their way into the pork chop. But the plane had malfunctioned and the bomb got stuck in its undercarriage. The fighters, who may have included the snipers, were free to spread out and enjoy another day of firing at marines from the maze of alleys, firing holes and roofs offered by the pork chop.

Captain Sparks couldn't sit back and watch them do that again. He ordered all available marines to put on their body armour and follow him. They would run eight hundred metres, mostly over uncleared ground, sneak on to a roof to the north of the pork chop and ambush the Taliban fighters as they became visible. I followed about thirty marines as they ran through the five buildings they'd cleared the day before, pausing briefly in La Mirage to work out their final route on a map.

'You good? You know what your job is … ? You good?' Staff Sergeant Young asked the marines as they waited at the gate. 'Four minutes until step time. Any questions?' There were no questions. Some marines furiously chewed gum or tobacco, others bounced up and down on their toes. 'Whoop, whoop, WHOOP, WHOOP', one shouted, each whoop louder than the last.

One of the Afghan soldiers couldn't get a magazine into his rifle. A marine grabbed it and did it for him. 'It's the same shit you were doing last night', he said, clicking the magazine into place. The Afghan soldier held his rifle horizontally. The marine grabbed it again, violently pushing it down. 'You're POINTING it at people. Leave it, you're good.' He walked away, shaking his head: 'Fucking guy, man.'

The route to the rooftop hadn't been cleared for IEDs. Where possible, sniffer dogs were let loose or the EOD team quickly checked a doorway or bridge with their metal detectors, but mostly we just watched our steps and hoped we weren't unlucky enough to step on anything. The firing holes in the walls we passed had been created so recently they still had piles of fresh dirt beneath. Every time the marines walked around a corner, they left one behind, lying on the ground with a SAW machine-gun. 'Keep your eyes on that building', said Young, quietly, 'anything moves, let 'em have it.'

Everyone was silent. A message came in over Young's radio: 'Be advised, there is mass movement around buildings two nine and one five, how copy.'

'That's on the other side of the pork chop', said Young, 'it shouldn't affect us any, unless they start moving towards us.'

'Are you happy?' one of the ANA soldiers asked me. 'These are the enemies of this country, we should finish them.'

They reached a compound with a high-roofed building, kicked the gate down and walked through. Three ANA soldiers went in first, ordered to clear an outhouse that looked like a stable. They timidly looked through the glassless windows and stepped through the doors, pointing their guns as they went, just like the marines. One saw what looked like the top of an anti-tank mine. He pointed it out to me with his left foot, then kicked. Luckily, it was just a pot lid, with hard ground underneath it. He smiled, let out a theatrical sigh of relief, and moved on.

I followed a marine to the staircase. He stopped halfway up and stabbed a huge spider against a wall, then crawled out on to the roof. 'Look, over there', whispered one of the Afghans, pointing to a man casually walking away from the northern tip of the pork chop. I fully expected the marines to start shooting but they let him go. Another young man stood about two hundred metres away, staring at us, carrying a shovel on his shoulder, in a very obvious way. (Months later, I showed this footage to some Afghan friends in London. They laughed out loud: 'That guy's so Taliban', they said, incredulously, 'he's laughing at you.') Another man walked away across a field, slowly and nervously, glancing up at us every few steps.

Young crawled to the edge of the roof and looked through his rifle sights. I crawled to the edge too; the lip surrounding the roof was only a few inches high, offering no protection. More marines came up the stairs, dropped to their stomachs and dragged themselves to the edge of the roof, like snakes moving across sand.

Somewhere close by, a battle started. Nothing came towards us. The fighters in the pork chop were attacking someone, somewhere, but they hadn't seen the marines gathered on the roof, further away from their base than they'd so far been, waiting. Occasionally, the fighting died down. I heard a dog, tied to a tractor, barking constantly. Its throat sounded as dry as the desert around us. It must have been tied there for at least three days, with no food or water. But still it wouldn't stop barking.

The marine on my left, Lance Corporal Blancett, adjusted his rifle sights with one hand and the two legs on which his rifle rested with the other. Every movement was delicate and precise and he appeared to have the touch of an old watchmaker. With his blond hair, bright white teeth and cocky smile, Blancett looked like Val Kilmer playing Iceman in *Top Gun*.

'See that building straight out in front of you? Look to the very end, the right edge of the pork chop', said Young quietly. 'See them?'

'Negative', said Blancett.

Whoever the Taliban had attacked was now firing air grenades into the pork chop. I heard the distant chopping sounds of grenades exploding and saw white clouds of smoke rising above the compound, one row of buildings in from the outer walls. I assumed the fighters were in those buildings. They must have known it was time to escape but they had no idea what awaited them on the route they had used to come in. I imagined the terror and panic they were about to experience. Blancett moved the legs under his rifle by millimetres. Other marines slowly screwed suppressors on to their rifles.

'THERE THEY ARE, THERE THEY ARE', screamed Blancett. He started firing. The marines next to him fired as well.

'ON THE CORNER', shouted Blancett, still firing. 'Hey, 240 gunner. You need to scoot up to the edge of the wall. You're on target but scoot the fuck up.' He looked up for a second. 'I HIT THAT FIRST GUY, HE'S FUCKING DEAD.'

'That's what I like to hear, baby', shouted Young.

'I hit that guy right in the fucking head', said Blancett. As everything went quiet, he took a breath. 'That was intense. They're behind that building somewhere. Hey – keep eyes in case they start egressing to the west; you'll be able to see them moving through that gap in the wall.'

Another marine saw movement in a building north of the pork chop. Blancett swung his gun around. 'Where they at? Building seven? Left or right?'

'Left but he's moving right.'

'I got him', whispered Blancett. He asked how far away the building was, adjusted his sights, put his finger on the trigger and let out two deep breaths.

'He's walking, behind the building.'

'I got him', said another marine.

'NO, NO, NO', said Blancett, 'that's the guy that I saw walking earlier, you asked me if he had anything in his hands. I said he's got a brown floppy jacket on. That's the same guy.' He took his finger off the trigger and pointed his rifle back towards the pork chop.

They spotted more movement along the north wall. 'It looks like a kid', said a marine. 'Yeah, I see him', said Blancett, 'he's got a little green man dress on.' They also saw an old man, standing next to the buildings, still full of white smoke from the air grenades.

The marines chatted continuously, sharing every snippet of information. Someone constantly relayed reports from the base and from marines nearby. And the terp had a radio permanently tuned to the frequency the Taliban used, reporting everything they said, which was often wildly exaggerated.

The result of all this information was, as the marines called it, 'a mindfuck'. It also left the constant impression that catastrophe was just a few minutes away: there were twelve suicide bombers in town (reported that morning); a sniper had them in his sights (reported the day before); and an army was marching towards them, intent on fighting to the death (reported every few hours). A machine-gunner opened up again, reporting muzzle flashes 'to the right'.

'To the right of what? You gotta be more specific', screamed Blancett.

'The right of the whole compound.'

'Same spot as before?'

'Same spot, that's the building they're consolidating in.'

A cluster of bullets crackled over our heads. Someone had finally spotted us. The machine-gunner opened up again. Young told everyone the Taliban had moved into the next building. 'Keep eyes on seven and eight', he said, 'give me a 203 gunner, let's go.' He wanted air grenades to be dropped inside the building's walls.

Marine Niemasz dragged himself next to me, on the other side from Blancett. 'See that building with the three trees behind it? That's what I want you to hit. I want you to pepper them', shouted Young. Niemasz popped a gold-coloured 203 (air grenade) into the tube beneath his rifle and cocked it. Air grenades look strange when they're fired; the popping sound as they fly out of their tubes makes them seem like children's toys. They are designed to be dropped on to their targets, not fired at them, so they're only pro-pelled by the force pushing them out of the tube, travelling like golf balls rather than bullets. Not until you see them explode do you take them seriously; their blast is big enough to kill anyone within five metres. Niemasz quickly pumped seven air grenades into the walls of Building eight, which disappeared beneath waves of white smoke. So much smoke that Blancett complained he couldn't see to shoot. Then the building caught fire, filling him with hope that the fighters would flee right into his sights.

A big group of people suddenly emerged from the furthest tip of the pork chop. A shout came for everyone to hold their fire; there were women and children among them. 'Man, they're not a family. Those fucking assholes are using those kids and women as cover to get out of there', said Blancett. 'Horse-shit man. That is … …' He couldn't find the words to express his frustration. 'ARGGGHHH GOD', he shouted, growling.

I saw at least two children, one woman and five or six men who could easily have been, in military language, 'fighting-age males'. But we would never know. Too often in the past, people on roofs, in jets or staring at computer screens had seen what we were seeing and made the wrong choice.

A burst of gunfire crackled over us. The marines on the far side of the building shouted, 'EGRESS, EGRESS.' The Taliban fighters weren't all in Buildings seven and eight and they hadn't all escaped using women and children for cover. Another group, far to the left of where the marines had been firing and much closer to the building where we lay, were shooting at us. As marines on the far side of the building ran from the edge of the roof and back down the stairs, an RPG hit the building, followed by bullets that seemed to almost skim the tops of our helmets. Perched on the flat roof of a single-storey building, I suddenly felt very easy to see.

'Where the fuck is that LAW?' shouted Young.

'We got two prepped sir.'

'The next shot that comes from Building seven you rip it right through that fucking window, you understand?'

'You want me to put one in there?'

'No, wait. I'll tell you when.' Young had moved to the back of the roof, standing up, to get a better view. More bullets popped above our heads.

'To your right. You know Building seven? The next little compound to your right, see it?'

'The left side or the right side?'

'The middle, he came up right in the middle, you can almost see a little dust trail.'

A burst of machine-gun fire was aimed at the little compound.

'Higher', said Young. Two more bursts, from two marines. About twenty came back, right above us.

After an hour, there was no movement in the pork chop other than the white smoke drifting. The white-bearded old man reappeared, with two young boys; all of them wore green *shalwar kameez*. They walked towards us, then stopped directly beneath the marines, staring up, their arms behind their backs. The old man pointed to the burning buildings, which had been pummeled for the last hour, and held out his hands in despair. One of the boys looked up at us on the roof, the other looked at the ground. One of the Afghan soldiers on the ground shouted at the old man: 'Lift up your shirt.' He looked even more despairing, as if to say, 'after all that … *this*?' The two little boys nervously copied him, first showing their bare stomachs, then turning to show their backs. It was the saddest thing I'd seen in Marjah.

The old man said everyone had now left the buildings. He and the boys slowly walked away. We got down from the roof as a Harrier jet approached to hit the smoking buildings with a gun run.

*   *   *   *

Back at the base, about thirty trucks from Charlie Company had arrived. It had taken them almost three days to clear five miles along the road to Marjah. On the way, they'd found more than twenty IEDs. As the marines jumped from the first vehicle, the driver almost landed on a large metal drum, just visible above the ground. He pulled out his knife and dug up the earth around it. Three other marines gathered around. 'Don't be a hero', they laughed. In the end, they decided it was the lid of an old anti-tank mine and left it alone.

Bravo now had a supply line, power and the reassuring presence of armoured trucks with huge machine-guns on their roofs. Captain Sparks hadn't requested the backup, nor had it been part of the original plan. But the relentless violence of the first few days and the content of the reports he'd sent back had made his commanders decide to send Charlie Company.

Some trucks were parked in a long line along the road into Marjah and some were at each end of the bazaar, pointing out, their guns manned. The bazaar, the commercial hub of Marjah, straddled the main road through Kuruh Charai, the same road where we'd been ambushed as the sun came up on the first morning. Now, its battered metal shutters were closed, a small blue lorry lay on its side in a ditch and abandoned boxes of fruit and vegetables had dried up in the sun. Other than a few distant figures who hovered outside, pretending not to look, the bazaar was deserted.

Charlie Company's arrival in Karu Charai hadn't been without incident. As they covered the area south-west of the pork chop, to help Bravo Company start moving north, they'd been caught in a gunfight and fired a rocket into a house where three families were sheltering. As they'd been told in the days before the invasion, the families hadn't fled, but stayed indoors until the fighting died down. The rocket had killed four people and injured seven, two critically.

'These dark figures kept running towards us. They would show up with a bundle in their hands and it would be a baby wrapped up, either alive or dead', said First Lieutenant Aaron MacLean, a lean and kindly-looking Platoon Commander. 'They just kept coming and coming. By the end we'd evacuated seven casualties and there were four KIA [killed in action]. They kept bringing them over the field. It was one of the worst things I've ever seen.' He struggled to breathe as he spoke. His lips were dried up and cracked and his startled, wide-open eyes darted around the room, not focusing for long on anything.

The seven injured people had been flown to a British hospital in Lashkar Gar. The rest of the family, and the bodies of the dead, sheltered in an abandoned store in the opium bazaar, now occupied by Charlie Company.

'You're looking at the definition of innocent people, there's no question about it, you know. Little girls', said MacLean. 'There's just no way to rationalise that this was in any way a good thing or justi-fied. It's just a terrible failing and a terrible sight.'

Of all the soldiers I'd ever met, both in Afghanistan and Iraq, MacLean was one of the most idealistic, in the best sense of the word. Commanding officers and generals always say honourable-sounding things about noble intentions; they have to. Grunts often don't care or even know about higher political aims. I'd asked Hillis about COIN and General McChrystal's promise of a 'government in a box'. 'I wasn't even aware that was the long-term plan', he'd replied. 'I didn't know there was a future part to it, just that there were bad people here.'

But MacLean had clearly read and thought a great deal about Afghanistan and the war on terror. 'The United States and United Kingdom have a responsibility not to let these people slide back under the thumb of these theocratic fascists', he said, softly but passionately. 'We've promised these people a lot over the years and we owe it them to see those promises through.' He'd just seen seventeen lives torn apart; he was in shock, struggling to hold on to the beliefs that had brought him to Afghanistan. 'War is a curse. I knew that intellectually before I came. But it's not the worst thing out there. That's the calculation you have to make to justify it; otherwise everyone would be a pacifist. And there's a good case to make for that, I could certainly make it more strongly having seen what I've seen.' What he'd seen had reinforced the arguments against his belief in military intervention. But he remained resolute: 'I have strong black and white moral views about people like the Taliban; they are just evil.'

I followed MacLean, several marines and a terp as they went to meet Abdel Baki and his father. They had both been in the house when it was hit; Abdel Baki's sister and her daughter had been killed. The family had fled Uruzgun Province following a dispute with the government about land; they'd come to Marjah because there was no government there. Now, they had to sleep next to their family's dead bodies, in two storerooms on one side of the opium bazaar. We sat down on the floor and MacLean asked the marines to introduce themselves. Abdel Baki interrupted them. 'I don't know what I'm going to do with the dead bodies', he said. 'I need to take them to Lashkar Gar, to the cemetery.' His hair, eyebrows and long beard, which curled out from the sides of his face, were thick and dark, extensions of his unusually solid frame. His eyes were almost black and he had a graze across his forehead. Although Abdel Baki struggled not to break down, he spoke without anger or hyperbole.

'I've had a very difficult life. I kept moving from place to place. I took refuge somewhere and had to leave and then came here. I'm

a farmer working on somebody else's land. I get a sixth of everything I make. I have nothing except the clothes that I'm wearing.
If I go to Lashkar Gar I have no place to stay', he said. 'We heard
on the radio that coalition forces were coming. And then we would
be allowed to leave. So we spent four days indoors waiting, as you
asked, waiting for you to say it was OK to leave, to take us to a safe
place. But then a shell hit our house, destroying my family. Two of
my family are killed: one from another family, and another family
had a member killed.'

'We're really sorry for what happened yesterday', said a marine,
addressing Abdel Baki directly for the first time.

'Right now, I don't have anything. No money, no clothes, no
food. When I'm done with the dead bodies I have to go to the
hospital, where the rest of my family are. You guys have to take
me there.'

The marines said they were checking with the military hospi-
tals in the area, trying to find out which one the injured had been
taken to. Incredibly, no one knew. But they couldn't promise to take
Abdel Baki to see them, or to bury his dead, because ISAF rules
forbade Afghan civilians from travelling on helicopters unless they
were escorting injured children or were themselves casualties.

'Why don't you do your piece?' said MacLean to Sergeant
Berwa, who knelt next to Abdel Baki.

'It pains us all here to know what you must be going through
right now', said Sergeant Berwa, a reservist working for the Civil
Affairs team. He coughed, struggling to get out what he'd been
sent to say. He looked at the floor and continued. 'You know, the
US Marines, the citizens of Afghanistan and the government of
Afghanistan, together can achieve great things to make Afghanistan
a safer and more prosperous place for all.' How he managed to say
that last line I don't know, nor did I have any idea what good it was
supposed to do. 'There's nothing we can do to bring back your loss.
But what we can do is try to help you out by giving you the very
least that we can, which is to help you in your travels to Lashkar
Gar for your fallen ones.'

'In future, if you guys have operations, announce them to civilians, tell them to go to you, then this won't happen again', Abdel Baki said.

'We're here to help out with everything that we can, with security and stability in the area', said Lieutenant Greenlief, Bravo Company's executive officer, who'd been entrusted with clearing up Charlie Company's mess. 'And because we're here for you, we never target ... or if there are any indications that civilians are there, we do not shoot. I've seen the cowardice of the Taliban, forcing women and children to walk with them, using them as shields so they can shoot at us and walk away. One of the most important things in our lives is family and taking care of our family.'

MacLean sat next to Greenlief, his arms around his legs, gently rocking back and forth. His jaw muscles twitched under his skin. He seemed to be struggling not to break down. (He was suffering from pneumonia, which he'd refused to be evacuated for, and had lost nearly ten pounds in weight in five days.)

Abdel Baki said his family could easily have been saved. 'I was waiting inside my house for four or five days, I was waiting for you to call me to come out and for you to take me to a safe place. There are lots of people like that, if you ask, they will come out.'

MacLean thanked him for the information, saying he didn't know families were waiting inside their homes like that. (ISAF messages had specifically told people to stay in their homes and had even claimed they wouldn't fire anything powerful enough to penetrate their compounds' mud walls.) 'The majority of the people in the Taliban are poor, helpless Muslims', continued Abdel Baki, 'who have been forced to be there. You have to give them a chance to switch sides. Only the core fighters will stay, the others will come over.'

'Sergeant B?' said Greenlief, prompting Berwa to finish.

'It's not the most that we can do for you right now but we want to try and help you out with a payment for your losses ... to help you out ... with your travels to Lashkar Gar, the burial process and any other type of alleviations. We all feel deeply saddened by this incident and we hope to try and avoid these in the future using the information that you have been telling us.'

Abdel Baki explained exactly who in each family had been killed or injured. One family had just a single child left. His wife and four children had all been injured.

'There were four deceased, bottom line', said a marine.

'Check', said another.

Sergeant Berwa continued. 'I'll present him with the … with the condolence payment.' He coughed again and turned to the terp. 'Like I said, it's the absolute least that we can do because there's … obviously you can't bring back someone you love.'

He pulled bricks of Afghan notes out of his backpack and piled them in a stack. Abdel Baki's whole body turned away. He didn't touch the money. He just stared at it, at the final confirmation that this was really happening.

Sergeant Berwa placed the stack of notes, roughly $10,000 altogether, $2,500 for each life lost, on the ground in front of Abdel Baki.

Abdel Baki picked up the money, his face twisted away from it, as if he were carrying one of his dead relatives.

'My heart still bleeds from what happened yesterday. I'm suffering a lot', he said. Next to him, his father, Abdel Kareem, wiped tears from his eyes.

As I walked out, I looked into the next room. I saw four bodies on the floor, covered with a single, pale blue, sheet of cloth. Over two bodies, blood had seeped through the cloth. A man invited me in, motioning that he would lift up the sheet so that I could film the bodies. But I already felt I'd intruded too much. I bowed my head, put my hand over my heart, and walked away, failing to do my job properly.

Later, sitting on the concrete floor of the small room where he slept, half-way down the opium bazaar, MacLean was admirably frank when describing what had happened.

'We'd been engaged all afternoon by an enemy team and they'd taken a few RPG shots at us. At one point, someone actually stepped out directly on the road and fired an RPG at one of our vehicles. Through the course of the afternoon we fired multiple rockets and the enemy fired multiple rockets at us. Either our rocket or their rocket hit this family's house.' He could have shed more doubt on whose rocket it had been but he didn't. 'We're here to provide security and last night we failed at that. It doesn't really matter whose rocket it was, the Taliban won last night because people got hurt and marines were in the area.

'I've been told this by Afghans before. "I don't mind Taliban and I don't mind marines, I just want everyone to leave me alone and I want to lead my life." There's something to be said for that point of view and certainly if you've lost family members I couldn't stand in front of you and tell you otherwise and that's not really my place. I don't know. If I was in his shoes … It's almost like there's two entirely different levels. There's the political level and there's the level on the ground and I'm not sure I've entirely reconciled them myself right now.' The marines under MacLean didn't have his sensitivity. And they had no doubt whose rocket had hit the family's house. They even knew who'd fired it and already nicknamed him 'Whopper'. I asked what this meant. 'Whopper – Burger King – BK – baby killer.'

That night, the bodies were buried, in coffins of wood and plastic sheets, in a vacant lot next to the opium bazaar. The marines watched as Afghan soldiers recited from the Qur'an and spoke a eulogy.

The massive restrictions on air strikes had been introduced because President Karzai, the Afghan population and the international public were appalled by civilian casualties. To a large extent, the restrictions had worked. In 2010, civilian casualties had been reduced and, according to the UN, over two thirds had been caused by the Taliban, not the American forces or ISAF. But the restrictions on air strikes were also a response to bad headlines. Rockets could be fired from the ground that were almost as powerful as those fired from the air. And because they were fired horizontally, these rockets could travel hundreds of metres before they exploded, increasing the chances of killing civilians if they missed their target. If the accidental slaughter of the people we were supposed to be helping was to stop, the restrictions had to go further.

Weeks later, Abdel Baki was still in Marjah. The marines hadn't been able to do the one thing he'd asked for – get him to his wounded family members in the military hospital at Lashkar Gar. When they couldn't get him on a helicopter, they'd stolen a car, hot-wired it and presented it to him. But he couldn't drive.

CHAPTER 10

There was surprisingly little damage to the building the marines had showered with air grenades the day before. The main rooms hadn't been hit and all four walls still stood. Only a storeroom in the centre of the compound had been directly hit; that was what we'd seen burning. Even so, a terp emerged holding two eggs, perfectly intact. When Captain Sparks came in, the marines had already cleared the compound, although one had shot two dogs in the process. Sparks called him over. 'We've got to clear the entire rest of the town without killing any dogs. You've killed two in the first two hours. Very simple, very clear; do not kill another fucking dog.'

He climbed a mound with Marine Anthony Piccioni – Picc – a stocky and jocular Italian-American with a cynical sense of humour. Sparks pointed to the roof we'd been on the day before. 'Those bitches didn't have a chance and they had no idea we were up there.'

'They didn't?' said Picc, who had called in the gun run that finished the rooftop ambush.

'It's a perfect position. We had them trapped and I think we got ten of them.' For a minute or two, Sparks was buoyant behind his sunglasses, albeit in a very controlled way.

The pork chop had still to be completely cleared of IEDs but it now belonged to Bravo Company. The operation had been chaotic and had taken longer than expected but they had achieved their objective. The fight for the control of Karu Charai village, Marjah's most densely populated area, appeared to be over.

145

Now came the hard part. Marines who had been trained to kill and, in the Captain's own words, be 'masters of controlled chaos and violence', now had to become social workers, policemen, community project managers, anthropologists and judges.

The aim was to show the people why they should side with the Afghan government and reject the Taliban's rule. But the only representatives of that government were the army and the police, who wouldn't even be there if it weren't for the Marines. The people were being shown what they already knew: your government is incapable of looking after you, so don't burn any bridges with the Taliban.

Even if the Taliban had been vanquished, there were few signs that the government would be embraced and plenty that it was hated and feared. People approached marines in the bazaar, saying: 'Please don't leave us alone with those guys', referring to the police. The same thing had happened in every town I'd seen cleared.

The fact that the people being liberated were asking for protection from those we were fighting to introduce ought to have raised obvious questions. But it was too late in the day to admit such a terminal flaw in policy. A perma-smiling lieutenant colonel told me that 'spreading GIROA' (pronounced 'ji-row-ah' – the Government of the Islamic Republic of Afghanistan) was going fantastically well and being embraced by the people.

* * * * *

Bravo had to clear their area of IEDs and drugs, so that people could return to their homes and the bazaar could re-open. The ANCOP (Afghan National Civil Order Police) appeared in the bazaar. ANCOP were supposed to be an elite unit, trained and blooded in Kabul, where they had been taught how to work with communities, rather than against them, as local forces had done. They wore ballooning light blue trousers made of what looked like felt, smoked a lot, carried machine-guns and looked unhappy. One carried a rocket launcher on his shoulder.

I asked Captain Sparks how he knew the police wouldn't be as bad as, or worse, than the Taliban. 'I don't,' he said. 'I just have faith that somebody has vetted these guys, that they have good leadership, they've been mentored properly and that they want peace and security in Afghanistan as much as we do. They have been deployed in other places successfully, so that adds a little confidence. But I don't know that for sure and that's definitely something I'll keep my eye on. I'll leave marines behind to make sure they're doing things the right way.'

The ANCOP commander saw two men approaching the bazaar. He shouted to them to put their hands in the air, turn round and walk backwards towards him. He sent two of his men to meet them half-way. One knelt by the side of the road and pointed a machine-gun at them, while the other patted them down. The two men were Abdel Baki and his father Abdel Kareem – the men who had just lost four members of their family to a stray rocket. No one had told the Afghan police.

In the bazaar, the marines greeted Abdel Baki and Abdel Kareem warmly. 'Did you have a good night?' asked Gunny D. 'Did the Mullah stay with you?' The two men, who looked genuinely pleased to see the marines, said the Mullah had stayed with them until ten o'clock. 'I'm working on the family names', continued Gunny D, 'and as soon as I hear word back, I'll tell you. I won't forget them.' Still, no one knew which hospital the injured had been taken to.

Gunny D was the face of the marines for this stage of the operation. He was a weapons platoon sergeant; his real name was Brandon Dickinson. Dickinson's thinning hair and round, friendly face made him look as affable as Sparks looked lethal but his ability to put anyone in the mood to talk was described as 'almost magical'. Accompanying him on this first important day was Lieutenant Mark Greenlief, Bravo's executive officer and Captain Sparks's right-hand man, who had similar people skills. He and Sparks shared an almost telepathic connection, communicating with a word or two, a look or a nod. Having such trust, without actually being the boss, meant he was more relaxed than most marines; at briefings, he'd often do camp little dances and voices, or creep up on people and slip sweets into their hands. I'd bought a badge at Kandahar Air Base, an American flag that said, 'We're gonna freedom the fuck out of you'. Greenlief wrote an entire song with that line as the chorus.

A few people had complained about damage to their homes; the marines helped them fill in compensation forms, then handed over money from their piles of cash. A man approached with his tiny son, whose face was covered in dirt and whose thick head of hair was red in patches, often a sign of malnutrition. The man said he'd been hiding in a field for two days and needed to buy some cream for his son's skin from the bazaar. The marines gave him some halal food and took him to see the medic. An older man, a tailor, and his two sons appeared, complaining that someone had broken into their store and damaged their property. Marines from Charlie Company were sleeping in the surrounding stores; it looked like they had moved in for a few nights. They had stolen some biscuits, slashed a *shalwar kameez* hanging on the wall and written 'I ♥ USA' on the breast pocket of another. 'You must have a bad name to do this', said the tailor.

Greenlief immediately offered to buy all the vandalised shirts. He and Gunny D also asked to be measured for bespoke 'man dresses' of their own. They negotiated hard but playfully, eventually agreeing $60 for two shirts. The tailor corrected them about the length, saying only women wore them that long, and told them not to have black, because it was too hot. The tailor asked for $70, to which Greenlief said, 'We'll send more marines down here. People will see me with my "man dress" on and they'll want to know where I got it.' The tailor had gone from being angry at the marines to being charmed, even if his goodwill was partly bought. A relationship had begun: Greenlief would have to come back to collect the 'man dresses' and a box could be ticked on the counter-insurgency checklist.

The marines had lots of ideas about building relationships and improving the bazaar but mostly they asked one simple question: 'What would you like us to do for you?' But the question proved very hard for people to understand. Most were convinced they would be thrown out of their homes, arrested, hooded and beaten. They were wary of co-operating with the marines, sure they would be gone in a few days. But even when they realised that the question was genuine, they didn't believe it was to do with the next few years, or even the next few months. So they asked for money, compensation for things that had happened over the last few days. The marines were willing to pay for any damage they'd done but many of the claims were far-fetched, which annoyed them. They wanted to work with the local people, even to become friends with them, not just offer hand-outs.

'Gentlemen. Good morning', said Captain Sparks in the first *shura*, to the twenty-three men who were there. 'I'm in charge of the Marines in Karu Charai village. We're very happy, it's a great day. The Taliban is gone and we can finally start to open your bazaar.' The Captain promised to repair any damage and get all the stores opened. What he didn't say – but everyone knew – was that the arrival of the Marines meant the end of the lucrative opium and heroin production business, which everyone in Marjah depended on in some way. If it did continue, as it surely would, it would have to be carried out away from the marines' eyes and probably needed the continued involvement of the Taliban. Yet another reason the people wouldn't pick sides.

Captain Sparks introduced everyone but, as he hadn't met him, he didn't know the name of the new ANCOP chief, who'd arrived and was quietly sitting in on the *shura*. One of the men in the crowd interrupted: 'Are we allowed to open the stores?'

'Of course you are', said Sparks, 'you can do whatever you want.' Gunny D appealed to everyone to work with the marines and report any suspicious behaviour or the arrival of anyone from out of town.

Abdel Baki said that the marines needed to push the Taliban right out before that could happen. 'We can't announce anything', he said, 'or they'll hear and come back and hit us again.' In one of the very first exchanges, at the very first *shura*, the challenge had been presented. The people couldn't co-operate until the Taliban were absolutely gone for good. And that hadn't been achieved in a single province or district in Afghanistan. Captain Sparks set out to reassure everyone.

'We and the ANA and ANP are not going anywhere. And we're watching the Taliban all the time. They can't hide from us. It's my dream for this to be the place that everyone wants to be in Marjah. The jewel of Marjah.'

Another man stood up, one of the sons of La Mirage. 'Since the war started we haven't been able to go to work. Are you going to pay us compensation?' The marines said they couldn't do that but they would pay men to clean up the bazaar. Gunny D said he'd give the money for this to the *malik* (community leader), pointing to an old man he'd met earlier. There was uproar. He *used* to be the *malik*, now *this* man was the *malik*. And more than one man was responsible for the bazaar; there were three or four. Gunny D sighed.

Mohammad, the twenty-year-old dwarf, arrived. He stood in the middle of the rectangle where everyone sat. An old man stole a dollar bill from Mohammad's back pocket, in full view of three other old men, all with long white beards and toothless mouths. They could barely contain themselves, writhing, trying not to laugh out loud. The pickpocket tapped Mohammad's back pocket and handed the dollar bill back. He snatched it, frowned and put his chin on his chest, as angry as he'd been when the ANA put him in the hanging basket.

After the *shura*, some of the men opened their stores. Marines and ANA soldiers bought cigarettes by the carton. Everyone smiled and shook hands. Afterwards Gunny D walked back into the base, threw his arms in the air and shouted, 'First store open, baby.' Another marine high-fived and hugged him.

Behind the bazaar, other marines, accompanied by Tim Coderre, slowly cleared every building in the pork chop. Tim's job was to treat every sniper hole, drug lab, or IED as a crime scene, collecting any evidence before it was contaminated. The first building where I saw him work was a small two-roomed outhouse that had been hit with an air grenade through the roof. Tim took a photo of the building's red metal doors, then pushed one open with his right foot. He rocked back slightly, and pushed the other door open. I saw the hairy lower half of a severed human leg, with shoe.

'Has a dog been in here?' asked Tim.

'There was a dog right out here', said one of the marines. Then, I saw a man's body, its left side blown open. Several yellow and red organs, swollen with fluid, hung out of the hole. The man had been killed by the grenade; the dog was eating his exposed muscle and fatty tissue. Tim put on his gloves and walked in. The man lay on his right side, his face buried in a blanket. Rigor mortis had set in, so as Tim pushed the left arm, the whole body went with it and the man was flipped on to his back. The right side of his face and head had been blown off. Tim searched him, pulling prayer beads from his shirt: 'Those didn't work, did they, motherfucker?' A rifle that looked about seventy years old was propped against the wall. 'It's very powerful, well-maintained and very accurate', said Tim. 'It's a 7.62 mm, .303 Enfield.'

He searched the man's pockets. 'Oh wow. Here's your prick', he said, pulling a string of shiny new bullets from the dead man's clothing. 'Get the fuck out of here', said a marine standing in the door. '556?' he asked.

'Oh yeah', said Tim. The bullets were NATO rounds; the bullets that Americans and Brits used and the ones that were issued to the ANA. They were also the bullets that had been fired at the marines, so the dead man was either one of the snipers or one of the marks-men covering the snipers.

'What are you gonna do with him?' asked one of the marines. 'Him?' said Tim. 'I don't believe we're gonna do anything with him, we'll just leave him there.'

Three people approached; two old men and a woman. They said the building was their house and they wanted to move the body. Lieutenant Greenlief asked if they were related to the dead man. One of the men said he was his nephew and his sister – the dead man's mother, who was blind – wanted her son to be buried near the family home, on the other side of the pork chop.

'Ask him if any more of his relatives are Taliban', said Greenlief.
'No one', they said.

'So the guy that's dead is the only Taliban in their family?' asked
Greenlief.

'He was not Taliban', said the family, all together. 'But they forced
him to carry a gun', said his aunt. 'If they give you an order, you
don't say no', said his uncle.

* * * * *

Charlie Company had also started work in Karu Charai. Their area
included the opium bazaar, where one of them noticed a wire coming out of a wall and disappearing into the ground. The wire linked
eighteen military-grade rockets and a fragmentation device ('like a
home-made Claymore [a type of mine]') in a daisy chain, that zig-
zagged for a hundred and fifty metres. It was the most complex IED
they'd found in Afghanistan.

'If a marine patrol had walked through [the opium bazaar] it
was designed to kill the whole patrol, all at once', said Lieutenant
Aaron McLean, the marine I'd met at the condolence payment
meeting. 'Walking round here', he said, 'is a bit like swimming
in the ocean. You'd never do it if you knew how many sharks
there really were. The number of IEDs we find, the number of
IEDs that malfunction or that we miss entirely, in this country, is
tremendous.' They'd detonated every IED they'd come across so
far. 'We're twelve for twelve right now', said Ski.

Elsewhere in the pork chop and bazaar, the marines found so
many bags of heroin and opium that they hadn't enough space to
store them. One house alone had somewhere between forty and fifty
kilograms of heroin in a few old sacks. The EOD team found tool-
boxes full of IED-detonating devices, mortars and recoil-less rifle
rounds. 'These are the best-looking pieces of ordnance I've found
in this country. Some of them are brand new', said Tom Williams,
examining some shiny Chinese rockets. They also found a hideous
device, a DFC (Directional Fragment Charge). This was a metal
barrel, three-quarters full of explosive powder, the rest packed with

nuts, bolts, broken china and ball-bearings. It worked like a cannon, firing the junk into whoever was in front of it when it went off.

Their ingenuity amazed me. Most houses I'd seen in Marjah didn't have toilets, beds, chairs, tables, cookers or a source of clean water. But if you wanted to make IEDs or turn opium into heroin, it was like being in Toys'R'Us.

However, after a few days, Tom and Ski, the most experienced of the EOD team, began to mock the bomb-makers. 'I thought this would be a hub for seasoned Taliban fighters but the IEDs we've found are simple', said Tom. 'Words can't express how Bush League these devices are. The daisy chain we found was command-detonated [detonated by wire] and the guy who set it off would have been …', he pointed to the roof of a single-storey building across the street, 'less than twenty metres away. It was shady. You think we'd not see a guy on the roof with a wire in his hand?'

It was surreal sitting in the sun, laughing at Tom and Ski insulting the Marjah bomb-makers. They chuckled slightly when I reminded them that barely a week ago, the streets where we sat had been described as among the most dangerous on earth. Staff Sergeantt Robert Dawson, from 1st Platoon arrived. In his thick, Long Island accent, he complained that getting here had been 'serious and hectic' (together with 'stoopid', these were the most dramatic phrases he ever used) but the Taliban had now 'punked out. We drove them right out. And now it's quiet and boring.' He was as dismissive as Tom of the enemy's actions. 'One dude with an RPG didn't have enough space. It bounced back and blew him up.'

The unsophisticated IEDs found in Marjah suggested that the Taliban here weren't part of an international network of criminal masterminds or even a pan-Afghan network that shared bomb-making expertise and equipment. The seasoned fighters and snipers may well have come just for the battle. There certainly was a criminal network in Marjah but its chief concern seemed to be the manufacture and export of heroin, not *jihad*.

* * * * *

Back at the base, Nascar and Picc were glued to the surveillance laptop, talking to some marines two kilometres away from the base, who thought they might have spotted four men placing an IED.

'You have PID?' asked Picc over the radio. PID — positive identification — is required before anyone can be targeted. There was silence.

'It's as close as we could be to an IED being placed. We've been watching them for a while', said the voice on the radio. Picc was annoyed at their vagueness. Nascar smiled knowingly. 'It looks like it would be an IED to me', said the voice.

'So ... based on pattern of life and their actions right now ...', said Greenlief, watching at one side. Picc repeated his words to the marines on the radio, encouraging them to say they had PID.

'PID is theirs', said Nascar, '*they* have to say they have PID.'

But the marines wouldn't say they were sure. Everyone was afraid of making the wrong call but not because of a horror of killing civilians. Most of the marines and soldiers I'd met, who spent their days at the sharp end, accepted the fact that civilians died in wars. They were scared of making the wrong call because everyone thought that the lawyers now decided how wars were fought. They were afraid they'd end up as the subjects of lengthy investigations, and could even face prison.

Greenlief and Picc shared a cigarette. They offered it to Nascar, who looked at it guiltily, then said 'one drag'. He was the only marine I'd ever seen who looked wrong smoking. He looked like a schoolboy trying to pretend he smoked.

'Scarface 6-4. It looks like we do have something going on here. Lots of individuals are coming up to it, walking away, looking at it like "oh wow what's this, check it out" so it is definitely not normal. I would say we do have PID on a possible IED', said the voice on the radio.

'He needs to have PID on an IED *emplacer*', said Nascar.

Picc spoke into the radio. 'Do you have PID on the IED *emplacer*. Do you have PID on the guys that are emplacing?' He put the radio down. 'FUCK.'

'Wait, wait, wait', said Nascar. 'You know, we don't want to put too much on them, I mean, they're telling us what they see. PID is ours. They've just got to build the picture.'

'FUCK', said Picc again.

'So if they say they have possible PID on an IED emplacer, that's right where we've had IEDs emplaced for the last three days', Nascar continued, hitting the map with his finger. 'We've watched it happen.' Two of Charlie Company's vehicles had been hit by IEDs at exactly the same spot the day before.

Picc put the radio to his mouth. He looked as close to a nervous breakdown as Nascar. 'Scarface 6-4 from Siege 1-4. We've watched them place IEDs in this vicinity for the last three days.'

'Scarface 6-4 has PID on the IED emplacer down in the hole, where the IED is', said the voice on the radio. Nascar nodded vigorously. 'Alright, let's go, we got it.'

'Let's do it', said Picc, smiling into his radio. It was a small triumph; Nascar reminded him they still had to get approval. The voice on the radio said he recommended a gun run, hitting the IED emplacers and the IED. Nascar agreed. Picc handed him the radio. 'I've been trying to give you this for half an hour, that's why I came and woke you up.'

The four figures on the laptop screen walked north, to a building they'd used for the last three days. They'd now been tracked for forty-five minutes. Picc and Nascar received initial approval, then set up a live feed to the general and his staff, back at Camp Leatherneck, so they could give the final approval. It took Nascar twenty minutes to make contact. Several marines had gathered around Nascar, Picc and the laptop. I asked why he couldn't get approval when they'd seen four men laying an IED. 'That's an outstanding question', said Nascar, not amused. The figures were digging the road again.

Greenlief said this was exactly what they'd been seeing, four or five times a day, for the last three days. He said that two guys buried the IED, while two stood sentry at either side of the road. As soon as something appeared in the air above them, they'd move women and children alongside, making it impossible to get air strikes approved. But this time, there were no women or children.

A pilot came on the radio. He'd seen two 'squirters' – figures running away from the IED. The pilot was flying an A10, a Warthog – 'basically a huge cannon with wings and a man sitting on top', said a marine – and had been given approval for a gun run against the target. Captain Sparks came to watch. 'Picc did all the work and now he's taking a shit. He's missing the gun show', someone said. Nascar pointed to the screen with the antenna of his radio and everyone watched in silence. We heard what sounded like a gigantic electric drill.

'We do have three individuals KIA in the field', said the pilot.

'Nice', said a marine, 'they got three.'

'How long did that take you?' someone asked Nascar.

'Two hours.'

There was movement on the screen. Three more figures walked away from the building that they'd used as a hiding place for the last three days.

'We're gonna slay some bodies today', said Nascar.

'Fuck yeah', said a marine.

'There's another one. There's two more, at the intersection.'

'These guys aren't real smart', said Nascar. He passed the grid references to the pilot and said again that the targets were confirmed IED emplacers. His eyes were locked on the map and the screen. Anything could have been happening behind him and he would have been oblivious. He asked the pilot for his altitude. No answer.

'Hog 5-1, siege 1-2, how copy.'

No answer. He said it again. Again, there was no answer.

'We should have just fired fucking Hellfires', said Picc, who'd come back.

The problem was that the sky above Marjah was crowded, especially at twenty thousand feet. At that level, the Apaches and jets made it difficult for the drones (Reaper pilotless aircraft, remote-controlled from a trailer in Vegas) to get the airspace below cleared so that they could fire the Hellfire missiles. The A10 warthogs flew at ten thousand feet, where the airspace was clearer.

'I don't know what they've got against Hellfires today. Those guys were out in the open', said Nascar.

He leant on his left elbow, the radio in his hand, an inch in front of his nose. His head dropped, his eyes closed and he pushed his forehead into the speaker, almost in prayer.

He called to the pilot one more time. 'Hog 5-1, siege 1-2.'

'Hog 5-1 go ahead', the pilot replied. The lives of the three men on the road hung on tiny details like how well the radios worked. There was no relief on Nascar's face, just an instant return to the furious concentration on killing the remaining men. Through no fault of his own and not because of any cunning on their part, the men had evaded him for the last three days. He was desperate to kill them.

The pilot and the marines on the ground confirmed that the men were still in the road and that one of them had put something into the ground, 'potentially the IED itself'.

Nascar turned to Picc. 'Alright, we got everything we need.' He didn't nod his head slightly as he said this, looking for consensus; he nodded his head five or six times, rapidly, as if he were daring anyone to stop him.

The pilot said he could still see the men. He prepared to turn towards them one last time.

'Roger. That is your target, we are awaiting approval', Nascar said.

'Mission approved', said Picc, who was talking to the Battalion HQ on another radio. Nascar nodded and spoke to the pilot. 'Final attack headings 3 6 0 to 0 1 5. Your mission is approved. Your airspace below is clear. Stand by for push.' Every muscle under the thin skin of his face strained towards his eyes, locked on to the laptop screen. A long furrow ran from his hair, across his forehead and between his eyebrows. A large vein was visible on one side of his head. 'He's inbound', he said and leaned closer to the screen. A minute passed. Nothing.

'What happened? What are we waiting on?' said Picc.

'We're waiting for him to call inbound', said Nascar. His head plunged closer to the screen. 'Come on buddy, push. Goddamn.'

'Hog. The emplacer has moved east, he is now moving south down the road. Your approval remains in effect.'

'Hog 5-1 copy. Still have eyes on.'

Nascar suddenly saw something on the screen. 'Who is that? Who is that?' It looked like a civilian had wandered close to the IED emplacer. For a second, Nascar looked ready to cry.

'Voodoo 1-4 what do you see in there?' Voodoo 1-4 was the drone controller in Vegas.

'It looks like the two IED emplacers. This is where we saw them bring back the objects and set them down on the east side of the road.' The other person on the screen had been deemed a target.

'Roger. Hog, confirm you are pushing at this time.'

'Moving in south to north, in about one minute.'

'What is this', said Nascar. Someone else had appeared on the screen. His thumb circled the press-to-talk button on his radio and he pushed his forehead into the speaker again.

His lifted his head. 'There's one PAX, coming from the south to the north, we don't know where he came from.' 'Pax', the abbreviation for passengers, had become a general word to describe a person. A civilian had appeared on the laptop screen, too close to the targets.

'Affirm Hog, hold for now, abort for now.' He released the speak button. 'FUCK.'

They had to wait for the civilian to leave. If he didn't leave, the IED emplacers would escape. 'Hog 5-1. I need you to stand by, ready for an immediate push.'

A few minutes later, the civilian walked off the screen. The pilot said he was 'hot' and ready to attack. Everyone moved closer to the screen, willing the plane to be able to attack. Even the chaplain was watching. He took off his sunglasses and whispered 'come on'.

'There he is.' The A10 Warthog appeared on the screen.

'5-2's in hot', said the pilot. We heard the effects of the first gun run, which sounded like the earth was being ripped open. Then came the sound of the cannon, a hideous roar that seemed too loud and deep to come from anything man-made. It sounded like the sky had split.

'East ten metres, east one five metres, in the canal, cleared hot.' Nascar corrected the second A10, even as we felt the roar from the first. We heard another burst of thunder, followed by the vicious belch of the second cannon.

'There he goes', said a marine.

'Wow', said the chaplain, as hundreds of 33 mm bullets turned the road into a huge cloud of smoke and dust. Some of the marines ran to the side of the building and looked over the wall to watch.

'Hog 5-2 good effects, good effects', Nascar said into his radio.

'Sympathetic detonation too', said Picc. The IED had been shot by the bullets and exploded. It was hard to imagine anything within a hundred metres had escaped being hit. Ants would have been directly hit by that many bullets.

'Finally', said Nascar. 'Hog, good shots, I need you to look for squirters to the south. Voodoo 1-4, I want you to look for squirters to the north.' After all that, he still wanted to make sure no one got away.

'There were two squirters to the east, I think we got them on the second pass', said one of the pilots. They reported that during the two gun runs, when the cannons had been used no more than a second and a half each, 460 bullets had been fired.

'They missed on the first one, we corrected them east and they *schwacked* the canal', said Nascar, turning to the marines who had gathered around him. One of them gave him a high-five, another sang the theme from *Team America*, 'America, fuck yeah!' without irony.

It was immediately reported that two squirters were still alive, probably tending to a wounded man lying by the side of the road. The Warthogs were told to climb back up to sixteen thousand feet and the marines on the ground were ordered to go and find out who had survived.

* * * * *

A deep canal ran through Karu Charai, cutting directly across the main road and cleaving to the eastern side of the pork chop. It would have been the long piece of fat on the chop, except it was perfectly straight. Someone at HQ had decided that 'pork chop' wasn't a good name for a place inhabited by devout Muslims whose hearts and minds they were supposed to be winning, so officially, it was renamed the 'lamb' chop. Everyone on the ground carried on calling it pork.

I followed Captain Sparks, Tim Coderre, Mark Greenlief, Ski and Tom Williams from EOD, and a few ANA soldiers as they walked about two hundred and fifty metres along the canal, then turned into the jumble of buildings, alleys and high mud walls, which had looked so mysterious and threatening until that moment.

The first building we came across looked like a small storeroom. Two makeshift gutters came off its flat roof. Water had run out of the gutters and down the walls, carving two channels, like tiny valleys, all the way down to the ground. The entrance to the room was on the other side of a long wall, so no one paid any attention to it.

On our way out of the pork chop, on the other side of the same wall, someone waited beside the small building. 'You gotta check this out', he said. Even when I went in, I still didn't know what I was looking at. Only when I saw Captain Sparks staring out though a slit in the wall did it click. A vertical line of sunlight striped him as he raised his rifle and looked through the sights. Someone had chipped away at one of the channels worn away by the water, until they'd gone right through the wall. The slit was impossible to see unless you stood right next to it, as Captain Sparks was. What he saw was a perfect view of the sandbags on top of the marines' base. They had found the sniper hole that had been used to inflict most of their casualties.

Captain Sparks stood in that shard of light for a long time, staring out. Eventually, he turned to a marine behind him and said,

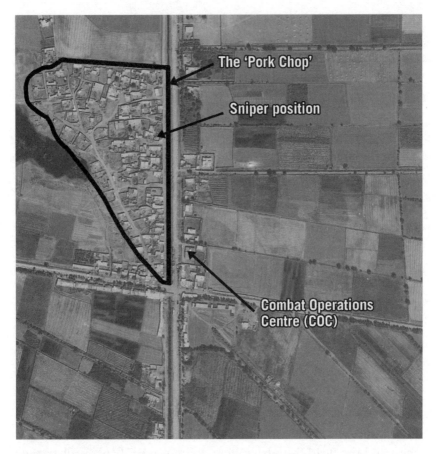

Figure 3   The Sniper Hole (© Google 2011; Image © Digital Globe 2011)

'Throw your ACOG [Advanced Combat Optical Gunsight] up there and look at our post.' The marine pointed his rifle through the slit and looked through.

'That's where Lamont was hit', said Tim Coderre.

'This is it. Perfect angle', said Sparks. He spoke into his radio: 'Roger COC, I believe we've identified the sniper position, break.' He gave the GPS position. 'There's a vertical loophole in the wall here, break. It has perfect sight alignment for the post, where Lamont and the snipers were hit.' He stared through the hole again.

He clenched a fist and gently punched the wall next to the hole. He looked angry to be standing where the sniper who had outwitted them for a few days had stood. The sniper had escaped and could shoot again. Tim Coderre picked eighteen bullet cases off the floor and put them in a plastic bag. There were 556 rounds, the same NATO rounds that had been found on the other sniper. 'He was probably using a weapon that we'd supplied him with in some way or another', said Sparks.

I asked a question but Sparks wasn't really listening; he was working out exactly how the sniper had stayed hidden for so long. He stepped back and looked at the wall opposite the slit. 'He was probably sitting back in the shadows where we couldn't see any indication of his weapon at all, shooting through this slit in the wall. Perfect sniper position.' I looked through the slit and saw three marines' helmets behind the green sandbags on the roof of the base.

I asked Captain Sparks how it felt to be standing there. He took a few seconds to answer. 'Um … I'm just a little upset that it took us three days to find it.' He spoke to someone on his radio for a second. 'But it's ours now, so victory is achieved.'

'He was extremely well-trained', said Tim Coderre, 'to know that he has to be this far back so that his muzzle flash isn't seen. And to engage targets … you know, he was hitting them in the chest and the head from back here, so he was probably well-trained military.'

I asked which military would have trained him.

'Possibly ours, at some point. But Al-Qaeda also could. There are lots of countries that could provide this level of training. The only thing he didn't do was pick up his casings.'

Captain Sparks was visibly aggravated that the man who'd shot four of his marines was getting some credit. 'So he's not a sniper, he's just a good marksman', he interjected. Tim followed suit. 'Exactly. He left target indicators [the bullet cases]. Eighteen of them to be exact.' 'A real sniper would have destroyed this wall or patched it up and picked up his casings and we'd never have known', added Sparks.

He'd done it again; found encouragement from nowhere. 'He's

just a guy that's a good shot and knows a little bit about conceal-ment. He's an idiot though.' In five minutes the man had gone from being a skilful, cunning and possibly American-trained sniper, to an idiot marksman with only a little knowledge.

'Alright' said Captain Sparks. 'Let's continue the game.'

CHAPTER 11

A week after landing in Marjah, just two days after the first stores in the bazaar had re-opened, two platoons from Bravo woke early to push east and clear another five kilometres of ground. This was an area they had regularly been attacked from and where they had identified an IED cell. I was surprised they weren't having a day off; they'd been clearing compounds and sleeping in them since the first day.

'We don't do days off', said Janofsky, without a hint of complaint, simply as a statement of fact. 'No days off', said Captain Sparks, with just a bit of braggadocio, 'there's no such thing.' Sometimes the marines acted so much like Marines it would have been easy to accuse them of thinking they were Clint Eastwood or Lee Marvin. But over time, I began to think it was actually the other way round and the Hollywood actors were copying the Marines. This was how they really were.

I told myself that I'd follow the marines as they headed out, then film them walking into another battle, which I thought would make a good ending for my film. But I stayed with them as they cleared one more building, then as they found an unexploded rocket sticking out of the ground, then another, then as they heard that a group of Taliban were watching them. I'd promised myself more than once that I'd had enough but I made no effort to keep that promise. I kept following until I'd come too far to turn round. I wasn't addicted to danger or excitement; each trip felt more like an endurance test that I had no choice than to pass. It was more that I was unable to say 'no' to seeing something new. It was impossible to feel I'd had enough. I was just watching and recording. I didn't need to kill anyone or save anyone's life. I didn't need to follow orders. And most of all, I didn't live there. I had a plane ticket home that I could use whenever I wanted. Of everyone in Marjah at that time, I had the easiest time.

The next three days were almost as bad as the first three. The Taliban only ever went as far as the marines pushed them. They were masters at staying just out of range. And no one pushed them from the other side, not from five miles away and not from any neighbouring town, province or country. The marines were attacked with mortars, found IEDs everywhere and were pinned down in fields and deserted compounds as they slowly made their way east. But there was a different atmosphere; I didn't see panicked and lost faces. Even in the worst moments, lying under fire in a field or sprinting between buildings with bullets zinging across their path, I could hear laughing and joking. Sitting in an abandoned building during a firefight, everyone told the marine next to me, who claimed to be a rapper, to perform for my camera. He was reluctant, but I told him not even 50 Cent had rapped under fire. What came out had neither rhyme nor any kind of rhythm. 'It was white people rhyme', he said. But it fitted the mood.

The ANA still did little except enter buildings first. Often they couldn't even do that. The marines watched in disgust as one soldier charged several times through a door too small for his backpack and rolled-up sleeping mattress. Each time, he dangled half-way into the compound, throttling himself, then re-appeared with a confused look on his face and tried again. 'GET IN THERE', screamed a marine. But he couldn't, so a corpsman went in first instead. 'Great, you just killed a corpsman', said Corporal Sanders, the squad leader. 'Stay here, stay here.' The ANA soldier wanted to try again. 'Sit. Sit the fuck down. Sit', said Sanders, usually placid to the point of aloofness. He pointed to the ground, as if he were house-training a dog. 'Sit, sit, sit', said Sanders and another marine, in concert. The ANA soldier took off his backpack and attempted to go through the door. 'No sit down. You …', they pointed to him and then to the floor. 'SIT DOWN. SIT DOWN.' He sat on his bag, smiling, but hurt and embarrassed. 'Sid dow', he said, trying to repeat his orders. Luckily, there were no IEDs or fighters in the building.

The mood suddenly changed. Corporal Sanders and his squad heard over the radio that their friend had been shot in the head and was not responding. Everyone assumed he was dead or at least badly injured. The men who had shot him were in a building just over a hundred metres away, across open fields.

Lance Corporal Rios, a young marine with a tattoo across his chest that read, 'I'd rather be judged by twelve than carried by six', found a hole in a wall. He saw one of the gunmen moving. 'I got good eyes on this cocksucker right here', he said, firing four shots. Two feet away from me a man was shooting at someone with every expectation of killing him. Yet there was no sense of drama or tension. Anywhere else, a gun would provoke terror, anger, increased heartbeats, policemen and news crews. Here it was humdrum, barely noticed. Rios cursed when his shots went over the man's head.

The building was hit by a Hellfire missile. They usually only took out a single room, so the plan was to run the hundred metres across open ground and storm it. 'You wanna do a *Medal of Honor*?' asked one of the marines, grinning. 'The fighters are probably still in that building and you're just going to storm it on foot?' I asked. Sanders looked at me with a pursed and slightly demonic smile and nodded. 'Alright, tell 'em we're pushing', said Rios. 'Alright fuck it, let's go. PUSHING', shouted Sanders. Everyone filed along a wall until they could see the field they needed to get across.

We sprinted to the building's outer wall and knelt, to get our breaths. The lead marine peered around the corner, then ran towards the door. I followed the marine behind him. We both fell into a deep ditch. As we struggled to climb out, the marine behind us saw a yellow jug hanging from a tree, above our heads. He yelled 'probable IED' but someone behind screamed at us to keep running towards the door. Others darted past, almost stamping on our hands as we climbed out of the ditch. There was another awful clatter of gunfire. 'GO, GO. WE GOTTA GET IN THAT FUCK-ING COMPOUND', screamed someone. I turned into the door and saw that half the compound had been reduced to rubble by the Hellfire missile. A marine came out of a small room, shouting 'CLEAR'. Another marine threw a grenade over a wall, scream-ing 'Frag out'. Everyone went down on one knee as the grenade exploded. Slowly, we realised that none of the fighters had survived the air strike. Their bodies lay somewhere beneath the rubble.

As the sun set, we waited to hear if we'd be sleeping there that night or would be moving on. Two marines argued about their Welcome Home parties. One's girlfriend was organising his and she had lots of friends, so the other, who was single, was desperate to be invited. But the marine with the girlfriend refused; he thought his friend would embarrass him. The argument went on until dark.

* * * * *

The next day, I decided I should try to see something different, to justify me still being there. So I tagged along with the EOD team, slowly making their way along the main road east, between the buildings that Bravo Company were clearing. Tom and Ski were working with Staff Sergeant Travis Gregrow and Sergeant Timo-thy Harrison, also EOD specialists. I joined them at 9.30 a.m., by which time they'd found and detonated four IEDs on just two hundred metres of road. I could see the craters spaced as regularly as lampposts, three or four feet deep and about twelve feet wide, big enough to use as trenches.

Occasionally, the EOD team were shot at, which only caused them to jump behind their trucks for a few minutes. After they had detonated their fifth IED, they attracted so much fire that we had to hide in an abandoned compound beside the road, where Nascar and Picc joined us. On their frequency, we heard the Taliban say-ing we were being shot at to keep us in the building until RPGs could be brought forward. No one wanted to wait for that, so they decided to take cover behind the truck as it drove up the road to the next building, where there were more marines. But the line of seven people – the four in the EOD team, Nascar, Picc and me – was longer than the truck. As everyone walked, pushed, pulled, slowed down and sped up, the people at the front or the back of the pantomime line-up kept appearing at either end of the truck. Not for the first time, only either our pure luck or the Taliban's poor marksmanship was all that meant none of us were shot.

The regular pattern of IEDs continued until we reached a cross-roads two kilometres from the base. There, a huge bunker had been dug at the corner of the intersecting roads, big enough for six men, with a concealed entrance and several firing holes. It was built from breeze blocks placed end up and plastered with mud, which exactly matched the colour of the road. Its roof, just a foot or so above the ground, had reeds planted in it. It was impossible to see until you tripped over it. The Taliban had spent a lot of time preparing this bunker but clearly, had expected the marines to slowly approach from outside. The plan to drop one company into the middle of Marjah had caused the bunker to be abandoned. Next to the bunker, the EOD team dug up a pressure plate, a simple device designed so that anything passing over it completed a circuit that detonated a nearby bomb.

'Oh really, this is a little different', said Ski, as he cut through the tape wrapped around the pressure plate to make it waterproof. He showed me a plank of wood, no bigger than a cricket bat, with three rectangular pieces of metal nailed to one side, connected with three pieces of wire. On top of each piece of metal was a small section of tyre, each lined with another rectangular piece of metal. 'When you drive over it', he said, pushing one of the pieces of tyre down and touching the two pieces of metal together, 'it closes the circuit, which sets off the IED.'

'You'd think they would have blown themselves up with that', said Staff Sergeant Gregrow, as he walked into the road to start digging for the bomb. He hacked at the ground with a small axe, pulling away the loose dirt with his hand and digging out stones with his knife. But the bomb was deeply buried, which meant it was big. This didn't inspire any fear in Gregrow. He was soon digging into the road with a shovel, pushing it into the ground with his foot as if he were digging for treasure, not for a bomb.

'Please don't film this part!' he shouted, as he swung the shovel once more into the ground.

'One question', I said, standing next to him and looking nervously down into the hole. 'Why don't you wear a suit, like in *The Hurt Locker?*'

He laughed. 'This close, a bomb suit isn't gonna do anything and er ... mobility I guess. You can't get around.'

'But you're digging, by hand, for a bomb that's big enough to blow up a truck', I said.

'Yah!' he replied, laughing again, not for a second stopping his furious digging.

'These fucks had a looooong time', said Tom.

Like every other EOD team I'd met, these men loved their jobs but not for the reasons you might expect. They didn't get a visible thrill from the huge danger they put themselves in and they didn't look like men with death wishes. They loved the technical challenge of discovering and dismantling bombs, of competing with the bomb-maker in a battle of wits. If it weren't for their obvious bravery, they could be described as nerdy. There was no doubt they were gun-carrying, Fox News-watching Republicans who could look after themselves in a dark alley. (At least, certainly Tom and Ski could; Gregrow and Harrison were more traditionally nerdy.) But I could also imagine them at home in their garages, spending hours on electronic or mechanical projects.

After a lot of digging, Gregrow eventually found a big yellow jug about a foot and a half underground. I asked how powerful it was.

'It would definitely kill us. We'd be little tiny pieces', he replied, smiling gleefully.

'What would it do to a truck?'

'It would probably rip a truck apart and everybody inside would not be happy.'

I asked him why he chose to do this for a living. He said he used to be a canine handler but 'I wasn't getting good results with it and I wanted to get out and help guys as much as I can, so this was the best option for me.'

They planted their charges next to the jug. We ran to a nearby compound and waited for the blast. It was much bigger than we expected. A plume of smoke, dust and debris went high into the clear blue sky. 'Wow, you think that was two jugs?' said Gregrow.

They also found a command wire, hidden in the reeds alongside a ditch. It ran for hundreds of metres up to, and under, the cross-roads. 'See how it's all chewed up at the top? It's like they threw a DFC in there', said Tom, pointing to where the canal disappeared under the road. I couldn't see anything that looked at all out of place. I walked around the reeds, where Gregrow soon found the DFC Tom had guessed was there.

'It's pretty much a cylinder', he said. 'A bunch of explosives and a whole bunch of nasty frag. And it's pretty much pointing right at you right now.' I took a few steps back.

We hid behind another building as they blew up the DFC. 'Pretty hot ... man, I love that!' said Gregrow, as rocks and dust rained down all around us. The reeds were gone and the 'nasty frag' had been blasted over and beyond the crossroads. It looked like the plan had been to defend the crossroads from the bunker for as long as possible, then flee after connecting the big IED to the power source. Then, when the IED blew up a truck, they'd detonate the DFC to hit anybody that came to help.

At the next set of compounds, the marines had to scream at the ANA until they handed over a small cache of Taliban weapons they'd found. One soldier offered a compromise: 'After we've fired the rounds we'll give you the magazines.' 'No, no, no', shouted Ski, as one of them reluctantly handed over an AK47, 'you cannot fire that, no. All the Taliban weapons have to be confiscated.' Someone offered a handful of bullets. 'We need one more one grenade', said Ski. A soldier moodily pulled a grenade out of his pocket.

'Tell them that the Taliban booby-trap this stuff', said Tom. 'Even bullets can be booby-trapped.'

Another gunfight began right outside the door. The ANA, still feeling mischievous after their weapons find, were in no mood to fight. While bullets cracked over the compound walls, one of them handed his rifle to his friend, showed me his knife and then pulled out a knuckle-duster with four spikes. 'Good', he said, 'for a Taliban boxer.' He grabbed his friend's head, raised his right arm and punched him on the helmet with the knuckle-duster.

When the ANA had gone, Tom, Ski and I were distracted into finding grain for some starving chicks we'd come across. Suddenly, we realised that we had been abandoned. There had been some marines and a sniper team on the roof of the building we were in but they'd left without us. Bursts of fire came from several different directions. Nervously, we looked through the door, trying to see where everyone had gone. 'You know what you said about never carrying a weapon?', said Tom, 'well, today might have to be the day that changes.' He tapped the pistol attached to his body armour. We eventually spotted some marines, who covered us as we ran to a large compound at a T-junction that marked the end of the road east.

We were five kilometres away from the base, as far as the marines wanted to go.

Ski was handed a pressure plate that someone had found. It looked similar to the one with the rubber tyres but didn't have the rectangular metal plates for completing the circuit. 'This is a low mag pressure plate', said Ski. 'See those carbon rods in there? They basically give off zero to minimum metal signature. These are bad little guys to have in the road.' Ski asked where it had been found.

'It was sitting on a shelf in their house, not connected to anything, right beside their teapot.'

'Fuck', said Ski, sighing.

He was also handed a WFP (World Food Programme) sack. He looked inside and pulled out five RPGs.

Someone else pointed out more bunkers, on either side of the main road east. They were fortified with sandbags and had breeze-blocks for firing holes. From the far side of the T-junction, the direction they'd assumed the marines would approach from, the bunkers looked like slight humps in the canal banks. If the marines had approached them on foot from the east, they would have been mown down in seconds.

* * * * *

A few days later, back at the base, everyone struggled with the sudden quiet. They had achieved their objectives and considered themselves lucky not to have suffered many more casualties than they had. But there was also a sense of anti-climax. Tim Coderre and Mark Greenlief started a workout routine that involved going through an entire pack of cards twice and doing whatever number of press-ups each card said. Gunny D and Picc held as many as five *shuras* a day, employing local people to pick up litter and rebuild the mosque but they were frustrated by how many people simply demanded cash handouts. They'd also been told that at several *shuras*, some men who hadn't spoken were Taliban representatives.

I wondered if there had ever been another conflict where one side had been handed so many advantages by the other. The Taliban had only to drop their weapons and they became invisible. Even the weapons, and the ability to use them, may have been handed to them, either when they fought the Russians or, more recently, British and American troops. There was such desperation to increase the Afghan National Army's numbers ('There's a certain quality to quantity', General Nicholson had said at the ROC drill) that just about anyone could get in, especially since the desertion rate was so high. Recruits received three months' introductory training, which for anyone with questionable loyalties meant three months of being taught how their opponents operated. Often, they used the weapons and uniforms they'd been given to attack real security force members or their foreign mentors. This happened more and more, suggesting both the police and the army had been heavily, albeit easily, infiltrated. But the problem was not properly addressed, because that meant admitting that the absurdly ambitious goal of having a national army able to secure every province of Afghanistan, on its own, by 2014, was a fantasy. But that goal was the exit strategy, so publicly, everyone had to say it was plausible. Shortly after Operation Mushtaraq, President Obama said something he could only have believed if he'd been badly misled: 'Not only have we succeeded in driving the Taliban out of Marjah but it also is a model of the partnership between US forces and Afghan forces.'

Marines wandered around the base or sat on the verandah, looking despondent and lost. 'Did we win?' asked Nascar, finally able to leave his laptop because the air surveillance now flew somewhere else. 'Is there a white flag flying somewhere? I don't actually know what I'm supposed to be doing right now.' He wasn't the only member of Bravo Company who found doing nothing very hard. 'The captain said we need to aggressively find something to do, otherwise it's going to become *Lord of the Flies* around here', said another. Even the captain himself seemed uneasy. He told me that one of the major potential pitfalls was if 'the government doesn't come in and establish control and fill a vacuum that we can't really fill'.

Three weeks into the operation, the chances of that happening looked low. There was still no sign of a 'government in a box'.

PART IV

US MARINE CORPS

JUNE 2010

1ST BATTALION

6TH MARINES

In May 2010, a week after President Obama claimed that Operation Mushtaraq had been a model of partnership between US and Afghan forces, General McChrystal was in Marjah. 'This is a bleeding ulcer right now', he said. 'You don't feel it here but I'll tell you, it's a bleeding ulcer outside. We have given the insurgency a chance to be a little bit credible because we've put more forces than ever in an area with a unique situation. We've said, "We're taking it back". We came in to take it back and we haven't been completely convincing.'

General McChrystal's claim that Mushtaraq was Afghan-led, a claim repeated by President Obama, a claim widely-spread and never seriously challenged, a claim backed by a massive media campaign, was the biggest fallacy of the entire operation. The Afghans were nowhere near ready to lead any military operation, leave alone in the Pashtun south. Certainly not one as big as Mushtaraq. Sadly, facing a public that had lost both interest and hope, it was too easy to say the Afghans had led and would soon be leading completely. That meant that the troops could come home.

I returned to Marjah just after McChrystal's visit, roughly four months since the marines had first landed there. Bravo Company was in the last month of its tour. The new district governor, Abdul Zahir, was revealed to have spent time in a German prison; he'd allegedly stabbed his son as he tried to prevent his mother being beaten. There were regular battles and IED strikes, and there were many reports of local people who co-operated with the marines being intimidated, beaten, or even murdered.

CHAPTER 12

Captain Sparks couldn't wait to show me what Bravo Company had achieved in the bazaar. Without helmets, we walked out of the base, past a refurbished mosque, complete with fancy minarets, a long ablutions block, a well and a little fenced area the marines wanted to call 'Freedom Park'.

The local people had re-opened many of their stores. Fresh fruit, meat, vegetables, cold drinks and even ice cream were available. The residents, I was told, were coming forward with reliable information about the Taliban. Children greeted us with high-fives and requests for more radios. The radios were still on their way, so they were given footballs instead. People were happy to be photographed laughing and joking with members of Bravo Company, with no apparent fear of reprisals. These things would have been unthinkable a few months earlier. I felt like I was on the set of an advert for counter-insurgency.

Gunny D created a 'Princess Diana' effect wherever he went. Kids followed him, chanting his name ('Ganna D', 'Gunna D', and even 'Kenna D'). Men embraced him, pressing letters into his hand and exchanging phrases in Pashtu.

'Gunny D is the Mayor, he knows everyone in town', said Captain Sparks.

Gunny D's popularity, which embarrassed him, was due to the fact he had spent roughly $675,000 on salaries for three thousand local people, for cleaning, repairing and rebuilding the bazaar.

'From the beginning we were always out there, always interacting with the locals', said Gunny D. 'We spend twelve to fourteen hours a day with them. We take off our sunglasses, the helmets, all the gear and it shocks them. But they feel very relaxed; they know who they are talking to. The Captain told them he wanted them to know who was in charge, who was taking care of them and who was here to kill the Taliban. Four months on, we've got genuine friends here. We regularly have breakfast, lunch and dinner with them.' A group of tailors, who had only re-opened their store five days earlier, complained that they didn't have enough work for their staff to do. 'Well, we're hiring', Gunny D told them.

'Yeah, they can make some new suits for the sanitation department', said Captain Sparks. A group of shopkeepers was told that anybody with a skill could use the marines, and their money, to set up apprenticeship schemes. Hard-working rubbish collectors could become apprentices, then receive micro-grants to start their own business. A man asked if he could be paid to train an apprentice moneychanger. 'I don't know if that's a skill', said Sparks, 'it should be for somebody that builds something or fixes something.'

Bravo had established two security 'bubbles': the bazaar, where Captain Sparks said there hadn't been a serious attack for three months; and a wider bubble around it, about eight kilometres across, where IEDs were still being laid and snipers and gun teams roamed. But although Marjah was one of hundreds of districts and sub-districts that needed to be secured, and it had taken roughly a tenth of the available resources to do it, Captain Sparks thought it showed that the policy could work. 'If you're just going through some checklist, you're never going to get anywhere', he said. 'You see Gunny D right there, he knows these guys, they're his friends. We establish relationships and figure out what they really need and want. That's really the key to this.'

Their goal was to create a self-sufficient economy, so that the people would choose to turn away from the Taliban. 'When we came in, the Taliban had a grip on the people; checkpoints, taxes,

sharia law, forcing them to grow opium', said Captain Sparks. If the
marines did the exact opposite, he added, the Taliban would lose
influence. 'The people are the objective. Eventually the Taliban will
become irrelevant, because the people don't want them here and
they'll push them out on their own.'

The only thing that hadn't re-opened was the opium bazaar,
although massive amounts of opium, heroin and methamphetamine
had recently been found. I asked how so much could be hidden in
such an obvious place; the police had been paid to keep quiet, I
was told. The marines talked about turning this area into a park or
a school but the local people were too afraid of the owners – drug
smugglers, who had not yet come back – to go anywhere near the
buildings. This was a reminder not only of how easily nefarious
interests could intimidate the local people but also how the invasion of Marjah had severely damaged the opium trade, the people's
main livelihood. This alone could have decided the outcome of
Operation Mushtaraq before the first shot was fired.

Gunny D spotted Mohammad, the dwarf, picked him up and
carried him over to us. Mohammed smiled but he looked awful. A
poor opium harvest, caused by a mystery virus (nothing to do with
the counter-narcotics policy) had forced him to go cold turkey.

I drifted away from the marines, to get a better view. Just a step
or two away from the handshakes and the high-fives, I noticed that
many of the men, especially the ones not directly engaging with
the marines, eyed them with suspicion and sometimes malice. As
we headed back to the base, news of another casualty came in over
the radio. A helicopter swooped low towards a field just beyond the
bazaar, sending the groups of kids sprinting away.

The situation was still precarious: 'fragile and reversible' in military euphemism. In just a few weeks' time, Bravo Company were to
be replaced, the close relationships they'd established would come
to an abrupt end and the residents would meet an entirely new set
of faces.

The remarkable progress made in Kuru Charai was entirely due
to the marines; the 'government in a box' still hadn't appeared. But

the changes had not yet spread to neighbouring areas. I was shown video of a riot that had occurred in April. Three hundred men on motorbikes and in the back of trucks, waving the white flag of the Taliban, stormed towards the bazaar from a nearby village, Sistani. The protest had been organised after rumour had spread that the marines had burned a Qur'an. Only after considerable diplomatic effort, including the donation of ten new Qur'ans, and the presentation of a marine who had recently converted to Islam to hundreds of ecstatic Marjah residents, did the crowds disperse. (The marine reverted a few weeks after returning home.) The marines said it could easily have gone the other way. Boulders were thrown and one demonstrator carried a hand grenade.

I saw footage of one of the ANCOP approaching a driver at a checkpoint and casually punching him in the face. I heard two ANA soldiers had collapsed from a heroin overdose, one in the corridor of the building where the senior marines slept. They were saved by the marine medics. And Captain Sparks had been involved in a stand-off with the ANA, when Captain Saed refused to make his men pick up their rubbish before they left. Saed said he wouldn't want to see his men firing on marines. Captain Sparks snapped, 'I'll back one of my men against any five of your clowns any day', and marched the ANA out without their weapons. Sparks said it had just been a clash of personalities.

The campaign to recruit residents of Marjah to the Afghan National Police was being re-designed; it hadn't pulled in a single volunteer. A local elder had been put on the payroll after he and twelve of his men had prevented the Taliban from entering their village, which was fewer than two kilometres from Bravo's base. They had captured some of the fighters and handed them over to the police. The elder, Commander Bosgul, a veteran fighter, was described to me as having been a 'Mujahadeen commander during the *jihad* and had serious co-operation with *every* government since then'. The emphasis on 'every' begged an obvious question, which was answered before I'd finished asking it: '... including the Taliban'.

'I'm sure that six months ago some of these guys were Taliban', said Captain Sparks. 'Now they're not. Now they want to protect their village and protect their family. The key to this whole thing has been proving to them that we're the winning side. Ninety-nine per cent of the population here, they're not really hard-core Taliban extremists. They don't like the foreign preachers that are coming in and influencing things any more than we do. Like anybody would, they side with the most powerful people to protect their family. The goal is to show them that *they* are the most powerful people.'

Bosgul had so impressed the Marines that they suggested he set up his own force, the ISCI (Interim Security of Critical Infrastructure). They announced a recruitment day when men recommended by Bosgul could sign up. They had to pass a health check: a marine corpsman asked, 'Are you in good health?' and they all replied, 'Yes'. Over sixty men turned up; the marines ran out of registration forms. Some recruits were elderly, others looked barely teenagers. But they all seemed willing. The $90 a month salary might have had a lot to do with it. 'It will be huge', said Captain Sparks. 'This turns into the police. Then we go to the next village, turn them into the police. And then we go home.'

The policy of creating local militias – *arbaki*, Afghan Local Police (ALP) – as they were known, soon became national policy. It was hoped that 30,000 local fighters would be recruited. There was a training programme, to teach basic policing and ethics and to discourage corruption, but it only lasted eighteen days. However, the plans had to be cut back after reports surfaced of robbery, warlordism, and even rape. Some of the militiamen attacked each other, the ANA and the Marines. Just outside Marjah, an alleged motorbike thief was beaten by militia members. In the subsequent brawl, a fifteen-year-old boy was shot in the head. Two militiamen argued over a woman; one was stabbed with a bayonet and another shot dead.

The Marines officers had a phrase they used when questioned about giving power to such men: it might not be perfect but it was 'Afghan good enough'.

*　*　*　*　*

I joined Bravo Company on a patrol to the east, along the road I'd watched them clear a few months earlier. The number of attacks had increased immediately after the poppy harvest, the traditional start of the new fighting season. Everyone stopped when we heard heavy gunfire three hundred metres south of our position. The ANA, which had advanced much further than it was supposed to, fired at us, somehow mistaking the marines for the Taliban. No one was perturbed; if anything, they seemed slightly bored.

The EOD team found a freshly-laid IED at the crossroads two kilometres from the base, where they'd found a bunker and two IEDs before. As they dug into the road, they were shot at first by a 'highly-effective' sniper, then from another direction by a machine-gunner hiding in a row of trees. At first, when the team heard the 'tsssszzzzup' of a bullet, they darted behind their trucks. Eventually, they gave that up, just lay flat out on the road, and continued digging.

When they'd uncovered the IED, I left my camera on the road to film it being detonated. We took cover behind the wall, exactly where we'd hidden before. After the explosion, I ran back to pick up my camera, thinking the dust cloud, at least fifty metres high, would conceal me. As I bent down, a bullet fired by the sniper zipped past me, louder and faster than any bullet I'd heard before. I grabbed my camera and ran back towards the truck.

'Oh my God', said one of the EOD team when I reached safety. 'He fired right into the fucking smoke man, holy shit. You'd say that just barely missed you, huh?' I felt shaken, even offended that the sniper had lined me up in his sights, followed me until I slowed down, taken aim and fired a shot. He wasn't supposed to single me out, I was just a witness, not a participant.

A group of men in black *shalwar kameez* ran across the road eight hundred metres away from us. Marines bounded across a neighbouring field in pursuit. 'This reminds me of day one', said a marine crouched next to me. Everyone scanned the trees for movement. A burst of fire came from the trees, no more than sixty metres away, but no one was hit. I asked how the gunman had managed to miss.

'I don't know', replied the marine, 'because they suck?' He sprinted to the next truck and banged furiously on the door. It opened, he climbed in, and slammed it shut. Marines were approaching across the fields north and south of the main road. The gunmen vanished; they'd decided it was time to retreat.

I'd had many similar experiences, both on this and previous trips to Afghanistan, when great numbers of the soldiers and marines I'd been with really ought to have been shot. I now regarded the idea that the Taliban were the best fighters in the world to be a myth. They were often terrible shots, used old and badly-functioning equipment and regularly wasted perfect chances. Their main strength was their ability to become invisible. The Russians had found things just the same; they called their enemy *dukhi* – ghosts.

As we approached the T-junction that marked the end of the road east, a drone above us filmed a man being dropped off a motorbike and eight others entering a mosque two hundred metres beyond the north–south road. 'Those are the guys that are going to shoot at us in a bit, so I'd like to padlock their movements. They've massed in the last short period of time, because it was a ghost town just a moment ago', Nascar said to the drone pilot. Soon, eight men became twelve, then 'upwards of twelve', then twenty.

The marines congregated at the petrol station at the T-junction. Although everyone expected to be attacked at any moment, many fell asleep in the shade.

The north–south road, and the canal that flanked it, formed the border between Bravo Company's area of control and the desert, where the Taliban had free rein. But the Taliban often crossed the canal, driving their motorbikes across shoddily-built footbridges. Captain Sparks wanted to strengthen the border and make it meaningful; he decided to blow up the bridges.

As we walked towards the first bridge, several local people came out of their houses. They wanted to know why the marines had abandoned a nearby base that they had established three weeks after they landed. 'When you had a post there security was very good. Now, every day, the place is insecure and the Taliban is coming', said a man who had recently moved to Marjah from Lashkar Gar. Captain Sparks said there would be a base there again 'very soon … We'll take down the bridges and that will provide security for you in the short term so they can't travel though here. That will allow us to build posts, then when security is better we'll build new bridges.' He told the man and his sons to go inside, to be safe from the explosions. 'And tell him to say "hi" to us next time we're on patrol', said a marine.

Listening to this conversation, I noticed that the terp had developed a curious habit, probably from spending five months listening to the marines, of inserting 'fucking' into every sentence he translated. This didn't make sense to the marines: 'did that old man really say fucking that much?'; 'is there even a word for "fucking" in Pashtu?' But the terp didn't stop, not until Captain Sparks told him that he didn't need to put the word into every sentence.

When I asked Captain Sparks why the post had been abandoned, he explained that having lost almost a platoon of marines, he had no choice other than to focus on a smaller area. One marine had died; the others had survived but their wounds were serious and they wouldn't come back. 'If you lose that many guys, it affects how much you can do each day. We have to accomplish the mission so it means that everyone gets a little more tired and a little more worn-out every day.' The squads Bravo sent on patrol had shrunk from thirteen men to eight.

Captain Sparks looked across the canal. He was as exhausted as I'd ever seen him. 'They're all over the place out here', he said, waving his hand across the desolate, flat landscape before us. 'This is the area where we stop trying to control. Our area of control fades a little bit about a klick [kilometre] away from here, it gets worse, but this is the edge of where we're really actively trying to secure the area. Literally right there, that road.' He pointed to the north–south road at our feet, then looked back over the canal. 'It might as well be a different country. This is probably one of the most hostile places in Afghanistan. There's two to three hundred Taliban out there.'

Sparks, who would later receive the Silver Star, spoke slowly and quietly. His eyes were dead. He looked like he could seize up and keel over on the spot, as did most of the marines. There is an argument that six- or even twelve-month tours are too short. That nothing can be achieved or understood in such a short space of time. But the look on Captain Sparks's face, like the looks on the faces of everyone in Bravo Company, suggested that for the infantry, six months was too much. They looked utterly hollow and ready to snap.

'It's probably just as dangerous as when we first landed', said Staff Sergeant Dawson, the marine from Staten Island, with whom I'd enjoyed the first quiet day in Marjah. He'd recently been shot. His radio antenna had become tangled in a tree; as he tried to pull it free, a bullet went through his hand, through the name badge on his chest plate and finally, pierced his throat, knocking him unconscious. But two weeks later, he was back in Marjah and on patrol again. 'I feel like I got hit in the face with a baseball bat. It knocked the wind out of me. If you let your guard down for a second, you get hit. I think that there are fresh fighters out there, with foreign advisory fighters. They're picking up their game.'

Staff Sergeant Dawson's experience was common. Three marines had been shot in the head, saved from death by their helmets. Lance Corporal Willis had been airlifted out after being hit by a DFC. He returned a month later, only to need an airlift out again when he was shot through both legs. The only real shock was that no one from Bravo had been killed since the first day of combat, when Corporal Jacob Turbott had been shot in the back by a sniper. As we got back to the trucks at the petrol station, the news came that two marines from Alpha Company, operating a few hundred metres south of Bravo, had been killed by a DFC as they entered a building.

The bridges were blown up. The next day, one of them had been rebuilt; men on motorbikes could be seen driving across it. Plans were made to blow it up again the following night.

* * * *

I wanted to catch up with Corporal Wesley Hillis, who'd been such a steady guide in those first few terrifying days. He was part of the QRF (Quick Reaction Force) – a small team, formed from the nine members of Bravo that you'd least like to get into a fight with. They were the crazies. Their job was to be ready to charge into a battle whenever anyone bad appeared. They spent their days driving around Marjah, praying to be ambushed.

I joined the QRF as they drove west from the bazaar, past a still-smouldering house from which they'd been attacked the day before. Hillis calmly scanned the buildings and trees around us. 'Come on motherfuckers, come out to play', he whispered from the seat in front of me. The truck knocked over a parked motorbike: 'What? What? What the fuck are you looking at?' the top gunner screamed at the stunned faces below him. The task today was to pick up a man who had tried to grab a policeman's gun – he wanted to shoot his own son, for theft – but Hillis almost got into a fight with the police commander. Hillis wanted to take the man in cuffed and blindfolded, but the police commander thought he'd done nothing wrong and Hillis should respect the commander's superior rank. As they argued, in front of a small crowd, Hillis held his helmet in his right hand. I thought he would swing it into the commander's face (later, he told me he'd wanted to do just that), but he turned and walked away. 'These people', he told me later, 'they're not like Americans. There's no way you can trust them. They let the Taliban beat them but if it comes to one of us saying the wrong phrase or anything, they lose their lid because we're Americans but "that Taliban was from the same tribe as me". It's ridiculous, it's a mind-fuck, it's frustrating and … that's a losing ball game.'

He was further sickened when he was told to take off the tiny American flag he'd attached to his truck; it 'sent the wrong mes-sage'. He told me that just before I'd come back, a local imam, who had been given more than $65,000 for repairs to his mosque, had helped a Taliban commander avoid arrest. The marines had reliable intelligence that the commander was in the imam's village; they searched every building except the imam's house. The imam agreed his house could be searched but asked if he could first usher the women into a separate room. The commander, the marines later found, was amongst them, wearing a burqua.

'This is nothing against the people of Afghanistan', Hillis told me, 'but I fucking hate the people of Marjah.'

* * * * *

The people of Marjah, four months after they had been liberated, also had plenty to say. Away from the marines, in front of large crowds who neither disagreed nor showed signs of disapproval, a succession of men, including some I'd filmed re-opening their stores, selling cigarettes to the marines and the ANA, smiling and shaking their hands, took turns to complain about life since the intervention.

'We are Afghans, we won't accept anybody else's rule', said one, summing up the entire problem in nine words. They kept coming, each more eager to speak than the one before.

'The situation is getting worse day by day. We are afraid. Our women and children are being martyred. Americans are entering houses. When they see someone with a beard they accuse him of being Taliban. America should pull out its military and leave us with our elders and with our Muslim way of life. We don't want them to be slapping this man or that man. Afghanistan is not going to be built this way. Where does the Taliban come from? The Taliban are the sons of this land, they don't come from outside. The situation in the bazaar is better but as soon as I leave there is no security. The Americans were driving their tanks, someone's stall was knocked over and dragged along the road. His money and his phone cards went everywhere. The marines drove on and didn't care.'

'When the Taliban were here it was fully secure. No one was allowed to steal or commit robbery. If anyone was caught stealing they would pour used engine oil on his head and parade him in the bazaar, so no one would dare commit robbery. I had a shop in this market, selling melon. I would leave them out at night and nobody would dare steal them.'

'If someone comes out of the house to use the toilet [a field] they are shot. Two people are not able to sit together at night.'

'I don't think it will be of any use if they build a bridge or a school. I think it will be very good if they pack up and leave.'

No one had anything good to say, no one suggested any of the speakers had gone too far or shown ingratitude. No one seemed surprised by what was being said. One man said there would be peace if Marjah were left to the Afghans.

'The solution is that the Americans leave us with the Afghan forces and the government enforces Islamic *sharia*. We would totally support it, co-operate and work together.' His reasoning was simple: 'I will say *jihad* is an obligation against the infidels but *jihad* is not permissible against Muslims. The Taliban would realise this and not fight against them [the ANA].' My translator laughed when he heard this; he said the man well knew that if the marines left, the ANA would be defeated, or flee, within hours and Marjah would once again be under the control of the Taliban.

It is an old cliché, often used by those who know very little about Afghanistan and one that I have often argued against, that the Afghans will first fight foreigners, then each other, and nothing will persuade them otherwise. Although every Afghan friend has proved to me, again and again, that a foreign guest is offered levels of hospitality and generosity that can be embarrassing, it is also true that as soon as a foreign soldier lands, especially in the south, the local men will reach for their guns. Perhaps it was a mistake to think that after all that has happened since we first arrived, even after we had re-defined our good intentions, we stood any chance of changing that.

Two months after Bravo Company 1/6 Marines left Marjah, their replacements found Mohammad, the dwarf, dead. He had been beheaded. No one knew why, nor who had done it.

PART V

US MARINE CORPS
DECEMBER 2010 TO JANUARY 2011
3RD BATTALION
5TH MARINES

Every few days during the summer of 2010, the same sentence kept appearing in the British newspapers: 'A soldier has died as the result of an explosion. His next of kin have been informed.' Taliban 'shadow governors' operated in all but one of Afghanistan's thirty-four provinces. The Taliban still conducted hit and run attacks but their most effective weapon, by far, was the IED.

In September 2010, the British forces quietly handed Sangin, the most dangerous district of Afghanistan's most violent province, over to the US Marines. The ceremony was described as a 'relatively private affair' by a British military spokesman. It was not a retreat or a withdrawal, we were told, it was a 'tactical realignment and rebalancing'. Several other problem districts were also taken over by the US Marines. The Brits moved to less volatile (but still far from secure) districts of central Helmand. US Marines now outnumbered British forces by almost three to one.

In late 2010, the Wikileaks site published previously secret communications that revealed that the American commander who had led NATO forces in Afghanistan between 2007 and 2008, and even President Karzai himself, didn't think the British were 'up to' securing Helmand. The official response from the UK Ministry of Defence was to say that UK forces had done 'a terrific job [in] an area which has always been and continues to be, uniquely challenging'. The bazaar in Sangin had been 'transformed ... more than eight hundred and fifty shops are trading, twice as many as the year before'. It was an impossible number either to calculate or confirm; it was the best they could do.

By summer 2010, the thirty-three thousand American 'surge' troops had arrived. General McChrystal had been sacked, after making inappropriate comments to *Rolling Stone* magazine. His replacement, 'King David' Petraeus, loosened the rules of engagement, giving the troops more freedom to fire what they wanted when they wanted, and to defend themselves more aggressively. Between July and November 2010, there were approximately 3,500 air strikes, the highest number since the war had begun and the number of night raids by Special Forces tripled. There were also 711 NATO casualties over the whole year, almost two hundred more than any other year so far. It was apt that the US forces taking over in Sangin, 3/5 Marines, were nicknamed 'the Butchers of Fallujah', because of the way they had fought there.

In Sangin, I was repeatedly told not to ask about the 'Wikileaks bullshit' regarding the Americans 'disrespecting' the British. 'Whatever we do here, we're building on what the British did', was a line I often heard. I also heard stories from the few Brits who remained in Sangin, who were absolutely sure they were being disrespected. Since my first visit, the British had established a team of 'stabilisation advisors' who had developed a rare and comprehensive knowledge of Sangin's tribal politics and built relationships with local elders, even with Taliban commanders, with whom they were negotiating peace deals. But their opinions weren't sought and their existence was barely acknowledged. A district-wide peace deal was possible, I was told by an aide to the district governor, who worked with the stabilisation team. However, the arrival of the US Marines had led to more civilian deaths and an increase in support for the local

Taliban, who wanted to keep fighting. There had been a recruit-ment surge, as young men joined the Taliban to get their revenge. The increase in Special Forces' kill-or-capture raids exacerbated the problem: if the moderate and reasonable local leaders were killed, they would be replaced by 'crazies from *madrassahs* in Pakistan'. The Marines thought a peace deal was only possible if the Taliban were beaten into submission.

Before arriving in Sangin, I'd spent some time in Kandahar with the 101st Airborne Division, US Army. In three weeks, I didn't see a single shot being fired but the list of dead and wounded from IED explosions was horrendous. Casualties, sim-ply described as double, triple and even quadruple amps (ampu-tations), had become common. My own colleague, Joao Silva, a much-loved and respected photographer, had stepped on an IED and lost both his legs, just days after we'd spent a few days stuck together at an airbase.

I'd also caught a glimpse of how the Afghan National Army was likely to operate after NATO forces left. A small ANA unit had charged ahead of the American soldiers and found all the IEDs in a small village in less than an hour. 'How did you do it?' asked the American captain, astounded. 'Did you offer the locals $50 for each IED they revealed, like we trained you?' 'No', said the ANA captain, excitedly, 'we told them "show us the IEDs or start digging your own grave".'

When I'd returned home, a colleague asked, with concern, why I kept going back to Afghanistan. I told him that Helmand no lon-ger revealed anything new and it was time to cover something else. But within days, I was given the chance to return to Sangin to film with the US Marines and I couldn't say no. A hundred and six British soldiers had been killed there, almost a third of all British deaths and I wanted to see how the Marines, especially a battalion with such a fearsome reputation, would cope.

The BBC manager who'd stopped me going to Marjah also tried to stop me going to Sangin because I hadn't completed the 'hostile environments refresher course' within the last three years.

The course was an idiot's guide to coping in a war zone. One section involved watching clips from my own films. On a previous course, I'd been made to run in zigzags while someone fired blanks at me. Eventually I was told I could go back to Sangin, as long as I completed the course when I returned.

CHAPTER 13

One of the first things I saw when I arrived at FOB Jackson, Sangin's District Centre and 3/5's Combat Operations Centre (COC), was the legless body of a marine carried into the medical tent on a stretcher. He was alive but unconscious. His legs had been blown off right up to the hips; his shortened body seemed more like a child's than a fighting man's. This kind of injury was becoming more common in Helmand as the Taliban worked out ways to get their IEDs to send the explosion straight up. Minutes later, another stretcher was carried in, but this time, the marine was dead. His body was intact but the way his head flopped around between his shoulders had an unmistakable lifelessness.

The marines had been struck by an IED; worse, one of them had been carrying a rocket on his back, which had also exploded. The marines who had carried them in stood outside the tent in shock, hugging each other, crying or simply looking down into the dust, unable to believe what had just happened. An ambush had followed the IED strike; the fighting still raged. After a relatively quiet trip to Kandahar, the sound of so much fire, coming from dozens of men summoning up every ounce of viciousness they had, in the effort to kill each other, was suddenly as disturbing as if I were hearing it for the first time.

Even before these casualties, 3/5 had learned what a deadly and defiant place Sangin was to those who were unwelcome. By the time I arrived, they had lost twenty-five men and more than 140 had been seriously injured. These were astounding numbers, worse than any other battalion's, anywhere in Afghanistan. They had been there just three months.

* * * * *

After landing, I'd been dumped in a long concrete and steel shed that somehow managed to be colder inside than it was out (and outside was already freezing) and ignored for days. The only contact I had was with a chubby civil affairs worker, who dressed to make everyone think he was Special Forces. 'BBC?' he said in disgust, 'you're like CNN – the Communist News Network. We don't like reporters out here.'

I walked to the COC every afternoon to find out if anyone had any plans for me. But the Public Affairs Officer, who had a sign behind his desk that read, 'Fighting the war on terror, one cake at a time', never had any news, despite helicopters and convoys coming and going every day. After a few days being almost hypnotised by the boredom, cold and loneliness of Sangin DC, I was eventually allowed to join a convoy to Lima Company, who were quartered in a dilapidated house on the edge of the Green Zone.

The convoy took the main north–south road through Sangin, right through the 'transformed' bazaar, which I was eager to see again. I'd walked through it more than three years earlier. Now I was in a million-dollar, twenty-tonne bomb-proof truck, looking through a tiny, bullet-proof window. The buildings on either side of the road were still crumbling shells, still sealed by warped metal shutters. The Afghans still sold what they could; a few piles of basic foods, old shoes, or bicycle and engine parts. Nothing seemed to have been brought in. It was as if the outside world didn't exist. I could expect that in a remote village in the middle of the Helmand desert but it was shocking to see it here, in a town that had been the focus of a multi-billion-dollar security, development, and governance effort. The eyes that followed us through the bazaar were hostile, just as they had been three and a half years earlier, when Major Martin David told me that the Taliban had been expelled from Sangin and were, 'reeling from the operations we've conducted against them, [and] low on morale.'

I was dropped off at Patrol Base Jamil, a skeleton of a three-storey house featuring pillars and a balcony. Once, it had been on its way to becoming something of a palace. Such buildings are assumed to be owned by narco-barons, so nobody felt bad about occupying them.

Lima Company had recently suffered three casualties from IEDs. One marine had lost both legs and an arm, one had lost both legs, and the third was considered extremely lucky to have escaped with just a fractured ankle. 'We had a guy that lost a foot. We considered him to be lucky.' I was told, 'Just losing a foot is a million-dollar injury out here.'

A *shura* was taking place in a large white tent. There were about sixty men attending, with about as many boys running around in the background making mischief and playing with the marines. Captain Matthew Peterson, the Commanding Officer of Lima Company, led the *shura*. Peterson, with fair hair, light green eyes and soft, boyish face that probably didn't need much shaving, looked more like his name than his title. That is, he looked like a friendly Scandinavian, rather than the leader of a company of marines in a battalion with a fearsome reputation.

Peterson welcomed everybody and told them he was there to be honest and help solve their problems. He came across as understanding and compassionate; he didn't try to look tough or intimidating. An old man complained that cars were being told to pull off the road or turn around when an ISAF convoy was approaching and even when they complied, as he had done recently, they were shot at or smashed into. Peterson started to speak but was interrupted by an angry man in a black turban, who spoke loudly and with enough venom to guarantee no one interrupted him. Six days earlier, the man's uncle had been shot, at ten o'clock in the morning, as he carried a bag of potatoes. No one had been allowed to go and help him until three o'clock that afternoon. Soon, the men around him were nodding in agreement. The terp translated for Captain Peterson; he nodded too.

'It's better to not be shot than it is to be helped when you are shot', said Peterson, summing up the man's point. 'Thank you for telling me that', he said. 'These are things that I need to know about.' He asked if the man's ankle had been treated. The man said they taken his uncle to Lashkar Gar by themselves; they had been held at a checkpoint and questioned about why he had been shot.

'I'm glad to hear he's doing better', said Peterson, understanding that the man had been talking about the uncle, not his ankle, even though the terp hadn't said anything about how the uncle was, 'but you're right, he shouldn't have been shot in the first place. As we continue to work together to make the community safer that's the kind of problem that we can avoid. But I'm afraid the truth is that people will still continue to get hurt, as long as the enemy is here. It's because of the enemy, not because of the ANA and the marines.'

The men at the *shura* disagreed. 'When there is a firefight, if someone gets shot, that's something that happens naturally', said an old man sitting in the front row, 'but when there is no firefight or when the firefight is finished and two or three hours later someone gets shot, that's you.'

'These are excellent points and I thank you for sharing them with me', said Peterson. 'But I want to tell you that there is a solution. If we wanted to get rid of the enemy in this area, we could drop enough bombs and use enough weapons to kill everybody and that would solve it. That would get rid of the enemy. But there's a reason we don't do that and the reason is because we care about the people here, so we're very careful. Sometimes people still get hurt but we do the best we can. We'll continue to try hard and it's important that you keep telling me these things.'

They eventually broke into small groups. People whose property had been damaged were given compensation forms. Captain Peterson sought out the old man who had spoken; he seemed to have authority. The old man told him there were lots of people in the area who didn't want peace and were giving false information, to prolong the conflict. He said Sangin had 'seen thirty years of war; tribal war, party war and governmental war' and that people had agendas that the captain didn't know about. 'People have tribal issues so they will use you to try and harm their enemies.'

'They're using us', said the captain, nodding again. He moved his hands between himself and the old man, symbolising an exchange. 'That's why this relationship is very important.' 'I'll give you an example: if somebody belongs to a specific tribe, they will come to you and say that all the Isakzai tribe are the Taliban; and someone from the Isakzai tribe will tell you that all the Alokozais are the Taliban. They will be following their personal agenda – they might be better off in a chaotic situation. You should be very careful.'

The old man took a compensation form. Captain Peterson agreed a figure the terp thought was far too high considering the damage. Peterson said he was happy to pay it, because with it, he was paying for a relationship with someone he wanted to talk to often, and learn about the tribal politics of Sangin.

* * * * *

The frosty treatment I'd received at Sangin DC continued at Patrol Base Jamil. The first sergeant I met threatened me with 'major, major problems', if I made marines look like 'baby killers'. I told him there was a simple way to prevent that happening; not kill babies. He still thought I was determined to paint marines in a bad light and needed to be scared.

The only way to get anyone to engage with me was to go out on every patrol, every day. Reporters, especially television reporters, often came to places like Sangin for only a few days and rarely ventured far from the bigger bases. It was easy to look good in comparison; the marines started to accept me and involve me in their conversations.

Out on those patrols, I came to understand how bad the IED threat was. Every patrol was led by a minesweeper; everyone had to walk in his footsteps. They left trails of bottle tops or sweets in case the footprints were too hard to follow. I was told that when we were ambushed, I shouldn't dive off the cleared path, instead, I should drop on one knee, because I was less likely to be shot than to step on an IED.

It took the first patrol I joined over an hour to cross the main road that ran past the base. It took other patrols hours to cross a field; one patrol needed five hours to travel one kilometre. The marines often froze, scanning the ground in front of them for clues, shouting ahead, asking exactly where their next step should be. They trod so carefully they looked like ballet dancers. They almost never went along the paths but walked through the fields, up to their ankles in freezing-cold mud. There was constant talk, from the terp monitoring the Taliban's radio frequency and the marines back at the COC. At the COC, they constantly monitored video from the drones and surveillance blimps above us. The blimps – like weather balloons with the latest long lenses and night vision cameras – reportedly cost $25 million and were described to me as 'game changers'; they could track someone on the ground for days on end.

To avoid obvious routes, patrols used heavy explosives to blast their way through walls and copses of trees. Every blast shook everything around it and half the patrol disappeared in the dust cloud. Each blast took up to half an hour to be approved; they had to take photographs of whatever they were blowing up, before and after the blast, so they couldn't be conned in compensation claims. Sometimes they blew holes in walls just metres away from a hole blown the previous day. On most patrols, the marines didn't make it to their destinations because they ran out of explosives and couldn't go on. The Marines had rejected the British forces' tactics of putting small groups of men in a large number of positions, abandoning over half of the twenty-two bases the British had fought to establish. They wanted to 'aggressively patrol', to keep the enemy guessing and limit their freedom of movement. But this wasn't aggressive patrolling at all: nothing is too disconcerting or disruptive if it's travelling towards you at two hundred metres an hour. If anything, it seemed to be a gift to anyone wanting to lay IEDs (now being laid in three minutes, I was told), set ambushes, or evade large groups of heavily-armed marines.

According the the surveillance reports, small groups of Taliban were always watching us, waiting to attack. Snipers with supporting machine-gunners were never far away and men with rifles crawled across roofs. We walked past murder holes and abandoned compounds and skirted orchards so dense you couldn't see through them. Marines had been attacked from these places before. In the distance, people moved, circling us, watching our movements, then disappearing.

On one patrol, the marines crouched in a field of cold, wet mud, dark as peat and crunchy with ice. The marines thought it was too dangerous to walk any further and decided to fire A-POBs across the field and up to a building with three walls still standing. A young boy, carrying a shovel across his shoulder, appeared within the walls.

'Delta rashah [come here]', shouted a marine, in Pashtu. But the boy turned and walked away.

'Shoot him, I don't give a fuck', shouted Sergeant Zeimus, the squad leader. He was a small, permanently angry Chicagoan, who had covered up a nasty neck injury so he could come to Helmand. A marine lifted his rifle and lined up the shot. Then, possibly remembering that I was there, Zeimus added: 'Don't just shoot him, shoot *at* him', barely a second before the marine fired two shots into the building.

'Don't hit him, alright?' said Zeimus, after the shots.

'I didn't', said the marine who'd fired. The boy had walked out of the back of the building. He re-appeared, waved nervously and slowly came towards us.

'Hey. Tell him to lift his fucking shirt up', shouted one of the marines. Another boy appeared behind the first. They both lifted their shirts, exposed their stomachs and chests, then turned and pulled them over their heads to show their backs. The first boy looked about fourteen, the second about nine; both carried shovels. They walked up to us and sat down in the field, suggesting there were no IEDs there. But the A-POBs were fired anyway, almost exactly along the route the boys had just walked. They said they only wanted to manage their fields and get water, then go home.

'Tell them to go home now', said Zeimus, 'today is a bad time.'

'NOW', he shouted, when they protested.

The boys, got up, walked, and then ran, away. They were the sons of a man who had been extremely helpful to the marines.

Marines went out on two or three patrols every day. They usually walked out of the base, across the main road and around the neatly-divided fields of the Green Zone, sometimes for as long as eight hours. They took a different path every time, to keep the Taliban guessing where they should place their IEDs. One patrol decided to blast their way through a wall on the other side of the road, rather than pass through the small garden they had crossed several times. Dozens of Afghans in cars and on motorbikes were forced to wait as the marines placed a charge and then sought approval to detonate it. There was soon a traffic jam in both directions, because HQ couldn't locate the wall on their map. 'Jesus Christ', snapped Zeimus, who was permanently high on Rip It® (a cheap American version of Red Bull, which marines drink by the crate), 'it's right across from the fucking base.'

Eventually the wall was blown and the entire platoon disappeared in a cloud of dust. The closest marines approached the wall and looked through the smouldering hole. 'Holy fuck man, son of a bitch', I heard Zeimus shout angrily. Beyond the hole was a thirty-foot drop into the field below. Nobody had looked around the edge of the wall, just twenty metres away. The drop was even visible from the gates to the base, where the marines had just spent twenty minutes waiting for the ANA. The Afghans waiting on the road were told to move on. I'd seen them looking utterly perplexed as marines inched slowly past, leaving their trails of sweets or bottle-tops. Now they looked at them as if they had finally lost their minds.

Embarrassed, the marines decided to go down an alley further up the road. They had avoided taking such an obvious route because it was so likely to be booby-trapped. Two marines nervously cleared a thin line down the middle of the alley, slowly combing the ground with metal detectors. Every time they got a reading, they dropped to their knees and delicately stabbed the earth with their knives.

An old man appeared at the far end of the alley and was told to lift up his shirt. He didn't understand, even after the marines gestured their order. Eventually the terp arrived. 'Tell him to show us his fucking chest', said one of the marines. The terp shouted but the man still didn't understand and turned to walk away. The marines screamed at him to stop; after a tense stand-off, an ANA soldier walked forward and explained what he was being asked to do. Panicked, the man frantically removed the shawl from his shoulders, undid his waistcoat and lifted his shirt. The ANA soldier patted him down in annoyance, saying 'God drown you', as the man raised his arms in the air, terrified and confused. 'There is nothing, nothing at all', the man pleaded and walked, sheepishly, up the alley, far away from the path the marines had cleared. As he passed me, an ANA soldier said to him, 'Don't do that again, they could have shot you.'

A little boy appeared, then a family of six. As we stood, rooted to our positions, they walked around us in perfect single file, with quizzical expressions on their faces, then quickly disappeared from sight. Everyone seemed to know where it was safe to walk but no one was willing to explain it to the marines. Instead, they had to concentrate on every step they took, which I found exhausting. The marines maintained a focus that only people who had recently seen several of their friends maimed or killed by slight mistakes could maintain. One marine, a young, skinny, boyish-looking lance corporal called Hancock, had had more close shaves than most. He had seen three marines from his squad hit.

'When we first got here I was in one IED blast', he told me. 'One of our guys stepped on one, Lance Corporal Billmyer. We were in a compound that we thought was safe, so we had our gear off. I was a couple of feet away from that one. And I've been close to four, or I think five, now. I was close to Lance Corporal Tinks and Lance Corporal Corzine.' Billmyer and Corzine were now double amputees; Tinks, whose real name was Litynski, was a triple amputee.

Incredibly, Hancock used these close shaves to give himself courage. 'Unless you're stepping right on top of it, it's just going to give you a concussion. Maybe if you're a foot or two away it'll rip off one limb or something, but if you're five feet away it's just going to rock your head a little. The first one dazed me a lot. It took a week or so to recover. But all the others have just been headaches, for like a week. Your ears will be ringing. You'll lose hearing.' I asked if seeing people killed or losing two or three limbs didn't make every patrol terrifying. 'It scares the crap out of you. I step just in footprints. Someone can say a route's been cleared and I'm still only stepping in footprints. I hate going in alleyways, choke points, intersections. Every intersection we've been in we've either found IEDs or been hit by IEDs. There's always going to be an IED, every day.'

One marine had asked his wife to send him some carbon-fibre underpants he'd read about on the Internet. All the marines took doxycycline so that if they did lose their legs, they wouldn't get an infection. Some seriously talked about duct-taping their testicles and penises to their bodies, to reduce the chances of losing them to an IED. Zeimus saw the look on my face when I heard that one: 'This is the way we have to think out here, man, this is the way we talk', he said.

A few months later, the Marines ordered twenty-five thousand pairs of carbon-fibre underpants, in response to the fact that many of those who were hit lost entire legs or suffered horrendous injuries to their lower bodies, including their internal and reproductive organs. One marine, they said, had 'his entire ass blown off', as well as his legs. Double amputees, I was told, nearly always ask the same two questions as soon as they can talk: Will I walk again? Will I fuck again?

*　*　*　*　*

On another patrol, the marines used explosives to destroy some trees that obscured their sniper's view. They also removed the long, grenade-filled sock from an A-POB and spread it across a bush. Only after they detonated it, sending a huge black and grey cloud hundreds of feet into the air, did the absurdity strike me; the special absurdity of blowing up a bush that would grow back as soon as spring came.

After a dozen or so blasts, the terp and an ANA soldier banged on the gate of the building we'd been crouching beside. It hadn't occurred to me that someone might be living there but I heard dozens of children's voices coming from inside. The gate screeched open and a woman's voice said, 'There is no adult male in here, you cannot come in', then pulled the gate shut. Sergeant Zeimus ordered them to knock again. He'd realised that the only roof where he could put marines to keep watch lay within her walls. Eventually, the woman opened the gate again and was persuaded to let some marines climb up on to the roofs of some outbuildings in the far corners of her compound.

'They're a cool family', said the terp. 'Many kids. We get permission to come in and use their compound.' The marines called the terp Rock, because he liked rock music. In among the marines, Rock looked like the happiest man in Helmand province. He sometimes tried too hard to please. Once, he ran up to me: he'd been ordered to tell the reporter what the marines were going to do. 'We gonna fuck right in asshole of Taliban right now. Got it?' he said eagerly, then turned back to the marines 'OK?' Rock was skinny, with bright, yellowy-green eyes and long eyelashes. Away from the marines, he revealed a sadness, at being away from his family and at seeing the suffering of the Afghans in Helmand province, that was heart-breaking. He was also sad that the marines and large parts of the rest of the world saw Helmand and thought 'Afghanistan'. He was from Mazar-e-Sharif, which, he kept telling everyone, was a beautiful place with no war.

I counted at least fifteen kids, who trailed behind the woman wherever she went and gathered behind her legs when she stopped. The kids were dressed in bright colours; none looked like they'd yet reached their teens. The woman wore a black veil that almost, but not quite, covered her black and grey hair. The small amount of hair revealed was shocking in a place as conservative as Sangin. It gave the impression that she was a lone renegade, looking after all those kids and speaking to Rock and the marines.

'Just tell the kids what we're about to do, because I don't want the kids to be scared', said Zeimus, who had more trees left to blow up. A dozen huge explosions had already shattered the compound's few windows and terrified the kids.

'Everything we do is controlled and they're not gonna get hurt', said Zeimus. 'And tell them that whenever they hear gunfire to go inside. Because sometimes the Taliban come here and shoot at us, so we shoot back. I'm gonna let the marines know there's a family in here so we won't fire in here.' He thought for a second, then corrected himself: 'We'll *try* not to fire over here. Tell her I'm sorry and I don't mean no harm to her.'

'It doesn't matter', said the woman, 'we have no options, God has made us helpless. We have many children here, we are scared.'

'Let her know that we're trying to help the country out', Zeimus replied.

'God sees all that we do', said the woman, 'God is kind.'

'We need it', said Zeimus. 'God is, you know … the answer, so … tell her thank you and I'm gonna go back to doing what I've been doing. Let her know we're just gonna clear some trees, then we're gonna leave.'

Rock, who looked desperate to offer her something, said that if there were any damage to her home, she would be compensated. 'I don't want anything. My son has become martyred and I want nothing, all we want is for you to leave', she replied.

The slow, grinding pattern of the blasts, and the headaches they produced, were depressing enough. Now I saw even younger children, who hadn't dared to come into the courtyard, hiding in an archway, wincing at each blast. Rock spoke to the woman for some time, then walked towards me and took off his sunglasses. He struggled not to cry. 'They're sad because of everyday blowing up, fighting, shooting … It's so hard … so … this is life in Afghanistan, see?' He swallowed and loudly exhaled a breath: 'I hope one day … become better.'

Zeimus walked back and shouted to the marines on the roof: 'Alright, let's roll.'

Rock waved at the woman and kids as they walked out of the gate.

'I can't hear shit', said one marine.

'Neither can I', said another.

* * * *

On Christmas Eve, as the calls to prayer echoed across Sangin and everything was painted blue by the last few minutes of daylight, the marines were told that the Taliban number two commander in the district was about to drive right past their base. Everyone grabbed their rifles and jogged to the gate, putting on body armour and helmets as they went.

Several marines got into firing positions on the road. Others leaned against the wide, gravel-filled Hesco barriers that protected the base and looked through their sights. Zeimus screamed at a boy walking across the road: 'Keep going, fucking idiot.'

'That's him, that's him!' said a marine. 'That's his blue sedan right there!'

'We see it.'

The car slowed, turned right and vanished.

'He went down the alleyway, man', said Zeimus.

'He saw us. That's why I told you I didn't want to stand here', said one of the marines in the road.

The light was about to fade completely but the marines wanted to go after the commander. Rock was told to call the ANA and get them to come out, in case the marines needed to search the compounds the car had driven into. They refused, on the grounds that they hadn't had a report on this mission. 'Jesus Christ, this just happened five minutes ago we don't have time to do reports', said Zeimus. A motorbike sped towards us. 'Slow down pal, before you bump into a 203 round', said Zeimus. The bike, carrying two little boys as well as the driver, stopped. Next a white estate car pulled up, then another motorbike. 'Tell them to fucking go', said Zeimus, 'they're not bad guys.'

'What a nice Christmas Eve, huh', he said. 'What's this guy's name?'

'Er …. Mullah Shithead', said Sergeant Giles, a tall, thin and quiet platoon leader who did yoga every morning. In many ways, he was Zeimus's opposite.

'He's gone by now I bet. If he's smart he's walking right now.'

'Those motherfuckers have got tunnels.'

'Please', said Zeimus, waiting for instructions, aching to be told he could go after the commander on foot, 'we got the A-team out here, know what I'm saying?'

'Can we go snatch his ass up?' said another marine into his radio.

'Negative. We're on op minimise', said the voice on the radio. 'Come back inside.'

'Roger', said the marine, 'request permission to enter friendly lines.'

'Horseshit', said another. They trudged back through the gates.

* * * * *

The marines weren't doing much mentoring of the ANA. Reluctantly dragging a few soldiers with them on patrols was as much as they would do. Even then, they barely tolerated them. Whereas the British OMLT involved a complete company of Brits living with a complete company of Afghans, the Marines just sent a couple of officers to the ANA base next door for basic training. I joined the ANA's first patrol. The two marines went out with them but the ANA were supposed to do everything.

Patrol Base Jamil was at the bottom of a low hill, which sat in front of a second, much bigger, hill. The marines had found almost twenty IEDs in the buildings on top of the bigger hill and been shot at whenever they were close enough to be visible from the other side. The ANA planned to walk in a small loop around the back of the base, going no further than the small hill. In other words, they wouldn't be going where anything was likely to happen.

The two marines clearly hated their job. They looked suicidal with boredom as they slowly explained the basic instructions over and over again. They told the ANA officer to give a briefing in front of a map, so that everyone would know the route. The ANA map hung next to an old British mural. That first OMLT must have gone through exactly the same process four years ago, although the goal of their mission – an Afghan Army capable of securing the country on its own – looked as distant as ever.

'We come out from here and walk this way', said the ANA soldier who eventually conducted the briefing. 'We go into this alley this way', he moved his finger across the map, 'and speak to the people in that house. Understand?'

That was just a translation of a script. They were supposed to pick it up from there and complete the briefing on their own. After suffering a few attempts, the marines gave up and delivered the essentials of the briefing: stay on the line of blue bottle tops or you'll lose your legs (the marines had supplied the bottle tops); stay at least ten or fifteen metres behind the guy in front of you; don't be lazy; don't leave your weapon on the floor, you need to be ready to fire; if you have to fire, don't spray, take your time, aim and don't waste your shots.

The ANA Executive Officer gave a speech before they left. 'Today, our own army is in command. When there is shooting, you should not move one step from your location.' He had authority and thought deeply between each sentence. 'Treat people properly', he demanded, 'and don't enter their homes for searches' – something the marines did constantly. I told one of the marines that the speech was impressive. 'He just did that because you were here with a camera', he said, wearily.

The ANA soldiers were handed tourniquets. They put them into the pockets below the knees of their trousers, still in their plastic wraps. One of the marines approached a soldier, took his tourniquet, unwrapped it and put it in the soldier's shoulder pocket. If they were hit by an IED, he explained, and lost their legs, they would also lose their tourniquet. The soldiers took out their tourniquets, unwrapped them and half-heartedly tried to clip them to their chests. Then quickly put them back in their trouser pockets when the marine turned his back.

One ANA soldier took off his backpack, complaining that the rockets in it would explode if he were shot. That thought had occurred to him exactly as he lifted the backpack and realised how heavy it was. 'These are mines', he said in protest and dumped the bag on the floor, with an expression of pain on his face, as if he'd been carrying it for hours. One of the marines lunged towards him, leaning his face forward in perfect position for a head butt. He stopped, took off his sunglasses, managed to contain himself and said, 'This is the world that you live in. Marines carry this stuff every single day, you have to accept the risk to do your job out-side the wire.' The ANA soldier wouldn't look at him; instead, he looked at the terp, waiting for him to interpret.

'If something happens to me, will you take the responsibility? They will explode if I'm hit by a bullet!' he said. The ANA dis-cussed whether or not the rockets would explode; eventually, he was persuaded to put the bag back on, reluctantly. As he clipped the shoulder straps together across his chest, he looked back at the marine and said, 'Fuck your mother', in Pashtu. That wasn't trans-lated. 'You're gonna be fine, it's not gonna blow up', said the marine.

Eventually, the ANA lined up and walked out of the front gate. An ANA sergeant, Samad, led the patrol. He waved a metal detec-tor over every inch of ground as he walked slowly forward. Two children were so bewildered as he walked by, followed by a US marine laying a trail of blue bottle tops, that one only just avoided falling off his bike. The other froze, his right hand on his hip and his mouth hanging open.

As the ANA swept through an alleyway, two more boys approached, ignoring the bottle top trail. They crouched and helped scrape the surface earth away from where a trace of metal had been detected. Further down the alley, the boys' father came out. One of the marines, Second Lieutenant Martin Lindig spoke to him. 'These guys', he said, pointing to the ANA, 'are having a *shura* on Friday and they'd really like you to come.' The man expressed interest and the marine nodded to the ANA sergeant, asking him, 'Do you have anything you want to say?' The sergeant shifted shyly, looked at his feet and said, 'You told all of the things.' Lindig sighed and shook the father's hand: 'have a good day.' He told the ANA to walk on.

We walked halfway up the first slope and waited for Sergeant Samad to clear a path ahead. An ANA soldier with a long bullet belt wrapped three times around his body approached me and posed for a picture. He was wearing strange, World War II-style, flying goggles but had pulled the head strap underneath his ears and across the bottom of his neck, so that the lenses pointed up into the sky, making him look demented. We waited a long time. We could see down into several families' compounds, effectively depriving them of their privacy. They looked up at us with contempt as they broke thin twigs for firewood.

As we walked back down the slope and towards the main road we passed a small, well-built mosque, with smooth, flat plastered walls and a new metal gate. The marines sent the ANA to knock on the gate and ask to speak to the mullah. A man emerged, wearing a bright white turban and with a huge white cloak slung over his shoulder. His sideburns were also white but his long, thick beard was black. The marines told the ANA sergeant to start a conversation but he just shuffled nervously and looked at his feet.

The man had no patience for training exercises but plenty he wanted to say. He started the conversation by saying his daughter had been shot in the shoulder by a stray bullet the day before and was now in hospital in Lashkar Gar. The family had taken her there themselves, with no help either from the marines or the ANA. This should have focused the marines' attention but the terp translated only a fraction of what the man said, saying only that everyone was scared of the fighting and the bullets, especially the women and children.

'Abduleem, why don't you talk to him about some of those things', said Lindig, nodding to the ANA sergeant, who still stared at his feet. He looked away, mumbling that he didn't speak Pashtu and the man didn't speak Dari.

A car pulled up. The man said it was his uncle, the mullah, who should be allowed through. The mullah approached, shaking everyone's hands, sizing them up as he went. He also wore a white turban and a long white cloak but with a dark green army jacket on top. The mullah looked unsympathetic as the conversation continued. Lindig said that civilian casualties were the Taliban's fault, because they used civilians for cover. He added that this was a good sign, because it meant they were losing control in Sangin and becoming desperate. It also meant that the marines and ANA were improving security.

The mullah smiled contemptuously, as if his suspicions had been confirmed, then spoke directly to the ANA sergeant. 'There is no security beyond the road. They are just saying this to make themselves happy. The Russians did the same. God willing they will suffer the same fate as the Russians.' The ANA sergeant started to look really uncomfortable. 'The Taliban are laying mines here and there', he said, without conviction.

'Yes, the Taliban are here but who are the Taliban? They are Afghans', said the mullah, waving his hand at the marines. 'Who are they? We two have to come together! Because my orphans will be left to you, yours to me. They …', he waved at the marines again, 'will be leaving.' 'Whatever God wills', said the ANA sergeant, looking at the ground. The terp interpreted none of this conversation for the marines.

'God will cause them such problems that they will forget about here', said the mullah, talking directly to Lindig. But instead of translating the mullah's words, the terp said: 'We used to live in the Green Zone but it was dangerous, so now we live here and it's very good, the children can play.' 'That's good', said Lindig. His words and tone sounded patronising; he was unaware how badly he was being misled. 'We are trying to increase security and I'm happy that you feel safer.' It was painful when the British or Americans talked to Afghan people as if they were idiots but this was especially excruciating.

The terp spoke directly to the mullah, explaining why he'd received such an odd response to his complaints. 'It's because I told him you said it was very secure here. I didn't tell him what you said, I told him the security was good here.'

The mullah argued that the three of them, the ANA sergeant, the terp and he, should unite against the foreigners. 'Yesterday they killed six people in a house, only two babies were spared. It was beyond the marketplace. Six metres beyond the bazaar there is no security. Can democracy be created by a cannon? Is that the meaning of democracy? We don't want this democracy. We don't want this law of the infidel. We want the rule of Islam. We don't want this government. We don't want the Americans. We don't want the British. It's because of them we have been fighting each other for thirty years.'

The ANA sergeant simply nodded in agreement, occasionally saying 'yes' under his breath. Lindig had given up being part of the conversation and was speaking into his radio. Everyone stopped talking and waited patiently for him to finish. The mullah was clearly annoyed. Lindig finished and asked what had been said. He got a brief translation about the six recent fatalities: 'Nothing special, the aeroplane come and explode lots of IEDs and three women, two child and one man is killed yesterday in the bazaar', said the terp.

'He's saying the airplane did that?' asked Lindig. 'Where did you hear this information?' he asked, sceptically. 'I saw it myself, the whole bazaar saw it', said the mullah. 'They dropped a bomb on the house, they killed all the adults, only two children survived. One was breast-fed, the other was three years old. It was yesterday at eleven o'clock.'

'Well, we do drop a lot of bombs', said Lindig, 'but when we do we are very careful where we drop those bombs and who we are dropping them on.'

'If you don't get upset I will tell you something', said the mullah. 'Sure', said Lindig, in a tone that suggested he was willing to endure the mullah's words, rather than seriously consider them.

'Whatever you have brought into Afghanistan, your people are here for killing. Your tanks are here for killing. Your cannons are here for killing. Your planes are here for killing. You haven't brought anything that we like. All you have brought are the things for death.'

He motioned towards the ANA sergeant: 'This man here is my brother and you've trained him. He kills me and I kill him. This doesn't do any good for us.'

'Nobody's here to kill you right now', Lindig replied. 'The majority of this patrol is made up of ANA and the reason they're on patrol right now is to provide security for you and your family and to come here and to talk to you and see how your day's going and see what you need and if there's anything they can do to make your life a little better.'

'We want nothing', the mullah snapped back, 'we have *Allah*. Is this security that a girl was shot in this house? Can security be established by a gun or by negotiation?'

For Lindig, this was the first he'd heard of the girl being shot. He said that at the marines' base, just two hundred metres away, there were medics who could have treated her. 'That's something that the Taliban can't do for you that we can', he said. 'I understand that you don't like us here because we attract bullets and we make a lot of noise and sometimes people get hurt because of us. But these things are going to have to happen before your country can become peaceful and if you help us and help the ANA and we win, we're not going to have to be here in your lives.'

'The Taliban will be here half an hour after you leave', said the mullah, smiling. 'They don't kill us. You have brought the things for killing. With them, we don't worry about going outside. They don't touch us. We don't touch them. Wherever you go you never leave us alone, whether we are inside our home or outside our home.'

It was difficult to tell if the mullah was on the verge of laughter or rage. 'Thousands of people have died in this area. As you can see, it's empty. All you have done is build one and half kilometres of road in the bazaar but against that, more than five thousand people have lost their lives: men, women and children. Now you can compare these two things against each other, which one of these do you say is better?'

The terp translated this as five to ten thousand people over the last ten years killed by marines. 'The marines have only been in

Sangin since last August', said Lindig, suddenly buoyed by what he thought was an open goal: 'We're the first Americans that have been here. It was Europeans. The Taliban tell you these things and they're not even true. They're not even based on facts.'

'It makes no difference', said the mullah, barely pausing for breath, 'if it's Pakistanis, Iranians, Americans or Japanese. Any foreigner is our enemy. They have destroyed us.'

Lindig was incredulous. Only someone insane, or brainwashed, could suggest that he'd come to Helmand with anything but the noblest of intentions. He was a modern-day Paladin. And yet here was an intelligent, articulate man, living in the shadow of an American base, expressing ingratitude. It pained him that anyone, especially one of the people being helped, could hold that view. Lindig seemed to shrink as the argument went on. 'We're not here to murder your people or to harm your family. We're here to make security and peace. If that wasn't true, I wouldn't be standing here today, talking to you, with a bunch of ANA soldiers providing security around your compound while I do it.'

'Do you have binoculars?' asked the mullah, equally disbelieving. 'Look at this area, where are the inhabitants? They have been killed, imprisoned or have fled. This revolution has brought no good for Afghans, it has just caused death.' Lindig tried to invite him to the Friday *shura* but the mullah continued regardless.

'I'm angry because if you look at my heart it's bleeding. The dangers I have faced during this revolution have not been seen by many. The truth is, as long as this government is there, I would never go to any of their events under my will, unless they force me.'

Lindig tried again. He said there were fifty people at the last *shura* and they needed men like him to come and share information and help them build a better community.

'But as soon I come outside the gate there is no security', said the mullah.

'That's why the *shura* is inside the gates', replied Lindig, accidentally confirming what the mullah had said about the lack of security everywhere else. The mullah laughed.

The ANA sergeant finally stepped in and spoke to the mullah in Dari. 'Even if you're not going, tell him you'll come.' The mullah stroked the long hair under his jaw and smiled derisively. 'I'm never going to tell a lie with this beard. Even if it meant getting killed I'd be the same. I just rely on God.'

While Lindig wrote down everyone's names, the mullah spoke again. 'I have lost two of my sons. One was killed inside his shop in the bazaar by the British, the other was killed by the NDS [Afghan intelligence]. Will I go to this *shura*? Even if my brother stands for this government, I will see him as an enemy.' The debate over, the mullah softened slightly. He said there was a small guesthouse inside the mosque and he invited everyone in for a cup of tea. Lindig looked at his watch: 'I would love to drink tea with you today but unfortunately I'm all out of time and I need to continue my patrol. But the next time we come down here I would be more than happy to sit down with you and drink tea and discuss things.'

If counter-insurgency (and Afghan hospitality) were reduced to a short list of pithy mottos, one of them would absolutely be 'never say no to a cup of tea'.

The mullah's smile turned back to a snarl. He gave up on whatever he thought talking could achieve. He shook my hand and asked where I was from. When I said '*Englestan*', he was surprised. He'd thought I was with the marines. I told him I worked for the BBC; he smiled, gave me a little wink, turned and walked away.

The next day, I followed Sergeant Giles and his platoon on patrol along the same route. There was no sign of the mullah but as we waited for the sweeper to clear a stretch of path, Giles motioned towards the mosque. According to what he'd been told, the guys inside 'were all Talibs'.

* * * * *

On Christmas Day, hundreds of welfare packages arrived at Patrol Base Jamil. They were stacked in shed-sized piles by marines, some wearing Santa hats. The company walked through the boxes, labelled 'to our American heroes' and 'America Supports You', searching for their names. Most of the boxes contained the same sweets or toiletries as they did every week. These were emptied into huge crates outside the main door and left for people to help themselves. Only when someone found smuggled porn or a few drops of alcohol was there a little burst of excitement.

Sangin was a hard place to celebrate Christmas anyway but Lima Company had also woken to the news that Lance Corporal Corzine, who'd had both legs amputated after stepping on an IED three weeks earlier, had died. He was the battalion's twenty-sixth fatality. Some of the marines speculated that he'd pulled the wires out of his life support machine. They said they'd do it, if they were in his position.

Next to the welfare packages, six dog tags hung from a cross, with the insignias of dead or wounded marines on its central column. Someone had placed a laminated card bearing Corzine's name and blood group at the base of the cross. Outside the front door, under a Christmas tree, a fluffy reindeer had been positioned to look like it was having sex with a toy puppy.

Zeimus, high on Rip It®, tried to cheer everyone by demonstrating exactly how he was going to teabag his wife when he got home. Although those nearest to him laughed a little, they soon went back to what looked like lonely, dark thoughts. Piles of ammunition boxes, rockets and explosives were dropped off at the gate, preparation for an operation that would start in a few days. That finally got everyone out of their morbid haze. For many, thoughts of revenge were the only remaining motivation.

Three days after Christmas, Lima Company left their patrol base to begin Dark Horse II, an operation to take Wishtan, an area of central Sangin. If I thought most of Sangin was bad, the marines kept telling me, Wishtan was much worse. It was the last piece of ground in Sangin where the Taliban had free rein. Where they'd had months to prepare defences and booby-traps.

Before they moved, marines from 2/9 arrived from Marjah to take over Lima Company's patrol bases. Within their first few days there, I was told, they shot at least three civilians dead. Two of the dead were well known to the men of 3/5: one had given them valuable information about IEDs, another often brought them chickens and cigarettes. Because of this relationship, the men were relaxed about digging in their fields, within clear sight of the base. The newly-arrived marines hadn't been told about them, thought they were planting IEDs, and shot them.

CHAPTER 14

A few months before they handed over Sangin, the British had cleared exactly that area the Marines now aimed at. It had cost them dear. In one incident alone, five British soldiers had been killed by a daisy chain of IEDs on Pharmacy Road, the main road through Wishtan. That was the biggest single loss of British life since the war began. Olaf Schmid, a bomb disposal expert and posthumous recipient of the George Cross, cleared thirty-one IEDs in twenty-four hours there, only to be killed soon afterwards.

The British had established three patrol bases along Pharmacy Road but these were abandoned by the Marines. This had given the Taliban several small valleys and a maze of alleys and compounds to disappear into if they attacked the remaining bases in the north and west.

The night before the operation, Lima Company travelled to the nearest remaining patrol base. It was the one I'd been in three and a half years earlier, when the Grenadier Guards were attacked with rockets and machine-gun fire. The plan was to slowly clear Wishtan before re-establishing the old British patrol bases. Pharmacy Road was to be cleared by ABVs (Assault Breacher Vehicles): 'super-tanks' carrying huge claw-like ploughs instead of gun barrels. These would be followed by armoured bulldozers, to flatten everything a hundred metres either side of the road. 'If it casts a shadow, it gets flattened', said Captain Peterson. 'I'd rather have a headache that costs money at a *shura* than one that costs blood.' If a house were occupied, he said, he would risk letting it stand, although the surrounding walls would have to go. He expected most buildings to be abandoned.

Before the bulldozers could start, the marines had to clear every building either side of Pharmacy Road on foot. It would be a painstaking and hazardous process; although the road was only a kilometre long, clearing it was expected to take three to four days.

The night before the operation began was miserable, so cold that some marines chose to stand, like skid row bums, around a burning oil drum, rather than sleep. Afghan winters are as punishing as the summers; a few hours in one made you nostalgic for the other. Only for a few weeks in between seasons is the weather bearable. The rest of the time, you have to make a massive effort just to survive. Wearing scarves around their necks, woolly hats under their helmets and sometimes, balaclavas beneath their woolly hats, the marines jumped up and down on the spot or chain-smoked to keep warm.

Just before first light, everyone put on their gear and congregated near the main gate. Captain Peterson and his officers formed a human tunnel, like basketball players before a game. As the marines streamed past, out of the gate, the officers patted them on their backs.

Every path, road, window and doorway was expected to be laced with IEDs, so the plan was to travel through people's houses or over their roofs, as much as possible. After a short walk up Pharmacy Road, the marines tried to blast their way into the first compound they came across, before they remembered the super-tank ABVs. Soon, one came roaring forwards towards the wall. When it was lined up, the driver changed gear; the engine snorted and spewed out thick grey smoke. It looked like the tank was psyching itself up. Then it moved forward, blades raised high, and pushed the wall over like a wave toppling a sandcastle.

The marines walked through the hole and saw a well-built white house, with a green, pink and blue border along its plastered walls. The floor was cement but piles of dust and twigs lay everywhere. The marines circled, then, crouched down, brushing the piles with their hands, looking for any wires. Lance Corporal Payne, the platoon's minesweeper, walked up the stairs and almost right on to an IED. 'It's a pressure plate', said Payne, 'right where we would have stepped.' It was also on the roof, where the marines thought they'd be safest.

Whether it was the large amount of equipment he carried or his absolute lack of swagger, Payne walked with a slight waddle and always had an apologetic look on his face. He spoke in short sentences, if he spoke at all. His slight speech impediment had earned him the nickname of 'Elmer Fudd'. These things – and the fact that he was doing one of the most dangerous jobs, in one of the most dangerous districts of the most dangerous province in Afghanistan and didn't seek the tiniest nod of appreciation or respect – made him one of the most admirable marines I'd ever met. But I'm sure if I'd told him that he would have shuffled away, looking for something to carry or a suspicious pile of dirt to start digging in.

There were black fingermarks on the walls, small piles of neatly-arranged rocks, like little totem poles and random mounds of dust all over the floor. The marines knew these were 'indicators' – warning signs for local people – but no one understood what they meant. Several times, moving to avoid one mound of dirt, I almost stepped on another. Soon, we were surrounded by voices: 'Hey, Payne, this is definitely something'; 'Hey, Payne, this is shady as fuck right here.' Around me, marines delicately brushed away layers of dirt with their fingers, trying to reveal what was underneath. It was odd to see them suddenly being so gentle, as if they were stroking a child's hair. Their muscle, firepower and aggression had suddenly been rendered utterly useless.

'Fuck my life', said a marine, nervously tiptoeing past.

The first compound cleared, the marines blasted their way through the next wall. They were about to walk through when a man and his two sons appeared in a doorway further up Pharmacy Road. The marines froze where they were. The man was so tall and thin that his body seemed to be caving in on itself. He walked towards us with a limp. As he came closer, I could see that one of

219

his eyes was almost closed by scar tissue; it looked like his skin had melted and slid down the right side of his face.

'There are mines there', the man said, pointing at our feet. Rock was right behind us. He confirmed what the man appeared to be saying; we were standing on IEDs. After some hurried dialogue, Rock said the mines were up against the wall, two feet behind us. The man's sons approached, then disappeared down an alley the marines had thought too dangerous.

The man said there were mines in the alley next to his house. 'We don't know where the mines are but they have piled rocks, implying no one should cross that point', he said. Pointing to another area, beyond the hole the marines had just blown, he said there were mines there too. The man was asked how he knew where the IEDs were. He offered to lead everyone to his house, show them the piles of rocks and tell them what he thought they meant. But the marines decided to keep going in the direction they'd already started, away from Pharmacy Road.

The marines asked if the Taliban ever fired from his house, in an accusatory tone that I thought was unfair. The man said they hadn't, but they had been close by. 'Thank you, bye', said the man, walking back to his house. 'Thank you, bye', said Rock.

The people with a little money had fled Wishtan; those who remained were the desperately poor and the powerless. They were exactly the people the marines should have been helping and who they could have built relationships with. Not helping the man who had helped us felt like a moral failure. It also seemed a waste. If the marines had someone like him they could trust, they could have walked through Wishtan in twenty minutes.

I asked Lieutenant Grell, the most senior officer present, if the man's house would be bulldozed. His cheeks tightened, exposing his front teeth slightly, as if he'd just dipped a toe in cold water. 'That's what ... that's what's on ... I mean if we knock it down we're gonna offer him a ton of money, offer him some other place to live but ...' He was distracted by the man, who had walked to the end of the alley outside his front door and was pointing out exactly where the IEDs were. 'Thank you' said Grell, waving at him. The man waved back, walked inside his house and closed the gate.

As we moved from roof to roof, I heard children's squeaks and giggles and almost every chimney had smoke coming out of it. But none of the families were evacuated or told about what was happening.

Soon, every few minutes, there were explosions that sucked the air out of my lungs. Most came from the marines blasting their way through Wishtan, creating new routes with wall charges and A-POBs. Even the buildings that weren't to be demolished cracked and crumbled. Occasionally blasts came unexpectedly, producing different sounds and dark smoke. These were IEDs set off by the blasts or by the ABVs as they ploughed their way up Pharmacy Road. When that happened, everyone stiffened and waited in silence, until a voice on the radio told them someone hadn't just stepped on an IED.

A man carrying a weapon wrapped in cloth was spotted in an alley on the other side of the building we stood on. An air strike was called in.

We didn't hear a plane, just the whoosh of a missile almost on top of us. We braced ourselves. We heard a heavy thud, as if a boulder had just been dropped. A thin plume of black smoke rose into the air. 'Dude, that was weak', said a marine next to me, who had curled up into a ball and put his fingers in his ears.

'That was a dud?'

'It had to have been.'

'Do you think the dud killed him?'

'If it hit him right on the head!' said Sergeant Giles, sarcastically.

It was soon impossible to proceed without walking along a path that ran parallel to Pharmacy Road and across the front of the house from where the Grenadier Guards had been attacked. Its few remaining walls were pockmarked by bullet-holes and shrapnel spray. In the rubble, two white Taliban flags stood; either a sign of defiance or another indicator that nobody understood.

Outside the house, several large rocks looked incongruous on the path. Payne, on his knees, scraped at the ground with his knife. Hancock slowly followed, stretching each leg straight out and feeling the ground with his toes before he took a step. He looked like a madman who wouldn't step on the cracks, or someone wearing their best pair of shoes, avoiding puddles. Hancock thought the rocks were a guide for someone at the other end of a command wire. 'They see someone walk by it, they know that's when to pull the trigger ... Boom!' He fanned his hands out to demonstrate the explosion.

'See that hole filled with rock?' said Hancock, 'I'm not going there. That's like the one that hit McGuinness.' McGuinness had stepped on IED a few weeks earlier, on Thanksgiving Day. He had survived.

We approached an S-shaped bend in the path, a junction of four alleys. The marines were desperate not to walk there. There were four big dips in the path, filled with gravel. Payne climbed a wall and looked for an alternative route.

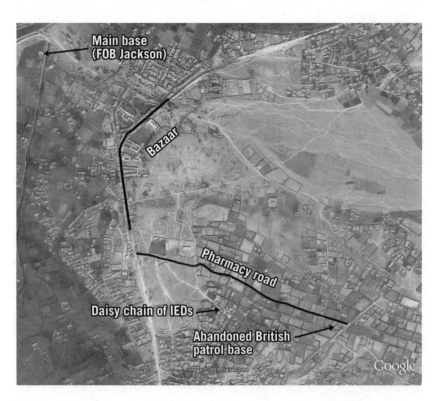

Figure 4   Pharmacy Road (© Google 2011; Image © Digital Globe 2011)

'Is there a better way to go besides this fucking choke point?' asked Hancock, hopefully.

Payne peered over the wall for a long time: 'No.'

'There have to be IEDs on this fucking corner', said Hancock.

No one knew it at the time but Hancock was absolutely right. A jug and a brake drum were buried just under the path, packed with home-made explosives. They were part of a seven-IED daisy chain, designed to kill or maim an entire platoon. Two command wires led down two alleys; at the end of one, someone watched, waiting to detonate the bombs. That person held the power source, prob- ably a battery, in one hand and the command wire in the other, ready to connect them and set off the daisy chain. This detonation mechanism left no metal for Payne to detect. Slowly, he swept the ground. Hancock nervously followed behind. I followed him; del- icately, we inched our way forwards, stepping right over the IEDs.

I didn't breathe until I got past the corner. Four marines came behind me, looking down each alley through the sights of their rifles. Payne put the ladder up against another wall, trying to find a way off the path – the 'fucking path' – as everyone now called it. As he reached the top of the ladder, a huge explosion roared behind us. I turned: two plumes of brown dust filled the alley and stones and rocks rained on us.

'IS ANYBODY HIT? IS ANYBODY HIT?' screamed the marines. I couldn't see around the corner but could hear some awful groans.

'That had to be a command wire.'

'Motherfuckers, man.'

I walked back to see what had happened. Everyone had fro- zen where they stood, their feet locked to the ground. The groans became horrendous begging sounds. As the dust cleared I saw a crater with the fragments of a yellow plastic jug in it. The jug was big enough to have held about forty pounds of explosives, enough to blow several people to pieces.

'Jesus fucking Christ, it was right there', said a marine. He pointed at the crater, about eight feet away.

Another marine was on his knees, his right hand reaching for something to grab hold of. But he couldn't even find the ground. The medic was screaming from far away; could he hear, could he see, could he crawl away from the corner? At least three IEDs had gone off together but everyone was sure there were more.

Payne appeared next to me. The marine who'd been closest to the blast said, 'You think we should step out this way, man?' Payne surveyed the corner for a second, then quietly walked forward. He stepped over the first crater and bent down to the casualty. It was Thomas, known as Big T; the other marines used to playfully mock him, because he flinched at any explosion, even small and controlled ones.

'Can you stand up, can you see?' asked Payne.

'He's blind! Big T's a priority!' someone screamed into a radio. Less than three feet away from Big T's head was another crater, full of a fizzing dark powder that sounded like a fistful of matches being scratched alight at once. It felt as if something else could explode at any moment.

Payne tried to get Big T on to his feet but he just patted the ground around him and groaned. 'Can you see? Can you stand up?'

'Huh?'

'Can you see?'

'Huh?'

'He can't hear you, man', the medic shouted. Big T was blind and deaf. Payne helped him to his feet but he collapsed, groaning. 'Arrrggggh fuck.'

'Big T, follow me, grab my shoulder', said Payne. Putting Big T's arm around his neck, he staggered back down the path.

I was suddenly alone, standing between two smoking craters. 'Stay where you're at, don't move', yelled a marine in front of me.

'The blast was right here', someone shouted from around the corner. But the marine who'd told me not to move was also temporarily deaf.

Big T was lowered to the ground. He groaned and his arms hung lifelessly from his body, like a stuffed dummy. The black powder in the crater was now on fire, crackling ominously.

'Do you remember what happened?' the medic asked Big T.

'Huh? What?'

'Did you lose consciousness?'

'Huh?' Big T put his hands to his ears. His mouth was wide open and his glasses were covered in thick dust, hiding his eyes. It was a disturbing image that reminded me of Francis Bacon's painting of a screaming pope.

'We have to get him out of here', said the medic.

I shouted to the nearest marine that the powder was still burning. 'Could it explode?' I asked.

'I don't know, I'm not going over there', he said.

The daisy chain had been made of seven IEDs but only three of them had gone off. Miraculously, none of the marines had been on top of them when they did. No one had been seriously injured. The people at the front of the patrol – Payne, Hancock, me, and four marines – had been standing on top of the IEDs for about ten minutes before we walked round the corner.

Payne came back to continue sweeping the path until we could get on to another roof. He was annoyed that he hadn't found the metal brake drum that one of the IEDs was made from.

An old man, leading a donkey pulling a cart full of firewood, appeared. 'Why don't we just follow him?' said one of the marines. But nobody dared. The old man guided his donkey and cart around us, beyond the edge of the narrow path Payne had cleared and on down the uncleared path ahead, without saying a word.

A marine pointed down one of the alleys. He was sure that's where the triggerman was hiding. 'It's alright', he said, 'he'll be dead soon.'

Eventually, we climbed on to another roof. We sat down and stared into space. Payne pieced together what had happened. I asked if it was simple human error that had saved us. Payne thought the triggerman probably hadn't had a perfect view and had misjudged where the marines were when he connected the wire to the battery. 'They usually try to time us but they don't always get it right on. It's harder to find command wires [IEDs] but there's less injuries from them. But Big T is lucky.' He looked down for a few seconds: 'We're all pretty lucky we walked over it.'

Sergeant Giles, who'd been behind the blast, said that five IEDs had gone off and one 'was a fucking pressure cooker and it had a bunch of big ass gears and shit in it. Only half the jug actually blew.'

'So they were either poorly made or really old', said Hancock. 'How did we walk by all that?' he asked despondently, holding his hands out, almost begging for mercy.

'It wasn't where we swept, it was off to the side of the road', said Giles, reassuringly.

'Except that one we walked right over', said Hancock, who wouldn't easily be convinced.

They talked about belts of IEDs, which I hadn't heard of before. 'There'll be a line', said Sergeant Giles, 'like this whole fucking line of IEDs.' He drew circles in the air with his hand, 'so that no matter where you go, you're gonna run into one.' Everyone let that sink in for a few seconds, then Giles tried to lighten everyone's mood: 'Thomas can't hear shit, he's like Twombly in *Black Hawk Down.*' 'I'd say I'm happy for him', said Hancock. 'He's lucky and he's gonna get out of this shit, probably for a while.' He looked overwhelmed, as he had done since I'd seen him on that first patrol. He let his head drop back until his helmet hit the wall behind him. 'Dude, I just don't know how we're gonna find these things', he said, talking more to himself than anyone else. 'This place is the fucking wild wild west.'

Later, I asked him how he kept going. 'It sucks, mentally', he told me, 'but I signed up to do this job, I'm gonna do it and get through, one way or another. There's not really much I can do about it now. We all volunteered. We weren't drafted or anything, so you can't say much, whether it's good or bad. Whether people are dying or not, it was our choice.'

As the light began to fade, we were told to lie down. The marines on Pharmacy Road were about to fire a MIC-LIC (Mine Clearing Line Charge). MIC-LICs worked on the same principle as A-POBs but on a bigger scale. Instead of giant football socks stuffed with grenades, MIC-LICs were more like one-hundred-metre-long sleeping bags, stuffed with shoeboxes full of explosives. 'It's a great end to the day', said Giles, as everyone put their fingers in their ears. 'I'm scared', said a marine. We were much closer than was thought safe. And there were families in at least two of the compounds between us and Pharmacy Road.

'I forget. Is it eyes closed and mouth open?' asked a marine as he curled up into the foetal position. 'Definitely keep your mouth open, 'cos of the pressure', said another.

I heard what sounded like a jet blast and saw a rocket spiralling up, then down, leaving an arc of dirty brown smoke behind. Everyone waited for the explosion. Ten seconds passed. Twenty seconds. Thirty. A minute. A blast came from the corner where the daisy chain was. 'Oh hell, no', said one of the marines, echoing what everyone was thinking – that one of the remaining two IEDs in the chain had gone off. It had, but in a controlled detonation. The EOD team had arrived and blown them up.

Another minute passed, then a long stretch of Pharmacy Road was filled with a line of fireballs the size of hot air balloons, which soon turned into a long, dark mushroom cloud. The compounds around us filled up with so much dust they looked like they'd been lined with explosives.

'It was like Jesus came down and punched the earth', said a Japanese-American marine called Futrell. We climbed off the roof and went back down the path, to sleep in one of the cleared compounds.

The marines found twelve IEDs on that first day, some with highly complex counter-tampering devices; decoy command wires or fake pressure plates. These drew people close to the mines, believing they'd disconnected them, then the real trigger was pulled. But no one had been killed or lost limbs and although three marines were concussed, one very badly, the marines would have gladly accepted those statistics at the start of the operation. Nor had any civilians been killed or wounded, although that seemed to have as much to do with luck as planning.

Before everyone had bedded down, a man came out from behind the house with the white flags. 'What does he want?' asked one of the marines.

'What's the matter?' Rock asked the man.

'The matter is that the children are screaming when they hear the explosions, they fear the planes will come and bomb. I say to them, "It's night, we are fifty people in this house, where can I take you? It's winter, it's cold".' He pointed out his house and begged to be left alone: 'Please take care of us, please do not shoot us.' 'Hey man, it's the Taliban placing all these IEDs up and down these alleys. That's what's been blowing up all day', said the marine in charge of intelligence.

Two men said they wanted to get to their home, a compound alongside the one the marines planned to sleep in. Lieutenant Mike Owen, who didn't disguise his automatic contempt for the men, didn't bother to listen to their request . He assumed they wanted to walk right through Wishtan. 'Check this out. Let them know this', he said to his terp. 'We have a weapon pointed down this direction. If anything's moving, we're going to shoot it, so if they want to get shot ...'

One of the men interrupted, 'I am not going there. My house is here. You see the gate in that corner?' He motioned towards a building less than thirty feet away.

'Tell him we're done talking', snapped Owen. 'If they walk up there, they're gonna get shot. We have an operation to kill all the Taliban and make this place safer. If they come in here we're gonna think they're Taliban and we're gonna shoot them.'

Sergeant Giles appeared behind Owen and politely asked what was happening.

'These guys are trying to sneak in here', Owen said, 'they say they fucking own this place.'

Sergeant Giles explained that he'd met the men already and that they were telling the truth.

'So we're just letting people occupy right behind us?' asked Owen.

'Yes, we already talked to them today', said Giles.

'Like no shit! Right behind us?' asked Owen again. He made it clear he thought this was a stupid idea.

'Yes', said Giles. He spoke to the men in Pashtu: 'Delta rasha [come here].' But they were now too petrified to move. 'You can go to your house if you want', said Giles, in English. But Owen had walked away, taking his terp with him, so the men stayed where they were, too afraid to walk back to their house. Eventually, Rock arrived and told the men they could go home.

* * * * *

The next morning, the marines woke at dawn and walked back to the roof where they had finished the day before. They waited there until enough walls had been blown for them to move to the next compound.

A young boy walked along the path below. 'Ask him if he's seen any Taliban', said one of the marines. There was a lengthy back and forth exchange, which the marines took to mean he was avoiding the question. Eventually, Rock said that the boy had come to get some stuff from his family's house, which was on the corner where the daisy chain had been. The boy said that he usually spent all day in the bazaar and only came here at night.

'Hey, if he goes to the bazaar during the day and comes back here at night, why is he here right now?' asked a marine. This was a typical pattern of meetings with local people – catching them out or spotting the tiniest of contradictions, even if they only arose from translation, was preferred to actually finding anything out, leave alone offering help or reassurance.

The boy was only about twelve but even children weren't above suspicion. A marine photographer, who told me he didn't think there was any such thing as civilian casualties, claimed to have personally seen little girls burying IEDs. He also said that little boys were usually Taliban spotters. Another marine told me about 'the Syrian Solution' that they'd been taught at military college. In the eighties, facing protest in the city of Hama, Hafez Al Assad had sent the military in, who'd killed at least ten thousand people, demolished the town and then – and this was news to me – spread salt everywhere, so that nothing would ever grow there again. I didn't need to ask if the marine thought that the Syrian solution would work in Sangin.

The boy had a reasonable answer as to why he'd come back during the day: he was moving as much as he could from the old family house to the house they had just moved to. 'Will you come back?' asked Rock.

'I am going and coming back frequently.'

'Why?'

'Because there are foreigners here.'

The boy was told to crouch down. Another wall charge was about to explode, not far from where he was walking.

'Don't trust anyone in this fucking area', said Rock. He was capable of one minute saying he thought that everyone was Taliban, then being reduced to tears at their plight the next. A marine said he'd been told about a fifteen-year-old Taliban kid. He thought the kid, now curled up in a ball below us, looked about fifteen and was probably the one he'd heard about. The boy put his elbows on his knees and his fingers in his ears, waiting for the explosion. When it came, he picked his nose, got up and walked away. He sprinted back again a minute later; his goats had escaped through the hole that had just been blown in the walls of his compound.

'I wonder where their Alamo's gonna be?' one of the marines asked Sergeant Giles.

'I don't think they're going to be stupid enough to have one', Giles replied. 'It would make sense for them to just continue a war of attrition. Basically, they have a defence in depth set up throughout the whole city where they can continuously fall back, then swarm back around and attack from different directions.'

A member of the marines' Psychological Operations (Psy-Ops) team arrived. He set up a speaker on the roof where we had moved. He had two Pashtu messages, he said, 'a friendly one and a call out one.' One message of reassurance and one challenge to the Taliban. He waited for an A-POB blast, then played them. First came reassurance:

'People of Sangin, peace and the blessings of God be with you, The national forces and their international allies are conducting an operation in the Wishtan area to establish sovereignty in this area, remove dangerous mines and destroy the houses which these criminals use for hiding weapons, bombs and mines. If these criminals have hidden weapons and bombs in the Wishtan area, the Afghan national forces and their allies will find these places and will destroy them in order to establish government control. Help your Afghan brothers and show them the places where the criminals have hidden weapons and bombs so that we can destroy these destructive weapons. If you don't do this these forces will have no choice but to clear the way with bombs. It's your choice, it's up to you. Show the places of the bombs to the Afghan forces and their allies or if you know where the mines are, cut the wires and bring them to our post. Thank you for your help.'

'And if you don't have bombs in your house or can't disarm them yourself and bring them to us', they could have added, 'we will blast our way through anyway.' As for the Afghan national forces, supposedly accompanying the 'international allies', I hadn't seen any yet.

The challenge to the Taliban was played next:

'Listen, oh, enemies. The national forces and their allies are conducting an operation in this area. Cowards, you are taking money from these poor people, you attack these innocent people and lay mines beside their houses. Oh cowards! The Afghan National Army and Police are taking pride in fighting you. To fight you and finish you! Leave your cowardice and do not use these innocent women and children. Stay and fight like men.'

I'd started to get some feeling back into my toes, and in a few muscles, but my bones had yet to thaw, making my legs feel like badly–microwaved spare ribs.

As the marines cleared another building, a group of old men appeared through a gate and walked towards us, waving cautiously. The marines didn't want to leave the building and meet them half-way, because the ground between hadn't been swept. But when the men stopped and gestured for us to approach, the marines reluc-tantly walked forwards.

The oldest man had a thin white beard and eyes as bright blue as Peter O'Toole's in *Lawrence of Arabia*. But the skin underneath sagged heavily, making them weep constantly and giving him a look of painful sadness. The marine's intelligence officer also noticed how blue the man's eyes were but couldn't put whatever he was thinking into words. He just pointed to them and said, 'Wow.' Then, remembering his job, he struggled to think of a question. In the end, he managed to say: 'Tell us about this area.'

The men said they didn't understand what he wanted to know. He then asked where they lived. The men pointed over their left shoulders.

'Will you walk us through the compound to show us a safe route?' asked the intelligence officer.

'Yes, yes', said one of the men, 'but you cannot stay there.' 'The women and children are scared', said another. 'We came here to ask what shall we do? When you come to our house will there be damage?' A third man asked, 'We want to know whether we will be harmed or not. When we leave the house, the women and children start screaming and they can't keep calm anywhere. When there are explosions, it rocks our rooms and we are so scared we don't know which way to go.

'If there are women and children in a house, will you still go on the rooftop and sit there? Will you still blow your way into that house? We have come to find out. If you leave us alone we will not move out, because it's cold. If it makes no difference to you whether there is a family in there or not, then we will have to leave.'

'Are there mines?' asked Rock.

'We will not tell you if there are or not. If we say there aren't, it's possible that there are. If we say there are, then you will ask us to show you and we don't know where they are. The Taliban places them and hides them, how are we supposed to know where they are?'

The marines asked about one house, higher than the rest, with a flat roof that looked like a good place to keep watch and spend the night. The old men led us to that compound, waved the women inside and walked up an outdoor staircase and onto the roof. The marines immediately set up gun positions on the corners while Lieutenant Grell radioed back to base to ask how much rent he should pay the owner.

As we climbed, a small boy, with a disability that made him look like he'd had a stroke, pushed himself backwards into the corner at the top of the staircase. His mouth fell wide open and his right hand gripped the wall as the giants filed past. His eyes could only just move fast enough to take in all the strange things he was seeing. Another boy crouched next to Doc St Louis, the dark-skinned Haitian medic, examining his face as if he were trying to work out a puzzle. I half-expected him to rub the doc's hand to see if the colour came off. The boy pulled a green shawl over his head; other than that, he barely moved, staring in wonder. 'It's fucking Yoda sitting right there', said Hancock.

Everyone was told to walk to the back of the building, as two more MIC-LICs were fired, shattering the compound's windows. The marines had two more walls to blast. It was getting dark quickly, so they used three times the normal amount of explosives to make sure they wouldn't have to do it twice. I knew they weren't checking compounds for civilians and could be disturbingly casual about where they placed explosives but I assumed they knew what was on the other side of the wall. The final blast was supposed to reveal a clear view across a field to the old British patrol base, Lima Company's final objective.

But when I walked over the first pile of rubble and towards the second hole, I saw a small garden and behind it a house, cracked across its entire face, with two shattered windows. 'Hey, we got a building right here', said one of the marines. 'There's definitely a fucking hole though, a nice fucking hole. I'm proud of myself.' He stopped smiling and sighed. 'Now we got a building, fuck it.'

I was overtaken by a small boy, wearing a skullcap and a brown shawl draped over his shoulder. He was followed by a much younger boy. Both walked straight across the garden, eagerly calling for their friend. 'Saifullah? Saifullah?' they shouted, in voices that hadn't yet broken. Two boys appeared from a small stairway that led to a basement, one no more than six years old, the other about twelve. Behind them two more children appeared, a girl and a boy, just six or seven years old, with impossibly innocent-looking faces. They all looked shocked; unable to express either fear or anger.

'Hey, this is the guy that lives here', said Payne, as the older boy walked towards us, smiling nervously. He nodded 'salaam', so quietly he was barely audible. The boy in the brown shawl stood next to his friend and turned to look at the marines.

'Does anyone know how to say "I'm sorry"?' asked Payne. Nobody did.

The boys talked among themselves. 'Did they destroy your other house?' said the one in the brown shawl.

'Yes, they destroyed everything', replied Saifullah.

'They will destroy this room as well.'

'Why?' asked the younger boy, who looked about seven years old.

'Because they want to be able to see from there. They can see the road from that position.' The boy pointed to the compound from where we had come and then to the roof where the rest of the platoon had set up machine-gun positions.

The boys walked through a gate in the wall and into the field the marines had thought they were blasting their way to. 'Did they make two holes in your house?' asked the younger boy.

The boy in the brown shawl nodded. 'They are going to make a bigger hole over there as well', he said, pointing to the gate they had just walked through. 'They think our doors are no good for them.'

The younger boy had a pained expression on his face. It looked like all this was new to him. It was the face of a child walking past a man asleep on the streets and asking why no one was willing to help. I walked up to the two young boys and flipped over the little viewing screen on my camera so they could see themselves. It was a pathetic attempt to make them feel better. They giggled and pointed at themselves, then became suddenly shy again. Behind them, the little girl was clearly eager to see herself too but she froze at the top of the stairs. I wanted to take the camera to her but I froze, too.

Beyond the compound walls, the bulldozers and ABVs strained for a few seconds as they came to walls and buildings, then exhaled as they flattened them.

As it got dark, we all put on every piece of clothing we had before we got into our sleeping bags. I tried to get to sleep before it got too cold but it was impossible, even wearing two pairs of thick socks, boots, trousers, gloves, a jacket and a woolly hat. By 2 a.m. I thought I'd got frostbite; my toes were so cold they felt as if they'd drop off if I flicked them. At 4 a.m., half-mad with tiredness and cold, I got up, hopped across the roof in my sleeping bag, emptied the contents of my backpack and put my feet in, pulling the zips on either side up as far as they'd go. But it didn't make any difference. At dawn, everyone woke and immediately lit cigarettes. It was impossible to tell whether they were exhaling smoke or cold breath. Two marines held a serious conversation about how handy the cold would be if they stepped on an IED. Frozen stumps, they thought, would bleed less.

'We're moving in one minute, so if you want to follow a cleared path, get your shit on', said Lieutenant Grell, who was already packed up and ready to go.

'Let's go destroy some more people's walls, man', said the marine who'd blown the last two walls the night before.

We walked down the stairs and out of the compound. Before the sun had crept over the horizon to offer a tiny promise of warmth, we walked a hundred metres up Pharmacy Road, turned right, climbed through what had been a window and entered a building that looked close to collapse.

Not until I'd walked around inside and read the graffiti did I realise we were in the old British base, FOB Wishtan. Lima Company had reached their objective.

*　*　*　*　*

Sergeant Giles and his squad started conducting patrols to the neighbouring buildings. They all had to be cleared and if they were uninhabited, demolished. At the first gate, a tiny old man greeted us. He looked surprised when the marines asked permission to enter, as if he weren't used to having a choice. The man had a feeble, buckled frame, with huge ears, pushed outwards by his black turban. His thick, white beard curled back in a long S-shape under his chin but his moustache, and the hair on his cheeks, starting just below his eyes, was black. His eyes were pleading, and the expression on his face was at once sad, kind, wise, and pertified. He led us into his home – four rooms off a cross-shaped corridor – and started to walk up the stairs to the roof. The marines asked if it was safe. The man stopped. He didn't know, he said; he hadn't been up there for months.

'We have no other choice, there are so many mines in this area. We have no choice but to sit in here for hours.'

'How long have you lived here?' asked Rock. 'Six to seven months', said the old man.

Another old man appeared, even more frail and bent-over than the first. The green turban on his head, and the once-white shawl that hung over his back, were so big on his emaciated body that it was almost impossible to see where his shoulders might be. 'We are so scared because of all the explosions', he said, slowly walking towards us. 'I am a poor person. I have nowhere to go, what can we do?' He squatted on the floor in the corridor, next to his friend. They pointed to their shattered windows. Rock promised they would be compensated, then told them that there was about to be a big explosion and they shouldn't be afraid.

'You are better than the others, we can talk to you', the second old man said to Rock. I assumed that 'others' meant the Taliban. In places like Wishtan, people saw both sides almost every day. The idea that they would be anything other than as pliant as possible was ludicrous, especially considering how helpless most of the people were. 'I have some military experience in Kabul, I know how government works', the old man went on. 'These others, we don't know where they come from; we cannot go out at night. If someone is screaming outside no one will come out because they are afraid.'

'Yes, I know, it's very difficult', said Rock, sadly. 'Life in Afghanistan, especially in Sangin, is very difficult. I don't know how you live in this area.'

'What can we do? We have no choice', said the old man.

'We pray to God for peace in Afghanistan', said Rock.

'We are so poor we can't even afford to pay the fare of a vehicle. I have no children, it's only me and my old wife', said the first man. 'He has one son and three or four girls', he gestured towards his friend. 'They are all ill. All the doors and windows have been blown up by mines.' I'd guessed the men were in their seventies or eighties but the mention of children made me think. I was shockingly bad at working out Afghan people's ages, often overestimating by several decades.

A third old man joined us. His right eye was badly infected; it looked like it was cast from creamy-coloured, misty glass, like a prized marble. The three men chatted with Rock, who tried to interpret highlights of what they said to the marines, so that they might show some sympathy. He said, almost begging, that they were 'Persian people, very good guys. Their knowledge is family but they are so poor. If they had money they would go back to their homeland, in Ghor province [in central Afghanistan].' He said that because they spoke Farsi (Persian), no one spoke to them, so they trusted no one in the neighbourhood. 'Tell them I don't either', said Sergeant Giles, as he walked past. Another marine pointed into a small room, with long brown finger marks on the wall. 'So you shit in here, wipe your ass with your hand and then wash your hand here', he said, laughing, pointing to the wall.

The explosion Rock had warned the men of shook the house. The man with the diseased eye flinched, gasping slightly, as if he had been slapped hard on the back. I didn't know how he survived a single night in that house.

I followed four marines as they put ladders between roofs to a neighbouring mosque, where they set up a couple of machine-gun positions and kept watch for a few hours. They could see the building on top of the hill where they had taken one of their first casualties, who'd needed a double amputation after an old IED exploded. 'That's Building 47', said Giles. 'Whenever you came up on that hill and exposed yourself to this side of the hill for longer than five minutes you'd start getting shot at from over here.' We now sat on the buildings the Taliban had disappeared into after such attacks but Giles was under no illusions about how much effect that would have. 'They'll still operate in this area, just not as freely', he said. 'They'll just move east, towards the desert and into the wadis they had used to transport weapons.'

Even if the marines could completely halt the Taliban's ability to operate in Sangin, it was one of only a handful of towns and districts that had anything like the manpower and resources needed. On maps of Afghanistan – even just of Helmand province – these towns were mere dots. It was easy for the Taliban to move on, as they had since the initial invasion.

'Holy shit, that's big as fuck, dude', said a marine, digging out a huge bullet from the wall with his knife. I asked if it had been fired by Americans: 'I hope so', he replied. Some kids in the courtyard below asked for chocolate and offered to sell us what looked like chillies. 'I ain't eating your pepper, it'll give me the shits', said the marine.

I asked Giles what he'd been told about Sangin before he came. 'We went on YouTube and there were hundreds of videos from the British. It was mostly air strikes and huge firefights. All the news articles we read, it was all "one of the worst places in Afghanistan" so we knew it was going to be a tough deployment. Marines like to fight, so we were excited to go somewhere that we knew there'd be plenty of fighting.' I asked if there had been fear too. 'You're definitely scared too, scared and excited. I'd say before you get here, mostly excited and once you get here, a little more scared. It's a mix of both.'

He said the Taliban were very good at guerrilla warfare. 'We have way more guys than them, much better weapons, supplies, all that stuff, and they still manage to make it a good fight. So they're good at sneaking around, they're good at ambushes, they're good at IEDs.' I asked the question I'd often asked: have you actually seen the Taliban? 'Actually seen them, no. Most of the time you'll just see muzzle flashes or the dust signature from where they fired but I haven't actually personally seen any. There's only a couple of guys in my squad that have actually seen them.'

I asked how he kept on going out, when so many of his friends and colleagues had been maimed or killed. 'It's just ingrained in the marines or in any military: you just keep going, you have to get the job done. It's scary. But it makes you want to go out and get the guys that have hurt your friends or tried to hurt you, so it's a mix of things.' I told him that things had got worse every year when the Brits were here and that by the end of their time someone was blown up every few days. Giles said he hoped the marines could win in Sangin. 'If we give them [the people] a better option than the Taliban, then hopefully they'll choose us.'

* * * * *

Back at the old British patrol base, I climbed on to the roof. The bulldozers went back and forth on either side of Pharmacy Road, flattening every wall and building in sight. Sergeant Giles was on the roof next to me. I asked if what we were watching made him feel bad. 'Er ... not really', he replied, without elaborating. The marines had several arguments for anyone who did feel bad. The people here probably didn't own the shitty houses they were living in, they'd be given far more money than they were worth and some of them would be rebuilt by the marines much better than they were before.

The rest of the marines were inside, eating, resting, enjoying having reached their objective in one piece.

'This is our shitty new patrol base', said one with a smile.

'We've still got ninety days though. Ninety days to keep our legs', said another, smiling. 'Three days of hard fighting and now we can masturbate in privacy.'

'This is where we jerk off and shit', said Zeimus, as he disappeared into a tiny room with a camouflage sheet for a door, the closest thing they had to a private space.

'This is our new place. It's great, a lot of concrete', said another, stamping his foot on the floor. 'We like concrete, so it's mission accomplished.' 'Yeah!' screamed another marine and the two embraced. It was indeed a massive relief to step on concrete; the only surface in Sangin which couldn't conceal an IED. The physical sensation of hard and flat ground under my boots was so soothing. It was difficult to understand how we'd walked on soft earth for so long without breaking down.

Back on the roof, I could see the house the marines had mistakenly blown their way into the day before. The three boys and the little girl who had emerged from the basement in shock were there. The wall that separated their field from Pharmacy Road had been demolished; their house, and their family, was exposed, probably for the first time in their lives. Seeing Afghan houses without their high and impenetrable walls is like seeing western houses without windows, doors, curtains or blinds. But much worse, because a lot of Afghan family life happens within the compound walls but outside the main rooms. Without the essential privacy the outer walls had given them, the children looked naked and pathetic, afraid even to move while so many people could see them.

One of the older boys was walking slowly and nervously towards the building where we were. I jogged down the stairs and grabbed Rock, telling him that the boy was outside and needed to talk to someone. The bulldozers were getting closer, destroying everything on either side of Pharmacy Road. It looked like the boy's house was next and I wasn't sure the marines had told their CO – or the men in the bulldozers – that there were at least four children inside. That was one of the few times when I felt sure the tiny role I played in the world was important; that I was in a unique position to report something essential. Suddenly, I had the courage and conviction that I assumed other journalists always had and that many others thought I had. We met the boy at the edge of the field, about twenty metres from the old patrol base. Curiously, the boy had a broad smile on his face, something I'd often seen local people often do in Helmand – look as unthreatening as possible to anyone strong and potentially violent. For most people, it was all they could do.

'They will destroy the whole house?' he said, still smiling. 'There are children in these houses and they are scared, it's cold outside.'

'No, no they will cause no destruction', said Rock, 'they will just destroy that wall.'

'My father is coming. He is very upset.'

'I know this must make you angry. If Americans came to my house and did this, I would be angry and I know you are.'

A stocky, bearded man walked towards us. He looked scared as he watched the bulldozer flatten a wall on the opposite side of Pharmacy Road. He was sweating; his movements were jittery and panicked but as he approached, he also smiled broadly, and shook our hands. He wore a long, light blue *shalwar kameez*, with a small label stitched to the chest pocket that read 'Lucky'.

'What is happening here?' he asked, so terrified that the words came out somewhere between a chuckle and a whimper.

'Sorry, but this is how it is. They will compensate you', said Rock. He made it sound as if the bulldozers would indeed flatten everything we could see, as they feared.

'All our belongings are there in that house, are you destroying it?' the man asked. Rock didn't know what to say. Buildings with people in them were supposed to be safe but no one was checking. And the man's house was right next to the old patrol base. 'Tell them that our stuff is there, we are poor people, what should we do? Tell him that our children are there!'

The Marines' Civil Affairs Officer arrived. Rock began explaining to him that the man owned the house we were looking at.

'All our stuff and our children are in there', the man said again, his panic increasing. He struggled to remain calm. His smile had gone and his expression was desperate. 'Do you want to destroy my compound?' he pleaded.

'No, we're not going to destroy your compound', said the Civil Affairs Officer. 'Tell him it's just the walls. It's for the security for everybody because this whole road has been laced with explosives and we're getting rid of it so we can keep security down this whole road, so his family can feel safer.'

'At the back of my compound there's another with a family ...', the man said.

'As long as there's people in it it's not going to get destroyed.'

Behind him, as he spoke, bulldozers flattened walls. When they reversed they bleeped loudly and repeatedly, an absurd warning, far too little and far too late.

The man was asked his father's name and his tribe. No one made an effort to address his obvious fears, no one apologised for the destruction or for the terror his children felt. As the Civil Affairs Officer made notes, Rock tried to reassure the man.

'You are a poor man, you mind your own business. It is good for you to have a base here.'

'But we are worried that if there is a base and someone takes a shot at it that we will be held responsible.'

'Our presence is good for you, you live in this area, so no one can shoot at you.'

Rock told the Civil Affairs Officer what had been said. 'Tell him I'm sorry for the inconvenience but it's going to be safer for everyone and he's going to get reimbursed at the end of this', was the reply. Two more men approached from the other side of Pharmacy Road. Both wore dark green *shalwar kameez* and turbans. One wore a brown waistcoat, the other a brown blazer. They were ordered to stop and show that they weren't carrying weapons or wearing explosives belts.

'Nothing! There is nothing!' they said, lifting up their tops to reveal bare chests and stomachs, then pulling up their loose-fitting trousers to reveal bare legs. They gestured towards an electricity pole that had almost been pushed over as a wall was flattened. 'It didn't knock down the line, just the pole', said the Civil Affairs Officer, smiling.

'This is our house, this is our area', the men said, pointing to several buildings just off Pharmacy Road. It looked like they were next for the bulldozers; the walls surrounding the first house had already gone and large white crosses had been sprayed on the other buildings.

'The engineers will come and rebuild it', said Rock. 'You will be compensated for all of this. Come here tomorrow, we will talk and we will assess the damage and they will pay you accordingly. Come tomorrow, every problem will be solved.'

'Give us the compensation and we will rebuild it', said one of the men.

'That house was full of stuff', said the other, pointing to another building that had been flattened.

'No problem', said Rock, 'when the owner comes he can speak with this man. OK?'

'OK', said the man. He knew there was nothing they could do.

An ANA soldier with a long dark beard, green woolly hat, and thick lines on his face stretching from the corners of his eyes all the way down the sides of his cheeks, approached. 'Were there mines in these houses?' he asked.

'No', said both of the men.

They looked at the bulldozers and held spare cloth from their turbans over their mouths and noses to keep away the dust that filled the air.

'Was this was a mosque?' asked the soldier, pointing to a single storey building across the road. Its speakers were still there but the windows and doors were badly damaged, as if someone had attacked every straight edge with a hammer.

'Yes, it was our mosque.'

The Civil Affairs Officer asked who the mullah was. The men said there was no mullah, just them and an old man. Between themselves, they looked after the place and prayed inside. As the men talked to Rock and the Civil Affairs Officer prepared compensation forms on his little notepad, Rock sighed with frustration and said, 'Bullshit.'

'What's he saying?' asked the Civil Affairs Officer.

'He's saying "when they give me money?" I said, "tomorrow, tomorrow".'

'Tell them tomorrow they can come up here but until then they have to go back to their compounds for their safety', said the Civil Affairs Officer.

The ANA soldier spoke to the mosque owners again. 'It is because of the divisions between us, Pashtun, Tajik, Uzbek and so on, that we are seeing this and it could even get worse.' The soldier said he was a Pashtun but had moved to Herat many years ago and only spoke Dari: 'If today a mosque here is being demolished, maybe tomorrow a mosque in Herat will be demolished.'

One of the men approached the mosque. The pole holding the speakers that sent the call to prayer was bent and only just upright. The man looked nervously at the rubble in the doorway, then cautiously stepped forward. Without going in, he pulled out a Calor Gas heater and a prayer mat; he snapped the mat in the air and slapped it to get some of the dust off. He told Rock there were Qur'ans inside but he didn't dare go in and retrieve them.

The other mosque owner watched, his arm around the home owner we had spoken to, gently rubbing his back. The men had been told to go back to their compounds but they stayed, squatting outside the old British patrol base, watching everything around them being effortlessly turned into dust.

Fifteen minutes later, the mosque was dust too. As the bulldozer turned to flatten the piles of bricks and cement, two explosions went off beyond the next wall due for demolition but no one seemed to notice.

I asked Captain Peterson how demolishing homes, and even a mosque, was supposed to win over the local people. It didn't seem like good COIN. 'I know that most people in the world probably wouldn't understand. You're trying to build a country up by destroying it and it seems like a paradox but those are people who have not been to Afghanistan. They don't understand that the nature of conflict inevitably includes destruction before you can start to build it the way it should be, in a way that's secure and provides a better economy for the people in the future.'

He thought the Afghan people would be more pragmatic: 'I think they understand, after nearly four decades of war, that damage is unavoidable. For a long time, we've been going about piecemeal destruction of things to open up new avenues of approach or provide freedom of movement. It's the same thing we're doing here, we're just doing it on a much higher scale and we're doing it all up front. Short term, there is a sacrifice of convenience to an extreme degree and that's not something that's lost on us. But I think what people understand is that to increase security on that route and to prevent the enemy from putting any IEDs there, these types of drastic steps are necessary.'

But the people of Wishtan hadn't been given a choice. The destruction had happened without notice, suggesting that the security of the marines was more important than the welfare of the local people. It felt like the era of 'courageous restraint', where foreign forces were supposed to be prepared to take more risks and more casualties, to protect the homes and lives of the people ('the people are the prize'), was over.

Everyone flinched and looked over their shoulders as another MIC-LIC exploded nearby. In the old patrol base, a marine screamed, 'Yee-ha.'

'So Monday, OK?' said the Civil Affairs Officer. Everyone whose compounds had been demolished was asked to go to the District Centre on Monday to claim compensation. There was a loud explosion in the middle of Rock's translation. Everyone flinched again. 'Tell 'em to get there early in the morning because a lot of people are gonna be coming to get payments', added the Civil Affairs Officer. 'Tell them also that tomorrow we've got a medical initiative going on, where they're going to be giving classes on how to use certain medications that they're gonna be giving y'all.'

Further away, some houses had been bulldozed along with their surrounding walls. I could just about see the house belonging to the man who'd helped us on the first day. To my relief, it was still standing.

We walked past the mangled shell of a British truck, so badly burned that it looked as if it were ready to blow away, like the ashes of burnt paper. A group of twelve kids, seven boys and five girls, approached and almost at once, said 'choc-a-let, choc-a-let.' 'Their fucking lives revolve around chocolate', said Hancock, not stopping.

'Me one dollar!' shouted one of the boys, as we walked back to the patrol base where we had started. Almost everything on either side of Pharmacy Road had been flattened.

* * * * *

The next morning, New Year's Day, 2011 (New Year's Eve had passed without a mention), I joined Captain Peterson on a walk through Wishtan. He wanted to see his platoon commanders, chart progress and give them a morale boost. But before we reached the first group of marines on the hill, the vicious crack of a sniper's bullet sent everyone to the floor. That snapping sound meant he had only just missed his target: probably Captain Peterson. People with long radio antennas were often 'bullet magnets', as they were assumed to be important. I was sure I heard the bullet hit the wall next to us. But within a few minutes, three other people, at three different points along the patrol, said they thought it hit close to them.

There was a brief discussion about where the sniper might be and what might be the best way to kill him. But soon, everyone was up on their feet and walking again, paying him no more attention. Someone had attacked a large group of highly-trained, heavily-armed foreign troops, while drones, jets, surveillance blimps and helicopters flew in the skies above. It should have been suicidal. But he had escaped with ease, without being spotted, shot at or chased.

Once he'd spoken to his men, Captain Peterson paused on the high ground and looked across Wishtan. 'We're denying the enemy any freedom of movement whatsoever. Now we're in the south and the north and they've got nowhere to run. It's a tactical victory but also an emotional one, because of the casualties we've taken. It feels good, personally, and it's going to make a big difference.' He explained why it had been so important to take Wishtan from the Taliban. 'As the noose tightened, this became his last refuge. We had to come here, as part of clear, hold, build. You have to clear effectively and completely otherwise you're holding areas and not holding other areas and it just becomes unmanageable.'

I mentioned that Wishtan had been cleared by the British. Was giving up the patrol bases they'd established a mistake? 'I don't know what the criteria behind the thought process was that went into that, I'm not sure what the reason for abandoning them was. You could spend a lot of time talking about what could have been done better and everything is clearer in retrospect. But I can tell you it's definitely the right decision to hold them now so I'm glad that we are.'

We walked to the old British patrol base. The marines were working in a long line, like a chain gang, filling sand bags. The Afghan soldiers sat in an outbuilding, three feet away from the marines, smoking and watching, not caring what anyone thought about them not helping. Someone had managed to light a small fire in a dustbin and cook a tray of powdered eggs. Squares cut from a cardboard box became the plates. Captain Peterson quietly served the marines this special breakfast treat, wishing them 'Happy New Year'.

Sergeant Zeimus appeared again, the inevitable Rip-it® in his hand. 'Hey, get all the snipers from the roof and downstairs. Hey, did you eat yet? Come on, let's go.' He sounded angry even when he was making sure that everyone got their breakfast. 'Hey, Reyes, let's go, dog.' Someone asked if the ANA got eggs too. 'They don't need to eat this shit, they got their own stuff.' He screamed at everyone not to throw the plates away but to pass them on. As early in the morning as it was, he was already high on caffeine and anger. 'Let's go, come on, hey, Lance Corporals, let's go, get the fuck over here, Jesus Christ.' He spoke so fast that seven words became two: getthefuckoverhere, JesusChrist.

Captain Peterson laughed quietly. But he punched Zeimus on the shoulder when he started impersonating a Vietnamese marine, Nguyen. 'The camera's on', Peterson whispered. 'Oh shit, sorry', said Zeimus. Then, not wanting to let even the captain have the last word, added, 'You just hit me and the camera's on.'

'That's not rated R material', said Peterson.

'That's not rated R material', Zeimus repeated. He walked away; he'd had the last word.

Captain Peterson went on ladling steaming powdered eggs on to dusty squares of cardboard. 'The beginning of a new year, you got hot chow, company objective three is secured, Operation Dark Horse II is almost over, there's only one or no casualties. Whatever you eat for the next New Year's breakfast is not going to be as good as this, I guarantee you.'

Zeimus ate last, putting his drink on to his piece of cardboard, so it looked like a breakfast tray. He simply lifted it right up to his mouth, shovelling every piece of powdered egg straight in. It was gone in seconds.

After breakfast, Captain Peterson and Lieutenant Grell made plans to erect a few tents, for families whose homes had been destroyed and who had nowhere to sleep in the freezing cold. Others finished fortifying the old patrol base or went on patrols to set up checkpoints or observation posts.

* * * * *

Captain Peterson was happy with the way the operation had gone, that the Taliban had nowhere left to hide and that the lower levels of insurgents had picked up on the marines' 'tenacity and determination'. 'People who were once thought of as irreconcilables are, as we speak right now, waiting to talk with American commanders to negotiate some deal where they're willing to bring in IEDs and identify higher leaders.'

The company's losses had been staggering. Peterson almost broke down when he told me about a marine who'd been killed the day before his son was born. But despite so many killed and injured men, he remained determined. 'We're never going to quit, we're never going to stop patrolling. There's not enough IEDs to keep us from patrolling. Not enough bullets to keep us from accomplishing our mission. We're not leaving, we're going to stay. When the enemy saw that, at the lowest level, it demoralised him and he said, "We can't continue to fight them, because they're better than us. We can't outlast him because he's not leaving. So we'd better figure out a way to carve our way into the future of Afghanistan or we're going to get left out in the cold". And if that's his analysis he's exactly right.'

I asked what he would say to people who were angered, scared or confused by the fact that Afghanistan had become America's longest war. 'If we put a timeline on it, well, then we've started to say that the time we spend is more important than the cause itself. And if that's the case we never should have gotten in in the first place. I don't think that is the case, I think the cause is justified and I would say to them: so what? This is America's longest war, so what? So it's taken us ten years to get where we are. If it takes another five, if it takes another ten, if that's the price of success, then who cares how long it lasts?'

AFTERWORD

It is now seven months since I was last in Helmand province. For now, I wake up each morning, switch on my laptop and read news from Afghanistan that cancels out the effects of my coffee. This weekend marks the tenth anniversary of the 9/11 attacks. The big story was that NATO troops have been ordered to stop transferring prisoners into Afghan custody because they were being tortured, mostly in prisons run by the NDS. Methods included electric shocks from car batteries and the use of a 'medieval-style rack'.

On Saturday, a massive truck-bomb killed five Afghans and injured seventy-seven American troops. One of the Afghans killed was a five-year-old girl hit by shrapnel almost half a mile away from the US outpost that had been targeted. She was somewhere around the 17,000th civilian victim of the war.

Yesterday, the Afghan Local Police (the *arbaki* militias, like the one I saw being set up in Marjah, with no vetting) stole the headlines, accused of gang rape, murder, torture and extortion. That news will not have surprised anyone who's been paying attention. There are currently seven thousand ALP, and funding has been approved for another twenty-three thousand.

As I write, groups of gunmen with rockets, and suicide bombers are taking part in an attack in Kabul. Fifty metres from a police checkpoint – part of a 'ring of steel' supposedly in place around the city's diplomatic centre – the attackers are occupying a tall building, still under construction, offering perfect views into the US embassy, ISAF headquarters, the presidential palace and the Ministry of Defence. The attackers had posed as labourers, stockpiling their weapons for two weeks. (The attack, which killed eleven civilians and at least four policemen, lasted for almost twenty-four hours.)

It's no exaggeration to say that every morning starts with similarly jaw-dropping news. A few recent examples: three senior government officials killed in one day; a third mass prison escape in Kandahar; a credible estimate that Afghans spent $2.5 million on bribes in 2010, the equivalent of twenty-five per cent of GDP; slightly-wounded soldiers dying because doctors and nurses at the military hospital in Kabul, who are mentored by American officers, only give food and treatment if bribed; and $910 million disappearing from the Kabul Bank in 'mysterious insider loans'. At the end of 2010, it was revealed that the senior Taliban leader, whom NATO had been flying into Kabul and showering with cash for peace negotiations, was just a shopkeeper from Quetta. I only wish I were making this stuff up.

This year, 2011, has also seen a string of high-profile assassinations. In May, the police commander for northern Afghanistan, General Mohammad Daud Daud, was killed. In April, it was Ahmad Wali Karzai, the President's half-brother, and a power broker in southern Afghanistan. In July, Ghulam Haider Hamidi, mayor of Kandahar, was killed. He and his daughter had returned to Afghanistan from the USA, believing they could help their homeland. A few months later, his daughter left Afghanistan again, saying it was in '360 degrees of chaos' and she had lost all hope: 'America came to Afghanistan and aligned itself with the very people who destroyed Afghanistan and who continue to destroy Afghanistan: warlords, drug lords, gun lords.' In September, Burhanuddin Rabbani, former president and head of the Afghan High Peace Council, was killed when a man entered his home with a bomb hidden in his turban. The assassin was offered a welcome because he pretended to be a Taliban commander who wanted to talk peace.

Despite this, the plan, for the time being at least, is to transfer every province in Afghanistan to the Afghan national security forces by 2014, when all foreign combat troops will return home.

Several districts have already been handed over, almost immediately becoming the target of symbolic, but none the less lethal, Taliban attacks.

2012 marks the beginning of the decline in our commitment to Afghanistan, as the thirty-three thousand surge troops leave. The peak of our efforts will pass, with little to show for it. Violence in 2011 was greater than the previous year, as it has been every year since 2006. There have been gains, for example in education and health, but only in some parts of the country and where foreign troops have little or no presence. Life remains grim for far too many Afghans, often in the provinces that have been flooded with troops and money. In lists of the world's most corrupt, violent, poor and illiterate countries, Afghanistan continues to come first, or very close to first; a situation that looks unlikely to change any time soon.

These basic facts, and what they say about the future, are so obvious they are barely discussed among those who live and work in Afghanistan. It would be unnecessary, gratuitous even, to point them out, were it not for the fact that, officially, the policy is work-ing. 'We are meeting our goals', said President Obama. 'We have basically thrown the Taliban out of their home turf in Kandahar and Helmand provinces', said the US Secretary of Defense, Robert Gates. This last claim was jaw-dropping several times over, because it was repeated by many journalists I had once admired and respected. And plans are 'on track' for Afghan national forces to take charge of security by 2014.

These, and many other dreamily upbeat claims, sometimes make me wonder if I ever saw the Afghan war at all.

In the war I did see, nowhere has been cleared of the Taliban. Armed men are no longer seen in the (literally) few square kilo-metres around the urban district centres that were focussed on but that is all. Even within those areas, the Taliban attend, unannounced, most of the *shuras* held by foreign troops. They have access to the population, often because they are the population, and they can still plant IEDs within a short walking distance of most bases, which they do with barely-believable frequency. They also allow the people to take whatever foreign forces offer them, as long as they also give the Taliban free passage, cover and food whenever they need it, ensuring a stalemate at best. Such a state of uneasy co-existence can hardly be described as 'holding', much less winning.

If I were Afghan, especially in Helmand, I certainly wouldn't be picking sides. Certainly not if the American Marines or British soldiers who were asking me to are replaced every six months, and will be gone altogether within two to three years. If someone built me a school or repaired my mosque, I would undoubtedly smile, shake their hand, maybe even make them a cup of tea or pose for a photograph. But this would be simple pragmatism. It would not mean I offered them my loyalty, much less that I had rejected the Taliban. The nature and detail of this pragmatism is entirely lost on idealistic foreign commanders.

The relationships that exist almost always exist because they have been paid for, which leads to yet another *even if.* Even if somewhere is cleared, held, built on and transferred to the Afghan security forces, what happens next? Currently ninety-seven per cent of Afghanistan's GDP comes from foreign aid and military spending, according to the World Bank. If the Afghan government is unable or unwilling to provide for its citizens when they are receiving such largesse, imagine what it will be like when the foreign money dries up. Until then, there is little incentive for the Afghan government to perform, or even behave, if that will hasten the foreigners' departure and stop the gravy train

In the years to come, I dread to think what I might read in tiny, two-paragraph stories buried in the middle pages of my newspaper. I fear that as long as we have a few secure and isolated bases from which to strike Al-Qaeda in Afghanistan and (mostly) Pakistan – I suspect that this is the only policy to which we are still committed – the Afghans will be left to suffer.

Three years after the Soviet withdrawal in 1989, the Communist government fell to the Mujahadeen. They went on to fight each other, reducing much of Kabul to dust and killing an estimated twenty-five thousand people. As dreadful as it sounds, as things now stand, that could be a better outcome than we have any right to hope for. For western policy-makers, desperate to avoid humiliation, a repeat of the Soviet defeat looks desirable, but unlikely. In huge swathes of the country, the government will not stand for twenty-four hours, much less three years, without foreign support. Every Afghan I have spoken to is convinced there will be another round of civil war as soon as we leave, with no rules of engagement or courageous restraint. They also think that the Taliban may well win. Perhaps the most damning indictment of our intervention is that there are also many Afghans who will think that if there is such a victory, the good guys will have won.

September 2011

RECOMMENDED FURTHER READING

I turned regularly to four books for inspiration while writing this one: Jason Elliot's *An Unexpected Light* is not only one of the most beautifully-written books I've ever read, it also offers an essential portrait of the Afghanistan we never hear about. Jon Lee Anderson's *The Lion's Grave* is such a pleasure to read that it's easy to forget how informative it is. David Finkel's *The Good Soldiers* and Evan Wright's *Generation Kill* are set in Iraq but are both brilliant chronicles of modern warfare. When I was in need of a boost, a small amount of time with one of these books got me straight back in front of my laptop. George Orwell's *Homage to Catalonia* had the same effect.

For a meticulous account of recent western intervention in Afghanistan before 9/11, Steve Coll's *Ghost Wars* is essential reading, as are Lawrence Wright's *The Looming Tower* (a history of Al-Qaeda) and Peter Hopkirk's *The Great Game* (Britain and Russia in Afghanistan from the nineteenth century). These three heavyweights are such masterpieces that I doubt they will ever be surpassed. For comprehensive accounts of the Taliban, I recommend Ahmed Rashid's *Taliban*, Antonio Giustozzi's *Koran, Kalashnikov and Laptop* and *Decoding the New Taliban* (as editor), and Abdul Salam Zaeef's *My Life with the Taliban*. Alex Strick van Linschoten and Felix Kuehn's *An Enemy We Created* and Giles Dorronsoro's *Revolution Unending* are also essential. We have no excuse not to have known better. For forensic insider accounts of western policy since 9/11, I commend Ahmed Rashid's *Descent into Chaos*, Sherard Cowper-Coles's *Cables from Kabul* and Bob Woodward's *Obama's Wars*. To understand how counter-insurgency is supposed to work, I recommend David Kilcullen's *An Accidental Guerilla*. Finally, Kate Brooks's *In the Light of Darkness: A Photographer's Journey after 9/11*, contains pictures that say more than all these words combined.

For the ultimate reading list go to http://www.foreignpolicy.com/articles/2009/09/08/the_ultimate_afghan_reading_list, where you can also subscribe to the excellent *AfPak Daily Brief*.

ACKNOWLEDGEMENTS

I would never have set foot in Afghanistan if it weren't for the support of several broadcasters. I'd like to thank Karen O'Connor, Paul Woolwich, Sandy Smith, Danny Cohen, Kevin Sutcliffe, Nancy Abraham, Sheila Nevins, Shane Smith, Suroosh Alvi, Spike Jonze, Tom Giles, and Daniel Pearl.

Rupert Chetwynd, Goran Tomasevic, Abe Sipe, and Bill Pelletier all helped me far more than I ever expected. Ismael Sadaat has not only been a brilliant translator, but also a trusted guide. Melissa Pimental stuck with me, even when yet another book on Afghanistan looked like an impossible sell. Mike Harpley and Oneworld decided to back me, even though the market was overcrowded. As copy-editor, Ann Grand gave this book a polish that I could never have managed on my own. My writing was often ugly before she scrubbed it up.

I would especially like to thank the following people, who offered me access to what they were doing long before they had any idea what I would do with it. The British, American, and Afghan fighters didn't volunteer to enter the Big Brother house, but, with very few exceptions, never stopped me filming or made me feel that there was a question I couldn't ask. In particular I'd like to thank Martin David, Jack Mizon, Carew Hatherley, Richard Westley, Simon Butt, Christian Cabaniss, Ryan Sparks, Mark Greenlief, Tim Coderre, Ben Willson, Wesley Hillis, and Matthew Peterson. Lastly, I'd like to thank my Mum and Dad, who I know hated to hear that I was going back again, but never said it.

INDEX

101st Airborne Division, US
Army 191

ABVs (Assault Breacher
Vehicles) 217–8, 221, 235
Accidental Guerrilla, The
(Kilcullen) 74–5, 258
Adin Zai 43–7
Afghan Development Zone 13
Afghan Intelligence Service *see* NDS
Afghan soldiers *see* ANA
air grenades 104, 116, 133–5, 145
air strikes 7–8, 11, 31, 33, 37–8, 41,
127, 167, 221
approval 130–1, 156
restrictions 101, 143
Alexander, Sergeant Simon 23–4, 26,
29
Ali Shah, Dur Said, mayor of
Gereshk 3, 14–17
ALP (Afghan Local Police) 181, 251
Alpha Company 185
American Marines *see* US Marine
Corps
amputations 191, 193, 195, 201–2,
215, 238
ANA 6, 8, 12, 18, 21–2, 25–7, 40–2,
52
at Adin Zai 43–4, 46
attack on Kakaran 30, 31, 34–7, 41
clash with marines 180

finding IEDs 191
infiltration by opponents 172–3
at Marjah 93, 102, 107, 111–2, 132,
165–6
problem loading rifle 131
in Sangin 200, 206–12
and Taliban weapons 170–1
training 49
transfer of power 252
ANAL (ammonium nitrate and
aluminum) 108
ANCOP (Afghan National Civil
Order Police) 81, 146–7, 180
ANP (Afghan National Police)
14–15, 49, 81, 180
A-POB explosives 106–7, 202–3
arbaki 181, 251
assassinations 252

Baki, Abdul 139–42, 144, 147, 149
bazaars 50, 52, 86, 109–10, 137–8,
146–52, 177–8, 190, 194
Berwa, Sergeant 140–2
Billmyer, Lance Corporal 201
Black, Sergeant 93–100, 104, 107
helping wounded 97
hit by rocket 106
shrapnel wound 23
Blancett, Lance Corporal 133–5
bombers, suicide *see* suicide bombers
bombings 3–5, 7–9, 37–8

Bosgul, Commander 180–1
Bravo Company 70, 83–137, 145–73,
    177–87
bribery 22, 252
bridges, blowing up 183–5
briefings before invasions 80–1
British Army 1, 10–4, 17–26, 28–57,
    59–60, 63, 73–4, 82, 172, 189,
    198, 206, 217, 233, 254
  civilian casualties 3–5, 7
buildings, clearing 112–27, 145–6,
    150, 164, 167, 200–2, 214, 217–8,
    227, 247
bulldozers 217–8, 235, 239–44
Bunch, Lance Corporal Brady 65–8,
    70–2
Butchers of Fallujah, the 190
Butt, Simon, Company
    Commander 20–1

Cabaniss, Lieutenant Colonel
    Christian 63, 73–4
Camp Bastion 13, 43, 46–9, 75
Camp Dwyer 83–9
Carter, General 82
casualties
  civilians 3, 5, 7, 32, 54, 64, 85, 94,
    138–40, 142–4, 210, 215–6,
    251–2
  soldiers 23, 160, 190–1, 193–5, 249,
    251
Charlie Company 137–44, 148,
    152–3
chickens 216
children
  in houses used by marines 233–5,
    240
  used by Taliban 229–30
Christmas 214–5
civilians
  Afghans on Americans 187–8
  bombing 3–5, 7–9
  marines interacting with 178–9,
    181
  marines using house 101–2, 203–5

Taliban use of 41, 155–6
  see also casualties
civil war 27–8, 255
Coderre, Tim 108–9, 127, 150–1,
    161–2, 172
COIN (counter-insurgency) 73–5,
    138
compensation
  for bombing civilians 3, 7–9, 142
  for damaging property 148, 196–7,
    204, 241–6
compounds, clearing 112–26
comprehensive approach 13–4, 63
condolence payments 142
  see also compensation
convoys 15, 24–5, 62, 194–5
corruption 27, 181, 252
Corzine, Lance Corporal 201, 215

Dark Horse II 215, 217–49
David, Major Martin 12, 26, 50–1,
    54–6, 194
  at Adin Zai 43–6
  and attack on Kakaran 29–30,
    36–8, 40–2
Dawson, Staff Sergeant Robert 153,
    185
deaths
  policemen 54, 252
  Taliban 151
  see also casualties
desertion rate, Afghan soldiers 21, 172
DFC (Directional Fragment
    Charge) 152–3, 170, 185
dickers 17–8
Dickinson, Weapons Platoon Sergeant
    Brandon ("Gunny D") 147–50,
    172, 177–9
drugs 51–2, 71, 108, 146, 152, 179
  and the ANA 21–2, 36
  see also heroin; opium; weed

Echo Company 60–74
Edgell, Company Sergeant Major
    Simon 23

EOD (Explosive Ordnance Disposal)
     team 112–5, 131, 152–3,
     167–72, 182, 227

flag, Afghan 111–2
flechettes 38
Freedom Park 177
Funke, Staff Sergeant 68–70

Gates, Robert, US Secretary of
     Defense 253
GDP 254
Gereshk 15–7
Gereshk, mayor see Ali Shah, Dur
     Said, mayor of Gereshk
Gereshk valley 10–2
Giles, Sergeant 206, 214, 221, 226–30,
     236–40
Godwin, Lance Corporal 105
Gomez, Lance Corporal 62, 69–70
Goolie, Lance Sergeant Adam Ball 55
Greenlief, Lieutenant Mark 141,
     147–8, 151–2, 154–6, 160, 172
Green Zone 10, 18, 20, 24–5, 28, 30,
     39, 43, 46, 53, 62, 194, 200,
     210
Gregrow, Staff Sergeant 168–70
Grell, Lieutenant 220–1, 233, 235,
     248
grenades, air 104, 116, 133–5, 145
Grenadier Guards 7, 10–2, 21, 23–4,
     28–47, 54–5
Gunny D see Dickinson, Weapons
     Platoon Sergeant Brandon
     ("Gunny D")

Haditha 84, 87, 106
Hancock, Lance Corporal 201–2,
     222–3, 225–6
hearts and minds 13, 73, 160
     see also COIN
Hellfire missile 33–5, 40, 64, 127.
     156–7, 166–7
helmet 26, 44–5, 70, 105, 111, 127–8,
     177, 185–6, 205, 218

Hennessey, Captain Patrick 7–8,
     30–3, 35, 37, 42, 47
heroin 86, 108, 149, 152–3
Hickey, Guardsman Daryl 47
Hillis, Corporal Wesley 92–3, 95,
     97–8, 100–5, 138–9, 186–7
homes, demolished by marines
     239–43, 245, 246
homosexual behaviour 21–2

IEDs (Improvised Explosive
     Devices) 15, 20, 55, 61, 64, 74, 80,
     88, 91–5, 131–2, 152, 189, 253
     in Kandahar 191
     in Marjah 113–5, 145–6, 150,
     152–9, 164–8, 182
     material of 108
     in Mushtaraq 178, 182
     in Sangin 193, 195, 197–9, 201–2,
     206–7, 215–7
     in Wishtan 219–29
infantry see British Army; US Marine
     Corps
injuries in combat 101, 202, 226
     see also amputations
invisibility of Taliban 70, 172, 183
ISAF operations 4, 7–8, 81, 140–3,
     195, 251
ISCI (Interim Security of Critical
     Infrastructure) 181

Jacko, Platoon Sergeant 18–20
Janofsky, Second Lieutenant
     Rich 103, 123–5, 164
Javelin missiles 44–5

Kabul, attack 251–2, 254
Kakaran 28–39
Kandahar 191, 252–3
Kareem, Abdel 42, 147
Karzai, President 4, 90, 143
Khanjar, Operation see Operation
     Khanjar
Kilcullen, David 74–5
Koenig, Lance Corporal 126, 128

Kuru Charai 109, 124, 137, 179
    under Bravo Company's
        control 129, 145, 149–50, 160,
        177–80
    and Charlie Company 138, 152

Lashkar Gar 13, 53–5, 137–45, 209
LAW (Light Anti-tank Weapon)
    rockets 103, 116–7
Lima Company 194–216, 217–49
Lindig, Second Lieutenant
    Martin 208–14
Lityinski, Lance Corporal
    ("Tinks") 201
Lloyd, Ryan 33, 46, 52
LTTs 18
Lucky (terp) 6, 16
Lutz, PFC Janos 71

MacLean, First Lieutenant
    Aaron 138–43
Mahayadin, General 81, 83
Marines see US Marine Corps
Marjah 78–173, 175–88
marijuana see weed
Massoud, Ahmed Shah 27
Mastiffs 20
McChrystal, General 77, 81, 94, 107,
    138, 175, 190
McDonald, Lance Sergeant Jason
    11–2, 23
McLean, Lieutenant Aaron 152
Meador, Captain Eric 72
Mian Poshteh 62–73
MIC-LICs (Mine Clearing Line
    Charges) 227, 233, 245
military police 49
militias, local see arbaki
Ministry of Defence (MoD) 1, 18,
    190
missiles 11, 34, 44–5, 87, 99, 166–7,
    221
Mizon, Lance Corporal Jack 11–2,
    23, 36, 39, 42, 46, 52–3
    impact of war 39–40, 47

Mohammad 118–20, 122–3, 150, 179,
    188
Morrison, Doc 94–101
mosques, demolishing 243–4
MRAPs (Mine Resistant Ambush
    Protected) 61–2
MREs (Meals Ready to Eat) 48
Mujahadeen 7, 180, 254
mullah in Sangin 209–12, 213–4
Mushtaraq, Operation see Operation
    Mushtaraq

Nascar see Willson, Forward Air
    Controller Ben ("Nascar")
NDS (National Directorate of
    Security) 6, 15, 17, 214, 251
New Year 246–8
Nicholson, General Larry 79–83, 172
Niemasz, Marine 135
Northern Alliance 27–8

Obama, President 59–60, 63, 72, 77,
    173, 175, 253
OMLT (Operational Mentor and
    Liaison Team) 21, 49, 206–7
Operation Khanjar 60
Operation Mushtaraq 79–173, 175,
    179
opium 15, 29, 35–6, 49, 51–2, 86, 108,
    149, 152, 179
Owen, Lieutenant Mike 228–9

Paserelli, Private 19
Pashtuns 27, 175, 244
patrol bases 17–9, 40, 195, 206, 214,
    217, 244
patrols 10–2, 65–71, 182–7, 197–205,
    206–14, 236–9
Payne, Lance Corporal 219, 222–5,
    234
Paz, Staff Sergeant 70
Peterson, Captain Matthew 195–7,
    217–8, 245–9
Petraeus, General 190
Pharmacy Road, Wishtan 217–49

Piccioni, Marine Anthony
    ("Picc") 145, 154–9, 167–8,
    172
PID (Positive Identification) 154–5
police 6–7, 40, 186, 252
    corruption 14–7, 179
    fear of 146
    military 49
    recruitment 180
    see also ALP; ANCOP; ANP
politics, tribal 13–5, 190, 196–7
pork chop 109, 125, 127, 131–8, 145,
    150–2, 160
    controlled by Bravo Company 145,
    150
prayer
    before battle 89
    call to 205, 244
PRT (Provincial Reconstruction
    Team) 53–5
Psychological Operations (Psy-Ops)
    Team 231

Qadeer 107–8, 111
QRF (Quick Reaction Force) 186–7
Queen's Company, the Grenadier
    Guards see Grenadier Guards

Rahim Kalay 28, 42, 54
Rambo 93, 111
reconnaissance patrol 10–2
Rios, Lance Corporal 166
riots see Taliban
rocket man 30–6
rockets 11, 26, 36, 38, 44–5, 143–4,
    193, 208, 217, 251
Rock (terp) 203–5, 220, 228–30, 232,
    236–7
    and compensation 204, 240–5
Rocky, ANA Captain 34, 42
Romo 107–8
RPGs (Rocket-Propelled
    Grenades) 11, 36
Rules of Engagement 88, 94, 114,
    190, 255

Saed, Captain 81, 111–2, 180
Saifullah 234
Salaam, Lieutenant Colonel Awal
    Abdul 79
Samad, ANA Sergeant 208–11, 214
Sanders, Corporal 165–6
Sangin 28, 49–55, 189–249
Schmid, Olaf 217
security under Taliban 7–9, 187
shalwar kameez 136, 148, 182, 214–2
shipyard confetti see flechettes
shuras 3–8, 13–4, 50–2, 54, 80,
    149–50, 172, 253
    in Sangin 195–6, 208, 213
Silva, Joao 191
Ski see Stachurski, Rich ("Ski")
Slynn, David 54
Snazle, Company Sergeant Major
    Glenn 10, 24–6, 37, 43–4
sniper hole, finding 160–2
snipers 6, 63, 91, 126–31, 161–3, 182,
    199, 246
Soviet withdrawal 254
Sparks, Captain Ryan 83–4, 105–6,
    112, 119–20, 131, 145, 164
    on ANCOP 146–7
    blowing up bridges 183–5
    clash with ANA 180
    and Freedom Park 177
    interacting with civilians 178–9,
    181
Special Forces 6, 62–5, 190
stabilisation advisors 190
Stachurski, Rich ("Ski") 113–5, 152–
    3, 160, 167–71
surge see troops increase
suicide bombers 20, 23–4, 39, 54, 56,
    110–1, 134, 251–2
Sword strike 60
Syed, Sergeant 31–3

Taliban 6, 40, 63, 74, 149–50, 253–5
    ambush by marines 132–6
    attacking EOD team 167–8
    attack in Zumbelay 11–2

Taliban (*cont.*)
  attack on Adin Zai 43–6
  attack on Kakaran 29–39, 41
  and bombing of civilians 3–5
  challenge from Psy-Ops 231
  deaths 151
  and drugs 51–2
  helped by imam 186–7
  and incident with Charlie
    Company 142–3
  life under 122
  marines' opinion of 239
  at Marjah 94–101, 103–7, 109,
    114–8, 125–6, 165
  and Northern Alliance 27
  organising riots 180
  poor shooting skills 182–3
  reducing influence of 178–9
  in Sangin 53, 190, 199
  using children 229–30
  weapons find 170
Thomas, Marine ("Big T") 224–6
Tinks *see* Lityinski, Lance Corporal
  ("Tinks")
tourniquets 97, 207
translations, deliberately misleading 42,
  123, 208–10, 212–3
tribal politics *see* politics, tribal
troops
  decrease 252–3
  increase 59–60, 77–8, 190
Turbott, Corporal Jacob 185

US Marine Corps

1st Battalion, 6th Marines 78–173,
  177–88
2nd Battalion, 8th Marines 59–74
2nd Battalion, 9th Marines 215–6
3rd Battalion, 5th Marines
  193–249

weed 22, 69, 71, 81, 122
  see also drugs
welfare packages 214–5
Westley, Lieutenant Colonel
  Richard 3–7, 14–7, 22, 25
Wikileaks 189–90
Wilkinson, Sergeant Dave 23
Williams, Tom 113–5, 152–3, 160,
  170–1
Willis, Lance Corporal 185
Willson, Forward Air Controller Ben
  ("Nascar") 130–1, 154–9, 167–8,
  173, 183
Wishtan 215, 217–49
WMIK (Weapons Mount Installation
  Kit) 23–4
Worcestershire and Sherwood
  Foresters 3, 18–21, 28, 46
  see also Westley, Lieutenant Colonel
  Richard

Young, Staff Sergeant 98–100, 106–7,
  113–9

Zeimus, Sergeant 199–200, 202–6,
  215, 240, 247–8
Zumbelay 10–3